Civic Communion

Civic Communion

The Rhetoric of Community Building

DAVID E. PROCTER

ROWMAN & LITTLEFIELD PUBLISHERS, INC.
Lanham • Boulder • New York • Toronto • Oxford

ROWMAN & LITTLEFIELD PUBLISHERS, INC.

Published in the United States of America
by Rowman & Littlefield Publishers, Inc.
A wholly owned subsidary of The Rowman & Littlefield Publishing Group, Inc.
4501 Forbes Boulevard, Suite 200, Lanham, Maryland 20706
www.rowmanlittlefield.com

P.O. Box 317, Oxford OX2 9RU, UK

The author and publisher are grateful to the following for allowing the use of excerpts from: David E. Procter, "Placing Lincoln and Mitchell Counties: A Cultural Study," *Communication Studies* 46 (Fall–Winter 1995): 222–33, reprinted with permission. Illustrations by Mary Hammel. Used with permission from the artist.

British Library Cataloguing in Publication Information Available

The hardback edition of this book was catalogued by the Library of Congress as follows:

Procter, David E.
 Civic communion : the rhetoric of community building / David E. Procter.
   p. cm.
 Includes bibliographical references and index.
 1. Community development—United States. 2. Communication in community development—United States. 3. Rural development—United States. 4. Community organization—United States. 5. Community life. I. Title

 HN90.C6P755 2005
 307.1'4—dc22

2004021118

ISBN-13: 978-0-7425-3702-6 (cloth : alk. paper)
ISBN-10: 0-7425-3702-1 (cloth : alk. paper)
ISBN-13: 978-0-7425-3703-3 (pbk. : alk. paper)
ISBN-10: 0-7425-3703-X (pbk. : alk. paper)

Printed in the United States of America

♾™ The paper used in this publication meets the minimum requirements of American National Standard for Information Sciences—Permanence of Paper for Printed Library Materials, ANSI/NISO Z39.48-1992.

To my wife, Sandy

Contents

Contents

Preface

The Speech Communication Department at Kansas State University is housed in Nichols Hall, an imposing limestone structure nicknamed "The Castle." Working behind the thick walls of Nichols Hall, it is easy to focus strictly on abstract theories of communication and remain insulated from the practical consequences those theories have on the outside world. Yet I came to Kansas State University in 1987 excited to conduct a program of research which would extend beyond the academy walls. I looked forward to getting out of my office and working across the state with real people on real issues. Indeed, the work that interested me involved helping small towns in their struggles to carve out a positive identity and to chart a path for survival. I wanted to assist small towns as they struggled to build positive communities.

As it happened, a new agency at Kansas State—the Kansas Center for Rural Initiatives (KCRI)—was organizing with a mission to assist small towns in Kansas. I introduced myself to this group and told them I would be glad to "help out." The problem was, they could not really understand what a "speech guy" had to offer them—a group interested in the practical issues of rural planning, community service, and leadership development. I persisted, continuing to offer assistance, and finally they offered me a chance to help. Since that time twelve years ago, I have worked on many projects with KCRI. I have facilitated leadership seminars, economic development conferences, rural policy conferences, and county and community strategic planning sessions. I have served as a university liaison with numerous community service student teams as they have worked with rural communities on projects ranging from main street development to the creation of promotional brochures. I have helped historical societies promote local heritage museums. I have assisted communities as they organized annual festivals and have helped small towns develop frameworks for collecting oral histories. Through my work on rural community projects, I have become convinced that communication is fundamental to building and sustaining rural community.

This book, then, is about lessons learned in community building and the role communication plays in that process. This book draws on my time at Kansas State University, the research I have conducted, and the experiences I have accumulated working with small Kansas towns. The text specifically explores the ways that communication functions to build community. It examines the variety of rhetorical forms used by a rich collection of rural Kansas citizens as they work to build, sustain, and enhance their towns. In addition, I hope this book will also say much about the Kansas people and their rural towns. They are remarkable people and their communities are remarkable places. The community-building lessons learned are not specific to Kansas, but ultimately relevant to all rural communities as they struggle to survive and thrive.

Acknowledgments

Just as it takes a village to raise a child, it takes a supportive community to author a text. Many different communities helped support and nurture this project, some well aware of their contributions, others unaware, but helpful just the same. This text could not be possible without the unfailing support of my family, especially my wife, Sandy. I appreciate the support of my colleagues at Kansas State University. They were always very positive about the importance of finishing this text. I appreciate that support as I know this project took time away from other aspects of my job. I want to thank the graduate students in my "Field Methods" classes. They formed the invaluable research teams that traveled to and studied so many small towns. I especially want to thank Erika Imbody for her wonderful assistance and careful reading of the manuscript. I also appreciated her many helpful suggestions regarding manuscript preparation. There are several rural community folks that played a significant role in this text. I want thank the Waterville Victorian Days Organizing Committee. LuAnn Roepke, Pam White, and Sandy Harding were most positive and supportive of my students working in Waterville and assisting with the Victorian Days festival. I also want to acknowledge the assistance of Jeannette Bergquist and her invaluable help with copyright issues. You say we helped you all, but you helped me far more. In Halstead, I want to thank Eva Lee Butin, Carolyn Williams, and David Flask for their assistance and help in providing perspective on the heritage museum. I want to also acknowledge and thank the people associated with the Kansas Center for Rural Initiatives. Carol Gould and Beth Tatarko were the first who were willing to take a risk on a "speech guy," enabling me to go and talk with rural citizens across the state. I also want to express special appreciation to Bob Burns, my cofacilitator at so many community meetings. I learned a great deal about group facilitation and small towns from Bob, and he made the trips to western Kansas a very enjoyable experience. I want thank the Kansas Explorers at "the Barn." So much positive energy comes from that experience that it really helped make this book possible. The diversity of people, experiences, and ideas coming from this retreat enriched the ideas of this text. I especially want to acknowledge the ideas and support I received from Moss (#2). She introduced me to so many wonderful places, people, and ideas. Marci Penner was a constant source of wonderful suggestions and unfailing support. I appreciated our talks about bringing a book to print. Finally, I want to thank the editors at Rowman & Littlefield for their support and many helpful comments. I especially appreciate the efforts of Brenda Hadenfeldt, Erica Fast, Karstin Painter, and Sara Gore.

Part I

Orientations and Beginnings

1

The Connection of
Communication and Community

The Concept of Community

As one millennium has now closed and another opened, there continues to be much thought, writing, and analysis of community. This community talk and study spans a variety of academic disciplines and is discussed from community main streets to township back streets. As national and global events often appear to spin beyond our control, we turn to our local associations for stability and grounding. We lament the loss of community and are nostalgic for an older, simpler time when everyone felt a part of his or her community. Academics and private sector practitioners advise citizens how to "create a sense of community" and "build a better community." But "community" is one of those "feel good" words that is used in a variety of ways, meaning different things to many different people (see Cohen; Gusfield, *Community*; Kemmis; Poplin; Selznick). Kenneth Wilkinson calls the meaning of community "elusive" ("In Search of the Community" 1), while Marcia Effrat offers this colorful description of the concept's evasive nature:

> Trying to study community is like trying to scoop Jell-O with your fingers. You can get hold of some, but there's always more slipping away from you. . . . Not only is the subject matter broad but it is also divided into differing camps, whose debates with one another continue heatedly and underlie much of the research being done. But the Jell-O analogy holds in this sense too, because in the process of debate the controversial issues have become mixed together in a gelatinous mess of hypotheses, research, and value judgments. (1)

Indeed, numerous scholars have articulated various conceptual schemas to try and organize thinking about community (Effrat; Gusfield, *Community*; Poplin). My purpose in this text is not to offer another cataloging of community definitions. Rather, I will discuss how various perspectives of community might be marshaled together into the service of understanding a symbolic, community-building construct. The remainder of the chapter will explore a variety of definitions of community and then weave elements of those theories together to introduce a symbolic heuristic for examining community building. A useful starting point begins with the territorial perspective of community.

Community as Territory

Community conceived as territory is the original and most traditional strand of community research (Gusfield, *Community*; Hillery; Selznick; Wilkinson, "In Search of the Community"). Thomas Bender, for example, writes "The most common sociological definitions used today tend to focus on a community as an aggregate of people who share a common interest in a particular locality. Territorially based social organization and social activity thus define a community" (5). Likewise, George Hillery argues that a "community consists of persons in social interaction within a geographic area and having one or more additional common ties" (111). Wilkinson refers to the territorial focus of community as "local ecology" and argues this perspective of community "is the original referent of the concept and the topic of the oldest and best developed body of theoretical literature" ("In Search of the Community" 3).

There are two fundamental components to the territorial conception of community. First, there is the element of physical place. In the territorial sense of the term, community is thought of "in a context of location, physical territory, geographic continuity" (Gusfield, *Community* xv). Community is used to refer to "a spatial unit, as a cluster of people living within a specific geographic region or simply as a 'place'" (Poplin 9). Thus, proximity of existence is taken as the essential element of community, and research is conducted on the community from this initial starting point.

A second element of the territorial perspective requires that individuals living in a common locale also share common interests and work to meet common needs with one another. As Amos Hawley writes, "Formally defined, community refers to the structure of relationships through which a localized population provides its daily requirements" (180). This feature of territorial community is essential. For a group of individuals to be considered a community, there must be communication which involves "communityness"—communication with and between local merchants, talk with and about community leaders, interaction with one's neighbors.

Within this subdiscipline of community study, scholars begin with a segmented territory—an administrative district, local housing development, a neighborhood, a housing subdivision, or entire city limits—identify that territory as a community, and then explore various phenomena associated with that territory that either contribute to the growth or decay of that community. According to Joseph Gusfield, the "thrust of work in this area of study is to understand what is occurring to such community entities. What is the structure of authority, of class relationships, of political governance within that area? How are these entities changing?" (*Community* xvi). Specific research areas include, but certainly are not limited to: the correlation of natural resources and community, patterns of land settlement, the social and symbolic functions the territorial community provides, local planning decisions, local power and governance structures, demographic variables characteristic of differing territorial communities, and the interaction of one geographic community with others and with larger bureaucratic organizations (e.g., metropolitan cities).

Community from the territorial perspective has been criticized on a variety of fronts (see Wilkinson, *The Community*). The most powerful argument is that proximity of location is not inherently necessary for community to exist (Bender). Certainly, our mobile society and the power of mass media fuel this position. Internet groups, professional associations, and other forms of long-distance relationships are all examples of potential communities without propinquity.

I do believe, however, the territorial focus remains an important cornerstone in community research, but agree with Kenneth Wilkinson when he writes, "The locality is the starting place for analysis because it is the point or locus of empirical convergence of the multiple threads that make up a community; but it is only a starting place" (*The Community* 27). In my research, I am interested in how rural communities—read as small towns—communicate in a pattern which enhances their chances to survive and thrive. I am not interested in strict territorial boundaries, but rather am interested in talk which is structured around a particular locality. Thus, individuals who live in areas surrounding a town, but outside the city limits, yet still go to town for various services, attend and discuss that community's events, and in some way identify with that town, would still be considered part of that town's community. Thus, the concepts of place, location, locality, and territory are essential pieces in this discussion of community development.

Community as Relational

A second community perspective interrelated with the territorial focus is community as relational. In this usage, "community is a characteristic of human relationships rather than existing in a bounded or defined group. . . . Here studies are oriented toward the ways in which group members cooperate and conflict—to the existence or absence of bonds of similarity or sympathy" (Gusfield, *Community* xvi). Poplin defines this form of community as "a condition in which human beings find themselves enmeshed in a tight-knit web of meaningful relationships with their fellow human beings" (5). This perspective of community has sometimes been referred to as "psychological" (Jason), "community of otherness" (Arnett), and as a "moral or spiritual phenomenon" (Poplin).

There are several characteristics of this community perspective that need brief discussion. An important characteristic of this form of community is one's perception or feeling or consciousness (Jason; Poplin). The perception of feeling connected, supported, secure, fulfilled, and whole, existing in a place where people feel significant and valued, is the most fundamental characteristic for community as relational (Jason 72; Poplin 6). David Minar and Scott Greer explain that community "expresses our vague yearnings for a commonality of desire, a communion with those around us" (ix) while Poplin writes that this sense of community involves "a sense of identity and unity with one's group and a feeling of involvement and wholeness on the part of the individual" (5). Indeed, Bellah et al. define community as "a group of people who are socially interdependent, who participate together in discussion and decision-making, and who share certain practices" (333).

Whereas community from a strict territorial perspective is often a value-neutral concept, relational community possesses a moral dimension. In community as territory, analyses are often descriptive and objective. Relational community, on the other hand, is cast in normative language. Interdependence is perceived as the fundamental value of psychological community. But working together on mutual projects or toward intertwined goals is not enough. For relational community to exist, the "whole person" must be connected to others. Poplin describes this community perspective as "moral community" and explains that "members of the moral community regard each other as whole persons who are of intrinsic significance and worth" (6). In Philip Selznick's definition of community, he likewise argues that "A group is a community to the extent that it encompasses a broad range of activities and interests, and to the extent that participation implicates whole persons rather than segmental interests or activities" (195).

Additionally, the normative notion of interdependence moves beyond just working together, beyond incorporating the entire person to taking responsibility for the other. This community perspective is most clearly articulated by Martin Buber in his concept of "the narrow ridge." Buber argues that "the narrow ridge is the meeting place of the human community, where an individual does not ask what can benefit himself or herself or his or her group; nor does he or she quietly acquiesce to another. The narrow ridge is a communication style that genuinely takes into account both self and other" (quoted in Arnett 36). In this perspective of interdependence, one walks a tightrope of concern for self and concern for other, embracing a dual concern for one and other.

Also characteristic of the relational community perspective is that the "feeling" of community comes from a seeking/creating process as opposed to a state objectively given. Robert Nisbet, for example, argues that one of the fundamental themes of the twentieth century is a "quest for community." Gusfield contends that community is not just a concept for social analysis, but is a goal toward which people move or from which they are repelled (*Community* 86-87). Thus, one sees texts and book chapters entitled "In Search of Community," "The Search for Ethical Community," and *The Quest for Community*.[1] Also clear in this characteristic of relational community is that one can both "find or build" community as well as "lose or destroy" community. This form of community, then, is not a static concept. It is dynamic, evolving or devolving, and gives rise to the notion that community can be constructed or destroyed. This characteristic of community also highlights the argument that familial ties and small town ties built upon tradition and nostalgia do not necessarily translate into relational community. Family biology and small-town relationships do not inherently result in concern for the whole person, respect for differences, interconnectedness, or taking responsibility for one another.

An intriguing question, then, is "How does one build community?" How does one enhance this feeling of interdependence, the care for the whole person, this relational concept of community? Whereas economic community development occurs structurally as businesses or money interests move into a segmented territory and urban development occurs physically as a locale's built environment expands, relational community development must be built symbolically. I believe that language is a fundamental component in creating a sense of community. One can explore the ways citizens in a town instill a sense of interdependence, fulfillment, and concern for one another by studying symbolic forms and cultural performances used to create those feelings of interdependence, fulfillment, and concern. There is, in fact, a research tradition that argues community is essentially a symbolic construction. The following section reviews this scholarly area.

Community as Symbolic

Within the body of research examining community, particularly relational community, scholars representing a variety of academic disciplines have argued that language is fundamental to our understanding of community. Speech communication scholars such as Walter Fisher argue that "community depends on particular forms of communication" (199) while Mara Adelman and Lawrence Frey contend that, "Ultimately, community is a social construction, grounded in the symbolic meanings and communicative practices of individuals, that fosters meaningful human interdependence in social aggregates. . . . Communication is thus the essential, defining feature . . . of community" (5). Anthropologist Anthony Cohen writes, "in so far as we aspire to understand the importance of community in people's experience, [language] is the most crucial" element (12-13) while sociologist Hugh Duncan forcefully argues, "Society arises in, and continues to exist through, the communication of significant symbols" (30).

From these general theoretical pronouncements about the importance of communication to community, the question arises, "How precisely does community arise in and exist through communication?"

A powerful answer is found in the communication theories of "communication as symbolic form" and "communication as performance." The theory of language as symbolic form argues that communication is much more than a stylistic expression of underlying ideas or artistic dressing to enhance the power of thought. Instead, as summarized by James Klumpp and Thomas Hollihan, this language theory is conceived as a voice of a social milieu rather than the symbolic property of a single speaker. Further, language is viewed as epistemic or as a creator of social values and reality. And finally, in a theory of symbolic form, language is viewed as a force that creates motivation rather than merely reflecting motivation (Klumpp and Hollihan 87-89).

When contextualized in the rhetoric of individuals working to build community, symbolic form argues that as people talk about their town, they are doing more than expressing their individual support or disgust for their locality. Symbolic form theory argues instead that citizen rhetoric about locality-oriented events and acts is the materialization of a larger synthesis of community sociopolitical beliefs and values. Further, this citizen rhetoric functions to create community belief and motivation. Community rhetors thus enact community by organizing experiences and then naming those experiences, thereby feeling communal with one another.

Communication as symbolic form is useful for its focus on language and communication that both synthesizes and generates community attitudes, beliefs, values, and motivation. Still, symbolic form theory focuses primarily on textual data generated by individual rhetors and relies on a researcher distant from the production of that rhetoric. The theory of "communication as performance" both complements symbolic form and profitably extends our understanding of symbolic community building. Communication as performance expands the act of communication to include expressive modes of communication, "framed in a special way and put on display for an audience" (Bauman 41). "Virtually any act of communication can be studied as a kind of performance" (Lindlof and Taylor 7). Data from this perspective include not only what is said, but also how communication is performed, focusing on the setting, special paraphernalia, and occasioning principles (Bauman 46). Communication as performance also expands the notion of rhetor from symbolic form theory. Rhetoric becomes the collaborative effort of performers and audience (Lindlof and Taylor 6) as individuals perform, interpret, and enact cultural scripts and audiences view, participate, interact with, and evaluate those performances (Lindlof and Taylor 25-26). Finally, communication as performance alters the researcher/researched relationship, insisting "on face-to-face encounters, instead of abstractions and reductions" (Conquergood 187).

Still, communication as performance and the theory of symbolic form are interrelated in the study of community. Initially, Bauman argues that "cultural performances tend to be the most prominent performance contexts with a commu-nity" (46) while Fuoss argues that the concept of community "is continuously negotiated in and by cultural performances, as well as other *symbolic forms*" (Fuoss 93; emphasis mine). Kirk Fuoss goes on to explain that community-orientated performances:

transact the internal and external articulation of community in two ways: by inscribing particular interpretations of community in cultural performances themselves and by enacting communal relationships in the very process of gathering for and participating in the cultural performance either as actor, audience member, or both. (82)

Thus, a study of community from the interrelated perspectives of symbolic form and performance theory would suggest examining local cultural performances for activities, behaviors, interactions, and rhetoric that articulate and enact common experiences instilling communal perceptions, attitudes, motivations, and values about the locality. While community interactions available for study are potentially unlimited, community-building literature in sociology, political science, and communication studies points scholars to a variety of locally oriented interactions that have been found to articulate and perform community. Several of these theories are briefly detailed below.

Social Interaction Theory

At the most general level is "social interaction theory," most clearly articulated by sociologist Kenneth Wilkinson. Wilkinson explains that "people, by the nature of being human, engage in social relationships with others on a continuing basis and they have their social being and identity in [social] interaction" (*The Community* 111). Further, it is this "social interaction [that] is the dynamic, creative force that redefines and articulates the relationships among actors [and comprises] the structure of the community" (*The Community* 36). Wilkinson concludes by arguing that rural community depends on purposive social interactions and actions that express a "locality-orientation" which ultimately encourage and cultivate community development (*The Community* 117-18).[2] Wilkinson's research focus directs scholars to examine any interaction between citizens in which the focus of the interaction is on some local issue or project. Under Wilkinson, potential sources of data remain vast and potentially unmanageable. A more narrow scope of interactions profitable for community-building analysis is found in the work on civic engagement by Robert Putnam.

Civic Engagement Theory

This theory, expressed most clearly in Putnam's book *Bowling Alone*, argues that "social capital"—just like physical capital or economic capital—is a fundamental building component for strong communities. Putnam explains that social capital refers to the "social networks and the norms of reciprocity and trustworthiness that arise from them" (19). Putnam argues that social capital is positively correlated with an individual's belief in community and government and urges individuals be socialized into the shared norms and cooperative societal actions of local communities. Theda Skocpol and Morris Fiorina explain that "individuals who regularly interact with one another in face-to-face settings learn to work together to solve collective problems. They gain social trust, which spills over into trust in government" (13). Putnam specifically connects social capital to community through a statement from Lyda Hanifan, one of the earliest social capital theorists. According to Hanifan:

> If [an individual] comes into contact with his neighbor, and they with other neighbors, there will be an accumulation of social capital, which may immediately satisfy his social needs and which may bear a social potentiality sufficient to the substantial improvement of living conditions in the whole community. The community as a whole will benefit by the cooperation of all its parts, while the individual will find in his associations the advantages of the help, the sympathy, and the fellowship of his neighbors. (Putnam 19)

Putnam and other adherents to social capital theory believe community building, neighborhoods, schools, the economy, government, and even individual health and happiness depend on adequate stocks of social capital and that social capital is the outgrowth of dense small group ties (27-28). The small group ties that Putnam discusses are civic associations and connections, whether those be religious groups, labor unions, professional societies, volunteering, or even community bowling leagues. According to civic engagement theorists, then, community scholars might examine actors' and audiences' interactions and performances in civic associations.

Unfortunately, Putnam and others lament that citizen participation in these forms of civic associations are on the decline, that people are not joining these types of groups in the numbers of decades ago, and that membership in these groups is aging and not being replaced with a younger generation. Robert Wuthnow, however, offers an alternative interpretation for Putnam's lament. Wuthnow notes:

> As Americans sense the fragmentation of their communities, many are now talking seriously about making connections with other people. They talk of coming together for the good of their communities, either in informal personal networks or through larger and more formal organizational partnerships. But these connections are often looser than was true in the past. Instead of cultivating lifelong ties with their neighbors, or joining organizations that reward faithful long-term service, people come together around specific needs and to work on projects that have definite objectives. (7-8)

I believe that by following Wilkinson, who argues that community is constructed through locality-oriented communication, Putnam, who believes community is performed in civic engagement, and Wuthnow, who contends citizens now come together for specific moments of civic interest, one can identify specific and significant moments of community interaction directed toward civic issues. I believe these powerful community moments can be profitably explored to examine specific rhetorical processes and cultural performances that function to build community. I label these community interactions "civic communion" and argue they are fundamentally a rhetorical and performative civic sacrament functioning to bond citizenry around the social and political structures—local ways of life, community goals, and political operations—of a specific locale.

Civic Communion

Before examining civic communion as a community-building process, it is useful to examine the more general concept of communion. Historically, communion has been thought of in association with religious rituals which "establish a bond in between the worshipers themselves and between the community of worshipers and the sacred power, be it celebrated by a sacred meal or sacrifice or any verbal or nonverbal ritual of a human community sharing a special relation to a nonhuman counterpart" (Nubel). The most common religious communion is the Christian sacrament of the Lord's Supper.

Martin Marty, religion professor at the University of Chicago and the senior editor of *The Christian Century*, argues there are "two basic features of the Christian sacrament—words and elements, both received in faith" (37). Each of these features function to join parishioners closer to one another and to the message of God. Words are most often given by church leaders—ministers, priests, liturgists, or church elders—and used in a way to bring the faith community together. The words are expressed in prayers of preparation, thanksgiving, and reflection. Words are given in "ancient readings [that] serve to help develop the plot and draw people in it. Those who hear [the words] will therefore have more in common at the subsequent meal" (Marty 35). Words are also exchanged in moments "of offering peace to one another—greetings, small talk, hand shaking, embraces. These giving gestures of peace [bring] people into a vivid sense of union" (Marty 43).

When Marty mentions "the elements," he is referring to the communion meal—breaking bread and drinking wine. The congregation participates in the meal. No act brings one closer to others than this act of communing and participating in Holy Communion. Marty contends that the communion "meal is an activity. On one level, what follows is like a very slow dance, choreographed to match solemn movements. . . . The people have their steps to take, as do the leaders" (42).Likewise Emerson Colaw argues that taking communion in an attitude of prayer provides a moment of fellowship with the global faith community, both past and present. Communion participants remember the great company of Christians of all ages who have followed Christ. Communion is also a moment when church members recall and renew their own faith journey (80-82).

Holy communion, then, provides a moment of reflection and renewal of one's commitment to spiritual truths. Its purpose is to create a bond between the believer, the faith community, and spiritual deity. The communion is accomplished by an exchange of important words and participation in ritualized religious activity. I believe there are important similarities between religious and secular communion. In fact, the general characteristics of Holy Communion serve to assist our understanding of community building through secular civic communion.[3] Many scholars have, in fact, connected communion as a celebration of faith to the celebration of localized community (Kato; Schmalenbach; Wilkinson, *The Community*). In its most general form, then, civic communion is the secular analog to Christian communion.

It is a conscious, collective, and emotional secular response to existing community structures (Schmalenbach 332), a "consciousness of community and joyful response to the relationships that are realized" (Wilkinson, *The Community* 74). I believe that by examining the scholarly writings of sociologists, psychologists, communication scholars, anthropologists, and community planning scholars, a useful framework for exploring the community-building process of locality emerges. I label this community-building heuristic "civic communion." As a symbolic framework, civic communion is characterized by several structural and rhetorical elements.

Initially, civic communion is distinct from community. While "community" is some preexisting bounded locality or a state of relational or symbolic connectedness, civic communions are symbolic moments which create or celebrate those existing communal structures (Wilkinson, *The Community* 74-75). Civic communions are performative community moments that transform citizens' latent responses to a locality into collective, emotional, and rhetorical support for local communal structures that eventually become recognized as "community." For example, community communication is routinely organized into performances that celebrate the community and that citizens recognize as naturally appropriate to their town (e.g., local festivals, community debates, celebration of public works' projects, strategic planning). Citizens subsequently participate in legitimizing these performances by assisting in the creation and perpetuation of that form (e.g., volunteering to organize or assist with the festivals, parades, rituals). They further legitimize the symbolic structures of their community by participating in that symbolic activity (e.g., watching the parade, scouring festival booths for items to purchase, playing patriotic tunes in the city band, engaging in public debate, participating in community planning). As citizens work to create and participate in the community performances, they also communicate with fellow citizens. This communication displays their membership as a cultural agent in the community (Carbaugh 198). The performative civic communions possess both structural and rhetorical characteristics.

Structurally, civic communions are collective, public, yet transitory events. Just as religious communion involves the congregation as a faith community passing bread and drink from one to another, and listening and reacting to religious leaders, civic communions involve groups of citizens performing and interacting together to create and celebrate secular community. Civic communions are initiated, organized, directed, and facilitated by community evangelists—either interested locals or outside community agencies. These individuals may be political leaders, economic developers, leaders of a civic organization, or simply an individual with a passionate vision of the community. Civic communions are collective, however, and are thus dependent on the willful and emotional participation of a group of interested citizens (Schmalenbach 339). In fact, Wilkinson argues that a greater number of participating citizens, local groups, and associations leads to a greater sense of legitimacy for the communal celebration of local social and political structures ("Phases and Roles" 57).

Further, civic communions are segmented, yet transitory moments of community celebration. Just as Christian communion is a special and segmented moment in a church service, civic communions are likewise special and bracketed moments of community celebration. Bauman argues these cultural performances "tend to be *scheduled*, set up and prepared for in advance" (46; emphasis Bauman). These communions may be planned, taking the form of an annual public festival or community celebration or community strategic planning session. They may be more spontaneous and take the form of some emergent community conflict or communal response to a local tragedy. The communions are, however, not ongoing. According to Wilkinson, these types of community actions occur "intermittently, if at all, when a common interest in place-relevant matters is aroused" (*The Community* 37). Civic communions may take several weeks or months to plan and work through, but eventually they come to some public and recognized conclusion. They are, as Bauman suggests, "*temporally bounded*, with a defined beginning and end" (46; emphasis Bauman). A community festival concludes—its booths disassembled, the community banners put away until next year. Community strategic planning comes to a recognized conclusion and the community proceeds to implement the plan's action steps. Public conflict subsides, if only briefly, following some public community decision. While often intensely emotional during their existence, civic communions are not ongoing events.

Rather than conceiving of community as some preconstituted category, as some given thing in itself, as a static, unchanging condition, community is instead a rhetorically contested and emergent process, a phenomenon continually in flux (Gusfield, *Community* 30; Procter, "The Dynamic Spectacle" 130). Community is a concept that seems to need some "discursive common place" (Lohmann 138), a center of interest, or some nucleus to shape its character (Scott 75). Martin Buber, for example, argues that community is "a community of choice around a common center, the voluntary coming together of person's in direct relationship" (Arnett viii). Likewise, Michael Walzer argues that "civil society" names "the space of uncoerced human association and also the set of relational networks—formed for the sake of family, faith, interest, and ideology—that fill this space" (7).

Civic communions function as the organizational and rhetorical "space" where civic relationships occur, a "common center" where people voluntarily come together for civic association, and as a nucleus that gives shape to the performance of community. But essential to the "common center" characteristic of civic communion is the ethical nature of that space. In other words, it is not enough for communities to create discursive space or to establish some event where citizens come together for talk. Rather, civic communions are ethical spaces characterized by "multi-vocality," "voluntarily coming together" (Arnett viii), "uncoerced human association" (Walzer 7), "mutual respect" (Oliver 9), "openness," "noncontractual cooperation," and "the lack and removal of repression" (Bakan 15). Civic communions are thus community-coalescing events that establish an open and ethical rhetorical space for creating, crystallizing, and organizing community-building talk for brief and intense moments.

Importantly, these community events are also fundamentally rhetorical. Just as church leaders recall important texts and parables that function to connect the faith community and guide religious behavior, civic leaders recall important historic texts, people, and events that ultimately serve to solidify community identity and offer guides to appropriate civic values and practices. Civic communions are purposive, goal-oriented interactions, involving rhetorical choice as organizers and citizens celebrate some features of community while devaluing or ignoring others.

Rhetorically, communion is a means of connection. Communion has been variously described as "the sense of being at one with another organism" (Bakan 15), a "feeling of togetherness or of affinity" (Oliver 9), "shared reality" (Cooper 336), and as the "recognition of a mutual sense of belonging" (Wilkinson, *The Community* 16). Kenneth Burke talks of communion and connection as a process of identification. "Insofar as the thing and its name correspond," Burke argues, "in that very correspondence, there is a kind of perfect communication (or more accurately 'communion'). . . . It is the name for the principle of identity between thing and name" (*The Rhetoric of Religion* 166). In his essay, "Auscultation, Creation, and Revision," Burke again writes that "man desiring 'communion-in-absolute' might symbolize this by imaginings of junction" (42).

Civic communions function to both connect and solidify internal community groups. Schmalenbach, for example, argues that "every experience of communion has the effect of establishing communal bonds" (337). These communal bonds are created partly by the performative act of citizens gathering and working together on some group project and thus feeling a sense of connection toward one another and their locale. But civic communions also generate communal feelings through the emotional rhetoric produced in creating, sustaining, and/or participating in the event. Civic communions produce rhetoric highlighting certain symbols, certain histories, certain values, and certain experiences that causes citizens to feel a kinship or identification with some communal groups. Thomas Cooper calls communion "core creative communication" which fosters "a social camaraderie" and "increases bonding and group identity" (342) while James Mackin argues, "Epideictic rhetoric supports the joy of identification in ceremonial events that reify bonds of trust and sanctify the group" (251).

Aside from identifying and building communal groups, civic communions also function to organize those groups hierarchically. As Hugh Duncan argues, the creation of community is symbolic and always expressed in some kind of hierarchy (33). Civic communions are symbolic events in celebration of some community. In celebrating local community, it is impossible to equally value or validate all communities within that territorial locale. Economic interests, ecological interests, tourism interests, historical interests, and individual interests cannot be equally highlighted or valued in community celebration. While dramatically enacting community celebration, civic communions naturally value some local interests and devalue others. As one community is celebrated or created, another is denigrated or destroyed. Fuoss explains:

> When a social drama occurs, certain of the externally articulated communities or internally articulated positions within a community are highlighted . . . and imbued

with a heighted intensity. Participants in a social drama tend to distinguish between "us" and "them," "inside" and "outside," "ally" and "opposition." (82)

Civic communions are intense, yet transitory moments of collective and enthusiastic praise for desired or existing community ideals and sociopolitical structures. This praise of community functions to connect citizens, provide an identity to them and their community, spotlight local community groups, and organize those groups into some sociopolitical community hierarchy.

The Need for Research

Community Research

Sociologist Kenneth Wilkinson notes that some scholars "would argue today that *community* is only a romantic term for a way of life long since passed in the progress of civilization" (*The Community* 1; emphasis Wilkinson). Indeed, this area of research faces many challenges. For well over a century, sociologists have argued that the idea of community has faded with the rise of industrial society. Durkheim and others would argue that people now look to large metropolitan areas as places where social and economic needs are met. Scholars have further contended that as mass communications have proliferated, local networks of friends, businesses, and voluntary associations have diminished in importance, thereby weakening local community bonds. The conclusion of these scholars is that people no longer depend on local networks for any kind of need.

Despite these criticisms, I believe, our communities remain important to both citizens and scholars. People from around the world and from all stations of life mourn the weakening of community and work toward building a sense of community. Whether as local as organizing a neighborhood watch group or as global as writing a text that argues it takes a village to raise a child, it is clear people yearn for community connections. Wilkinson, for example, argues:

> [T]he community has not disappeared and has not ceased to be an important factor in individual and social well-being. People still live together in places, however fluid might be the boundaries of those places. They still encounter the larger society primarily through interactions in the local society. And, at crucial moments, they still can act together to express common interests in the place of resident. (*The Community* 6)

From Wilkinson's statement, there are good reasons to continue research on community development. Initially, the community is where individuals witness and establish important connections. While the primary interactional relationship remains the family, the community is the next most important arena of social interaction (Wilkinson, "In Search of the Community" 3). Community presents a broad range of interpersonal contacts in which individuals engage—communicating with one's neighbors, the banker, the grocer, the plumber, the city commissioner. The community is an important setting for establishing associational competencies.

Further, community helps develop one's sense of self. George Mead and other symbolic interactionists argue that "self" is an interactional phenomenon consisting of the identification of the person in specific interactional relationships with others and in relationship with the "generalized other" or community (see Denton; Wilkinson, *The Community*). A more clear understanding of one's own value system develops within community. As people work beside friends, help neighbors, and interact with local businesses, values of cooperation, friendship, trust, and service are realized. As citizens watch and participate in local life, other civic values are learned. Values such as tolerance of diversity, generosity of spirit, fairness to others, and grace are also modeled by their presence or their vacuity in communities. Civic education is also most immediately learned in community. Individuals realize that local government decisions can have a direct impact on their lives, whether governmental decisions come in the form of higher or lower taxes, attracting local business, or enacting environmental decisions. Citizens can also most easily participate in political activity at the local level. Writing letters to the local newspaper, voting in local elections, running for the school board or city commission, forming neighborhood watch committees, or organizing local petitions are all more accessible to people at the community level. Citizens have the greatest opportunity to effect political change at the community level and therefore are likely to view their community as more politically efficacious than their state or national political system.

Rural Community Research

While the general concept of community certainly demands further study, the specific arena of rural community also remains a critical research area. There is no doubt that rural communities face many difficult problems. Recent stories in the *New York Times* and *U.S. News and World Report* chronicle the challenges facing rural America. Seemingly intractable problems ranging from declining population bases to a lack of social services to school closings to an absence of job opportunities face many rural communities (Glasser; Kilborn). According to Janet Fitchen, "Many rural spaces, the settings of rural life, are now endangered by a variety of societal forces. Some rural places, the social matrices of rural life, are now in serious stress or decline, and some will disappear" (2).

Without a sufficient base of resources centralized in a particular locality, rural residents must either do without many services and opportunities or travel great distances to have those needs met. Health care, education, the arts, government services, recreation, groceries, and trade are just a few of the needs that are often in limited supply in rural areas. Physical isolation also presents its own array of problems. Face-to-face interaction is often limited; networks of friends and support groups are in short supply. As Wilkinson reports, "In some cases . . . outside contacts are limited for most residents, producing insularity and rural malaise" (*The Community* 114). Ruralness can also lead to a lack of diversity in terms of opportunities and people. Rural communities are often characterized by a homogenous population, which can lead to an intolerance of differences.

In addition, rural community continues to be threatened by outside forces. National and international markets reorganize the demands for local products and services. Increasingly, it seems, corporate America consolidates factories, moving plants, and personnel to larger metropolitan cities or offshore to some third world country. Small and family farms face increasing competition from corporate farming, finding it increasingly difficult to survive on land that may have been in their families for generations. As family farms disappear, the local feed stores, hardware stores, small churches, and schools also begin to disappear (Miller 65).

The urban environment also possesses many attractions in the form of the arts, sporting events, employment opportunities, varieties of food, and interactions with diverse peoples. It is not surprising, then, when some rural citizens decide to move to these more urban areas.

Despite these challenges, rural research remains important for a number of reasons. It is important to understand rural community for epistemic, symbolic, and pragmatic reasons.

Initially, it is possible to better know American society generally if we have a more clear understanding of the particulars of rural community. Our knowledge of American society is fundamentally grounded in rural community images. As James Robertson writes, "The norms of American society were rural and agricultural. The myths which have given vivid images, controlling metaphors, and substance to what Americans believe community to be are the myths of rural, small-town, agrarian communities" (218). Further, Eric Zencey argues for a cultural epistemology "rooted" in local place and rural community. Zencey wonders, "how can a student appreciate our [national culture] if they have no knowledge of how they themselves are tied to locale and time?" (17). Likewise, Thomas Averill argues that "to know a place intimately is to have a way of knowing. To learn respect for a single place is to learn to transfer respect to all places close to people's hearts" (9). Daniel Kemmis also makes a connection between a locale and particular epistemology to understanding political culture when he argues that "the strengthening of political culture . . . must take place and must be studied in the context of very specific places and of the people who struggle to live well in those places" (7).

But rural communities are also important symbolically. Rural America is very important in the mythology that is the United States. Robertson argues that "the almost monolithic view of society contained in the mythology of the rural small town, has served, and still serves, several important [mythic] functions" (219). Robertson argues that the mythology of rural communities symbolically functions in three interrelated ways. Initially, rural mythology serves as "a foil to individualism: the belief in a stable and fixed society makes it possible to emphasize near-anarchic individualism without risking the destruction of the social fabric" (219).

Robertson believes that by perceiving community as a relatively static, solid, and foundational concept, Americans have the zest to pursue individualism. He further contends that "tension between the belief in individual freedom and the belief in social conformity is one of the great generators of energy" in America (219).

The myth of rural communities also functions in a second way to "provide a sense of secure, unchanging rootedness in a society of the uprooted" (Robertson 219). Rural communities are perceived as less transient and more stable than urban communities, with families calling the same farm or the same area home for generations (Fitchen 253-55). It is the perception that rural communities represent a slower, calmer, and safer environment in which to live and raise families. Rural America stands as the symbolic refuge of stability—stability of family, of values, of dreams.

Finally, rural mythology serves as a constant symbol of the democratic nature of American society (Robertson 219). As argued earlier, democracy is viewed most clearly at the local level. Civic participation and the consequences of that participation are readily apparent at the level of the small town. Robertson argues that by participating in, or at least viewing, politics at this level, "Americans continue to believe that the whole society is democratic" (219).

Pragmatically, rural community demands study as there are a significant number of people carving out their lives in rural America. There are millions of rural people paying taxes, raising families, struggling to "make a life," and participating in the civic life of their small towns. Understanding and strengthening local community structures becomes one way to assist these rural citizens. Fitchen explains that "Though rural individuals will continue to struggle with the stresses of change that are sweeping across rural America, they can do so more effectively if they are embedded in and supported by a strong community, for the outcome of the struggle is often determined by the characteristics of the community in which the individual lives" (279).

Further, the rural living arena represents a special condition of the heart. It is a life created out of expansive dreams, rich histories, and sublime and rugged landscapes. Despite the significant hardships of rural life, Peter Kilborn reports that "the pioneer spirit still glows" in rural America ("Bit by Bit"). As Lynn Miller writes, rural communities "can be wonderful repositories for the intertwining lives of good people offering strength and collective forms and pieces of identity to all who are fortunate enough to be a part" and that small towns "offer [an] opportunity to reverse the conditions of collective human misery" (65). Fitchen concludes that "The preservation of rural America, not as a romantic 'living museum' but as a viable alternative to other patterns of living, should be an important issue for the nation" (280).

Imperative in this search to locate a path for sustaining rural community is the symbolic creation of a strong and positive identity (Fitchen 263; Selznick 197). Indeed, as Ivan Karp argues, "For communities, the struggle over identity is vital to their existence: they often feel that they live or die to the degree that they are accorded or denied social space" ("Introduction: Museums and Communities" 14). In his essay, "Rethinking Community Development," Jnanabrata Bhattacharyya argues that when working to develop community, citizens, scholars, and practitioners should look for ways to increase group solidarity, to enhance a group's "shared identity and code of conduct" (61). Bhattacharyya continues by arguing that any community development must promote ways for people to "define themselves as opposed to being defined by others" (61). I believe an examination of civic communion offers insight into how citizens create a strong rural identity. By studying moments of civic communion, one can not only specifically examine the symbolic process of community building, but can also view those communal structures—organizational, social, and symbolic—that form the basis of local community. Civic communions may be manifest in any number of activities or events, but those that are most successful celebrate community structures that enable to local community utilize its strengths and integrate itself into the social and economic forces of the new millennium. This text, then, is an exploration and examination of some of the civic communions constructed by rural Kansans as they seek to build and energize their communities.

Preview of Chapters

This text is divided into three parts. The first part, chapters 1 and 2, provides epistemological orientation. Chapter 1 has introduced the general concept of community, reviewing it from territorial and relational perspectives. This chapter has also introduced the theoretical perspective that guides this work, namely that community is fundamentally a symbolic construction. Further, this chapter has argued that the symbolic construction of community is best examined from the interrelated communication theories of symbolic form and performance studies. Finally, by combining theoretical work from sociologists, political scientists, speech communication scholars, and community planners, chapter 1 has introduced the idea of exploring specific and significant moments of community interaction—"civic communion"—which citizens use to perform, build, and strengthen their communities. Chapter 2 discusses my orientation to the study of rural community and ethnographic research. The chapter argues that ethnographic research is a journey toward knowledge and understanding. Chapter 2 highlights moments in my journey as a rural community ethnographer, arguing that critical moments in my history have been formative to the perspective I take in this research endeavor and to the methods I use when exploring rural community.

The text's second part, chapters 3 through 7, illustrates the symbolic process of rural community building through a variety of case studies. Each case study explores a different moment of civic communion through which rural citizens perform local community. Each chapter in this section offers: (1) a brief introduction to the central issue of the chapter; (2) a discussion of the specific field research methods used in that chapter; (3) an explanation of how the context functions as civic communion; and finally (4) an analysis of the community structures and community identity affirmed by the specific civic communion.

Chapter 3 explores the community festival as a mode of civic communion. Waterville, Kansas's production of their Victorian Days festival provides an exemplar of how community festivals might be used by women as an agency of community power. Chapter 4 examines the way citizens of Lincoln and Mitchell counties in Kansas tell their community story through a series of strategic planning meetings. Through the civic communion of the planning process, citizens in these rural counties use the unique geographical character of their region to create their community identity. Chapter 5 studies public conflict as civic communion. Manhattan, Kansas, engaged in a heated debate to determine whether a religious monolith could appropriately remain in front of city hall. That conflict has functioned to highlight competing visions of community. Each vision is really an argument for a different community identity. This community conflict was finally resolved through a recall election of one city commissioner. The creation and presentation of a historical museum is examined as an example of civic communion in chapter 6. The Halstead Heritage Museum and Depot is used as the case study. This chapter argues that the museum functions not only to build local collective memory in Halstead, but also functions to reify the national myth of individual success. Chapter 7 examines the spiritual community-building rhetoric of the Kansas Sampler Foundation. This private, nonprofit foundation is external to local communities, yet it functions as a powerful catalyst for civic communions.

The third and final part of this text, composed of chapter 8, synthesizes lessons learned from part II about the symbolic process of community building. The chapter summarizes civic communion as a cultural performance, explores the rhetorical commonalities that span the case studies presented in part II, discusses the importance of conducting this form of research, and ponders where future symbolic community studies might proceed.

Notes

1. See for example, Ronald C. Arnett, "The Search for Ethical Community," in *Communication and Community* (Carbondale: Southern Illinois University Press, 1986), 95-110; Joseph R. Gusfield, "The Search for Community," in *Community* (New York: Harper and Row, 1975), 83-106; Robert Nisbet, *The Quest for Community* (New York: Oxford University Press, 1953); Philip Selznick, "In Search of Community," in *Rooted in the Land*, eds. William Vitek and Wes Jackson (New Haven, CT: Yale University Press, 1996), 195-206; and Kenneth Wilkinson, "In Search of the Community in the Changing Countryside," in *The Community in Rural America* (New York: Greenwood Press, 1991), 109-18.

2. According to Kenneth Wilkinson, "an action process may be regarded as locality-oriented if (1) the principle actors and beneficiaries are local residents, (2) the goals represent interests of local residents, and (3) the action is public, as opposed to private, in the sense that beneficiaries include other persons in addition to the actors." See Kenneth P. Wilkinson, "Phases and Roles in Community Action," *Rural Sociology* 35 (1970): 57.

3. Holy Communion is not the only religious sacrament connected to a secular setting. Daniel Kemmis argues that many community gatherings and celebrations function as the secular equivalent of baptism. He argues that there exists a symbolic asking and receiving both of blessing new citizens and a commitment from the community to take responsibility for maturing the new member into a full member of the community. See Daniel Kemmis, *The Good City and the Good Life* (New York: Houghton Mifflin Company, 1995), 48-49.

2

In Search of
Rural Community

This work represents both an academic and personal journey. It is an academic journey in search of symbolic paths rural citizens use to build and sustain their communities. This academic argument explores how small towns and rural citizens use various language and rhetorical strategies to preserve, position, and promote their communities. However, this project also represents a personal journey, a journey that began long before I came to Kansas State University, long before I began to work with and study rural Kansas communities. My journey began early, even though I was unaware of it, as I grew up in rural communities in Kansas and Missouri, traversed through my graduate work at the University of Nebraska-Lincoln, and continues today through my work with the Kansas Center for Rural Initiatives, the Kansas Sampler Foundation, and my independent rural community work. The paths of my academic sojourn and personal journey, while circuitous, have ultimately intersected, affording me the opportunity, perspective, and skills to work as a rural community ethnographer.

In this chapter, I share some of the important mileposts of my life journey and discuss how these experiences speak to important field research issues. Increasingly, field researchers are writing explicitly about their personal history and that history's interaction with cultural investigation.[1] This fieldwork methodology, often referred to as confessional tales or autoethnography, "is an explication of lived experience and encounters within a specified cultural context which combines self-reflection of autobiography and the intense scrutiny of 'other' as found in ethnography" (Alexander 309).[2] These ethnographic texts candidly discuss "how the fieldwork odyssey was accomplished by the researcher" (Van Maanen 75), including an "explicit examination of one's own preconceptions, biases, and motives" (Van Maanen 93). Additionally, one's character—fixed demographic characteristics, life history, and personal choices—as it interacts with the culture under investigation becomes a component of that investigation. Autoethnographic scholars reflexively explore how interaction with the studied culture both facilitates and impedes one's ethnographic research.

Indeed, my academic and life journeys have often progressed schizophreni-cally—at once preparing me for and pulling me into the study of rural community while at other times my very preparation has functioned to separate me profession-ally and intellectually from the rural culture I hoped to study. According to Lindlof and Taylor, competence in "[o]bserving and participating usually work in concert, even if not always seamlessly. As a result, researchers' competence develops in two parallel paths: (1) They become increasingly skilled at performing in ways that are honored by group members, and (2) they create increasingly sharp, detailed, and theoretically relevant descriptions" (135). This image is not totally accurate. I believe skills in cultural performance and skills in cultural research often develop in obverse directions, locating the ethnographer in a fundamental liminality (Lionnet 92). As academics are trained to see and create theoretically informed descriptions of indigenous cultures, that very training can isolate the ethnographer and restrict the researcher's ability to relate and empathize with that culture. The language and performance necessary to navigate the academy is not the language and perfor-mance necessary to easily traverse a studied culture. Lyall Crawford speaks to this concern when he writes of his field research with a Taoist commune. Upon reflection, Crawford found his work "inhibited by too many 'received ideas' about the procedures of 'legitimate' fieldwork and my own unwillingness to surrender fully to the scene" (165). Kenneth Burke refers to this as "trained incapacity" or a condition he attributes largely to the ways in which received forms of knowing operate on the perceptions and understandings of its users (*Symbols and Society* 31).

In this chapter, I discuss my academic and rural culture interactions, hopefully illustrating how these two learning journeys have at times proceeded in a complementary fashion, and how at other times, these two education paths have served inimical purposes. Victor Turner writes that "Each of us has had certain 'experiences' which have been formative and transformative, that is, distinguish-able, isolable sequences of external events and internal responses to them" (35). This chapter is divided into three sections, each relating a formative and transforma-tive experience in my search for rural community. Embedded in these formative experiences, however, are grounds of tension between my academic training and my performance in and examination of rural culture. The first section is a recollection of my early rural experiences which provided a base of understanding for rural culture. The second section explores several critical moments in my graduate school experience which provided theoretical and methodological frameworks to examine and discuss rural community. The third section discusses a most timely encounter with a rural community-building agency and how my relationship with that agency illustrates the importance of role development in field research.

Eldon, Olean, and Spring Hill:
Experiencing Rural America

D. Jean Clandinin and F. Michael Connelly argue that "Experience is . . . the starting point and key term" (414) for social research. They continue by explaining more precisely that one of these starting points begins with the telling of "the researcher's own narrative of experience" (418). This section recalls my early salient experiences in rural Missouri and Kansas. Embedded within these narratives of rural life are stories of the beginning of an ethnographic life.

Some of my earliest memories are about traveling to my grandparents' homes to spend time on their farms and in the small towns of Eldon and Olean (pronounced O Lee ANN), Missouri. My family spent nearly every holiday as well as part of each summer of my youth in the hills of the Missouri Ozarks. I knew we were getting close to my grandparents' homes when the asphalt of State Highway 87 turned into the rock and dirt roads of Miller County. As we drove along on these narrow, winding, and hilly roads, my parents would acknowledge each family farm we passed as if we were greeting our extended Missouri family. "Well, there's the Max Atkisson place," my parents would announce. "There's the Thorsen farm." "There's Sullens. I wonder how those two ole' bachelors are getting along?" "Look at Val Farmer's place. It's a sin the way he takes care of that house." "Doesn't the Mount Herman church look nice? They've really fixed it up." "There's Elisha White's place. His farm always looks so neat." "There's Halderman's farm." "There's the Wilson place. Jack Wilson has been working on that house for years now. Is he ever gonna finish?" We're almost to grandma's now. "Hey, there's Luther and Maggie Hader's place. I wonder how Maggie's gettin' along?" It just seemed natural that my parents knew each farmer along this crooked stretch of rocky road. As they talked about each family farmstead, I came to view these families as old friends and part of our extended family.

I regularly visited my relatives in the Ozarks. I went everywhere with my grandparents, great-aunts, aunts, uncles, and cousins. I would watch, listen, and participate in what seemed an embracing community. Everywhere we went, people seemed to know my extended family and treated me like I was just one more part of this rural community. Whether we were putting up hay on the farm, building fence, eating Thanksgiving dinner, attending church socials at the Mount Herman or Greenridge Baptist Church, riding the Ferris wheel at the Miller County fair, cruising Eldon's main street with my teenage cousins, or sneaking into Ruby's Pool Hall and Bar in downtown Olean, there seemed to be a network of people who were helpful, friendly, and caring toward my family and me.

If a work project needed attention, a group of those same farmers we hailed on our way to my grandparents came by to lend a hand. As my Grandpa Bill often said, "Many hands make light work." And there were always many hands. Neighbors and relatives would help my grandfather build fence, butcher hogs and cattle, put up hay, and cut wood for winter stoves.[3] Likewise, Thanksgiving and Christmas dinners were major productions, and the homes were full of cousins, aunts, great-aunts, grandmothers, friends, neighbors, and farmworkers all working together to produce and enjoy a special meal.

The same group of people who assisted my grandparents with work were there for social events and recreation. Fishing, for example, was a communal event. My mother's family loved to fish in their farm pond. My Grandpa Roark, Uncle Kenneth, and Great-Aunts Drucie and Lois would spend a couple of days just planning the event. My job was to dig the worms from underneath the woodpile outside the farmhouse. My uncle's job was to bring the store-bought lures as well as a backup supply of "bait shop" worms in case I failed my worm harvesting task. My great-aunts would bring the handwoven cane stools for everyone to sit on while my grandmother would make sandwiches and a jug of iced tea. On fishing day, we would all meet at the grainery and walk the winding trail through a grove of towering oak and walnut trees. We would pass by the gnarly bramble of blackberry bushes, open the rusty barbed-wire gate, and spread out along the bank of the tree-shaded pond. We would spend all morning fishing a little and talking and joking a lot. After all the planning, catching fish was secondary to hearing the latest news and telling big stories. There was nothing I enjoyed more as a young boy than lying on the warm bank of the pond, watching the float bob slowly over the rippling water, listening to my relatives and their friends talk and joke. Still, as I relaxed on the edge of the pond, listening to the latest Eldon news, I was also receiving an education about appropriate and inappropriate values and behaviors. I heard about the latest deeds and misdeeds of locals. From the stories and jokes, appropriate and inappropriate behaviors were quite clear.

It seemed only natural, then, that my family would also live in a small town. My father worked for the Sante Fe railroad, switching boxcars at the Argentine rail yards in Kansas City, Kansas. Yet he decided that he wanted to raise his family not in the Kansas City suburbs, but in Spring Hill—a small community of about 2,000 located thirty miles south of K.C. Just as I felt embraced by the farming communities in Eldon and Olean, Missouri, I also felt a part of the community of Spring Hill, Kansas.

I often walked from our home on the far west side of Spring Hill to downtown Spring Hill—a walk of about one mile. On my way downtown, I recognized and would often talk with neighbors, teachers, classmates, and friends. Once downtown—a full one block of businesses—I could do business with the local merchants, all of whom I knew by name. I could buy tools at Cade's Hardware or deposit my lawn mowing money with Neal Janicke in the State Bank of Spring Hill. I could visit Mr. Neff's soda fountain and drink cherry phosphates or go buy aspirin and vitamins at Loren Locke's pharmacy. I could buy jeans and shirts at Poisel's Dry Goods Store or milk and bread at Kuhn's IGA. I could get my hair cut at

Brownie's barber shop, listening to the latest Spring Hill gossip, or go hang out at the Spring Hill Pool Hall.

Still, there were times I confronted the limitations and darkness of rural communities. Small towns and rural areas are limiting in many ways.[4] Educational opportunities, for example, can be limited. We moved to Spring Hill when I was a freshman in high school. As a freshman, I enrolled in a drawing class and loved the experience. The teacher was young, energetic, very connected with her students, and gone after one year. The art program was summarily cut. Spring Hill, we were told, could not afford the luxury of a peripheral academic program. I subsequently moved toward speech and drama, participating in debate, individual events, and theater. The debate coach, Mr. McCrory, was a wonderful man—fun, motivating, compassionate. I came to realize, however, that not only was he the debate coach, he was also the theater director, the English teacher, the scenic designer, the speech teacher, and the costume designer. He was also gay and ultimately fired.

In addition to being isolated and insulated, rural communities can be places of traditional and conservative gender, racial, and ethnic beliefs.[5] One of the most interesting traditions at my mother's family illustrates these very traditional gender roles. At every large family meal—Sunday-after-church dinner, Thanksgiving dinner, Christmas, etc.—females would prepare the food. They would cook, bake, and set the table. When all was ready, all the family males would take their place at the large dinner table and eat. I remember sitting at the large dining room table surrounded by my grandfather, dad, brother, uncles, and male cousins eating the hot, delicious food as it came out of the ovens and off the stoves. The youngest of boys to the most elderly of men ate first. Only when the males had finished eating and left the table would the females sit down to eat. This was a tradition that had started many years earlier when my male relatives and hired men worked the fields. At the prescribed mealtime, they would come in to a prepared lunch or dinner. They would eat and return to the fields. At that point, the women would eat and clean up. The goal was to facilitate the male time and work schedule. Interestingly, this tradition continued up until my grandfather died in 1983, long after the farm was no longer the primary source of income, and field workers were long gone.

I saw very few people of color as I grew up in in the rural Ozarks. The few black families who did live in the area lived in the shadows of Olean and Eldon, literally hidden both physically and socially. While my grandparents and relatives lived in very modest farmhouses, local black families lived in backwoods houses that could only be described as shacks and shanties. Socially, blacks were also barely recognized. As I grew up, these families were routinely referred to as the "nigger Jones family" or the "nigger Washington family." I remember my mother once chastising my grandmother for her blunt and racist language. Another time, I was at a service station in Eldon and a young African American boy came by and asked if he could get a drink from the water fountain. The response, "Be quick about it and then get outta here boy," was blunt and brusque.

My past rural community experiences are imminently relevant for my current scholarly work. They are part of a constellation of experiences providing attitudinal and methodological orientations to my rural culture studies. As Maria Gonzalez argues, "all experience . . . becomes related to [one's] ethnographic study" (16). Bud Goodall concurs, "We are, at any given moment, the sum total only of what we have become. Our past is always with us, our family dynamic always a source of what we see in relationships, what we believe to be true as much as any theory" (*Living in the Rock N Roll Mystery* 169).

As I now reflect on my childhood past and my experiences with small towns, I strongly believe these early experiences were part of my rural community research sojourn. My early family and social experiences now color my attitudinal orientation to rural culture. These early experiences provided me with knowledge, understanding, empathy, and access to rural culture. But these same experiences also foreground fissures of difference between rural culture and me. I have witnessed firsthand the strengths and drawbacks to rural life. From my experiences, I have an intimate understanding of the importance of rural family and a direct knowledge of the incredible hard work done by rural citizens. I know about the deep religious convictions held by rural Americans. My experiences have enabled me to empathize with citizens of rural areas, to understand issues salient in their lives, and have equipped me with the language of rural America. These same early experiences, however, have served to highlight an attitudinal difference existing between many rural citizens and me. As I grew up, I became more interested in traditional urban activities—debate, theater, golf—and less interested in traditional rural activities—hunting, 4-H, car racing. My relatives and friends would sometimes only half-jokingly chastise me for not participating in derogatory racial or gender-oriented narratives and jokes. I was also interested in pursuing higher education. As a young boy, I longed to go to college. Indeed, I was the first in my extended family and one of only six in my graduating high school class of seventy-three to attend college. Seeking advanced degrees, however, only further set me apart from my rural heritage.

Yet, by growing up in a variety of small towns, the rural community context—their issues, perspectives, attitudes, prejudices, and values—became a part of my self. I was socialized in small town life. I came to understand and respect, yet remain somewhat wary, of rural life. I acquired not only rural community experiences, but also a rural community language to articulate those experiences.

Beyond forming attitudes, my early rural experiences have also been important to my scholarly role as a cultural ethnographer. As Steven Taylor and Robert Bogdan write, "Participant observers enter the field with the hope of establishing open relationships" with members of the community (32). These scholars suggest a number of research techniques to establish open relationships including, "getting to know the setting and the people" (32), "establishing rapport" (36), "communicating a feeling of empathy" (36), sharing community's members language and perspective (36), and "paying homage to local routines" (37). Likewise, Van Maanen argues that "fieldworkers are expected by readers, if their accounts are to be trusted, to like and respect those they study (and vice versa)" (80). Growing up in rural communities facilitated these ethnographic processes. My early rural experiences have facilitated my research tasks of gaining access, securing trust, achieving credibility, and establishing informant relationships.

Sociopolitical Communication, Qualitative Methods, and Farm Auctions: Shaping the Research Perspective

Dan Rose writes that "one becomes socialized in graduate school to one's profession, to the conduct of ethnography" (14). Rose goes on to explain that the professional persona one grows into emerges from the "experiences . . . laid out by peers, professors, monographs, articles, and books" (14). Or, as Bud Goodall argues, "You are what you read" (*Rock N Roll* 205). Three powerful educational trajectories from my graduate school days at the University of Nebraska-Lincoln set in motion my rural ethnographer research agenda and methodological orientation. Course work in sociopolitical communication established by speech communication faculty interacted with a sociology course in qualitative methods, and both these trajectories intersected with a field research project I conducted on farm foreclosure auctions to point me in the direction of rural community ethnography.

My interest in debate and speech was a catalyst that drew me away from my rural roots. Out of high school, I decided I was going to be an attorney and politician. So, I moved from Spring Hill and enrolled in a university political science degree program. I continued to debate. I prepared for law school. I went to Washington, D.C., for a summer and worked as a political intern. I wrote speeches for members of Congress. Senator Bob Dole (R-KS) delivered one of my speeches on the floor of the U.S. Senate. I came back to Kansas and worked as a district organizational chairman for a candidate running for the U.S. House of Representatives. My plan was to ride his coattails back to Washington, D.C., once he won the election. He lost.

I suddenly began to question the whole job security issue with politics. And so, while still interested in politics, I looked for employment that would allow me do political work, yet provide a little more occupational stability. I matriculated into the speech communication master's degree program at Kansas State University. I served as a graduate teaching assistant and an assistant speech coach. I wrote my M.A. thesis on the relationship of voter/candidate homophily and voter decision making. After completing my M.A., I accepted a job as a debate coach and an assistant professor of speech at Hastings College in Hastings, Nebraska, a rural farming community of 22,000 people in central Nebraska.

I entered the Ph.D. program at the University of Nebraska-Lincoln in the summer of 1981. Merging my interest in speech communication and politics, I was interested in examining the speeches of politicians, exploring and critiquing the rhetorical strategies they used to build political coalitions and energize mass publics. When I arrived at UN-L, however, Dr. James Klumpp and Dr. Jack Kay introduced me to a "new" area of rhetorical studies, one they called "sociopolitical communication." They directed me to books, essays, and lectures by speech communication scholars Robert Scott, Ernest Bormann, Michael McGee, and Walter Fisher. They introduced me to language philosophers Kenneth Burke and Susanne Langer. They asked me to read sociological works by Hugh Duncan, George Herbert Mead, and C. Wright Mills. Their scholarly perspective fused sociology and rhetorical studies, exploring how rhetoric affects social and political relationships.

Their perspective shifted my study of language from a "managerial rhetoric" to a conception of "rhetoric as symbolic form." Historically, speech scholars have held that "language was an expression of underlying ideas and that humans reasoned and manipulated ideas to affect material reality" (Klumpp and Hollihan 87). This perspective of language viewed True Knowledge as residing within some elite such as a deity or monarchy or within the formulas of science. Within this model, the rhetorician was conceived as an individual orator who influenced society by translating the Truth as given by an elite into a language accessible and understandable to the lay public. Rhetorical language, then, did not create knowledge or understanding, but served simply as a vehicle to make Truth accessible to the masses. Rhetoricians were mere translators and rhetoric simply a medium of exchange—transforming an impenetrable Truth into an understandable and acceptable public language.

In the sociopolitical language perspective, "the focus of rhetorical studies . . . shifted from the immediate power of expression to the creation of social forms in human symbolic behavior" (Klumpp and Hollihan 88). In this view, symbols condense experiences into particular patterns or symbolic groupings (Procter, *Enacting Political Culture* 2). Symbols, then, function as "mergers, marvelous syntheses, which fuse in a single work, act, or work 'a complexity of factors'" (Rueckert 70) including experiences, attitudes, beliefs, and values. Language scholars have found these symbolic patterns and groupings in "myths"—rhetorical patterns of symbols, images, beliefs, and attitudes that are carriers of the cultural storehouse of social ideals (Robertson), "rhetorical visions"—shared group and community fantasies (Bormann), "ideographs"—special words or phrases that express public values that provide the "constitutional" commitment of a community (Condit, *Decoding Abortion Rhetoric*), and "rhetorical fictions"—the dramatic episodes people create to describe their world (Fisher). Each of these forms of symbolic clusters is important in the creation, maintenance, and destruction of community.

From my reading and work in sociopolitical communication, I came to believe that the rhetorical act does not exist simply within the persuasive speaker, but rather the words of a single speaker were the materialization of the social and political beliefs of larger rhetorical communities. I came to view the voice of an individual rhetor as representative of the voice of an entire sociopolitical milieu. Rhetorical language became not merely the expression of community values and reality, but the organizer and creator of those values and reality. I came to understand that rhetors perform community by summarizing experiences into mythic terms, rhetorical visions, ideographs, and rhetorical fictions. Community rhetors enact community by organizing experiences and then naming those experiences so that people feel communal and kinship with one another.

Studying rhetoric from a sociopolitical framework, then, provided me with the theoretical lens and organizing framework to view cultural and community symbolic structures. My speech communication program of study also provided me with an understanding of a variety of rhetorical methodological tools to use when exploring sociopolitical rhetoric. I learned how to examine the rhetorical use of metaphors, ideographs, fantasy themes, myths, and other symbolic forms. These language clusters became important rhetorical data units for analyses of community-building efforts.

I remained fundamentally a rhetorical critic, but was becoming increasingly interested in the "rhetoric of the streets." Instead of exploring the rhetoric of "the great politician," I was becoming more interested in examining the rhetoric of everyday people as they tried to organize and build various communities. Instead of focusing on "the great speech," I was more interested in exploring the symbolic forms communities used to sustain and promote themselves. Instead of hunting through *Vital Speeches of the Day* for research ideas, I looked to get "out of the office to . . . engage [what I] desired to know about" (Goodall, *Casing the Promised Land* 140). In short, thinking about language through the theoretical and method-ological lens of "sociopolitical communication" started me on a path that would take me back to rural community research.

As part of a rhetoric class research project, I took a first stab at sociorhetorical research and studied the way a campus religious cult used metaphors in its efforts to build campus religious communities (Procter, "The Metaphoric Worldview"). This actually turned out to be my first foray into field research. To collect data for this research, I observed, interviewed, and ultimately participated in the religious activities of this campus ministry.[6] I witnessed their evangelizing in front of the student union. I listened to their one-on-one persuasion with students. I interviewed members. I also attended their church services. This research, however, imprinted on me the realization that my academic journey also functioned to separate me from cultural performance.

I was at a Maranatha Campus Ministries revival meeting on a hot summer evening. I had not yet told anyone of my identity or research goals. I slipped into the back of their small, Spartan church, my audio recorder registering the fire and brimstone radiating from the preacher. The minister was swaggering back and forth across the chancel, working up a froth about saving lost souls on the UN-L campus. The minister thundered:

> The Lord tells us, "The harvest is plentiful, but the laborers are few." The Lord says, "I am the God of the harvest and I'm going to send you out for the harvest!" Amen.
>> We need to work the harvest on this sin-infested campus! Amen.
>> We need to proclaim the truth to the lost souls at this university! Amen.

And that truth is revealed in the Good Book! Amen.

The secular HUUUUmanists on this campus say the words of the Bible are metaphorical, that they are only figuratively true. These learned proFESSSSors tell us the stories in the Good Book can NOT be literally true, that God could NOT have performed the wonderful miracles that saved your wretched soul and mine from eternal damnation.

As far as I am concerned, Ph.D. might as well mean Post Hole Digger! Can I get an Amen?

"Amen!" the congregation shouted.

You show me one page in the Bible that is not literally true, the minister boomed, and I will, right here, right now, rip that page from this book. Praise God!

This story confirmed two truths about field research: (1) ethnographers face multiple roles in conducting field research, and (2) sometimes these roles are contradictory. Lindlof and Taylor write that "Participant observers occupy uniquely liminal positions, in which they are situated—both literally and existentially—between various social groups" (135). Not only must field researchers balance differing roles, but at times must deal with the fact that membership in one group separates them from the very group they wish to examine. When studying Maranatha Ministries, I existed in a netherland between actively and energetically pursuing a terminal degree and interacting with and researching a group that loathed that very career path. It seemed the more education I received, the more that education separated me from local cultures I wished to study.

The sociopolitical communication curriculum at UN-L required that Ph.D. students take an "outside concentration." This meant students were to find courses outside the speech communication department that supported their program of study. Traditionally, students took history classes, courses in the classics, or business courses. As students became attracted to the area of sociopolitical communication, it also seemed natural to take courses in the sociology department. I enrolled in a qualitative methods course to help my emerging interest in field research. This class provided me with a variety of theories and methods, a body of literature, and the opportunity to conduct field methods. This class allowed me to fuse field research techniques from sociology with my content interest in sociopolitical rhetoric. I came to understand the field research processes of participant observation, creating field notes, writing thick description, and collecting data through various forms of ethnographic interviews.

As part of the requirements for my sociology qualitative methods class, we were required to conduct a small field research project. I decided I would study the rhetorical and social dimensions of farm foreclosure auctions. The field study, although never published, was a dramatic and transforming experience. The project taught me several research lessons and pushed me down the path to assist small communities as they tried to sustain their way of life.

It was 1984. A significant and widespread farm crisis had engulfed rural America. Family farms were disappearing at an alarming rate. Foreclosure auctions were not hard to find. One only had to visit any local café to observe auction notices cluttering the windows. I found a foreclosure auction outside Sutton, Nebraska, and decided I would attend. From a scholarly point of view, a farm foreclosure auction was attractive for several reasons. Anyone can attend and participate. People come to these auctions from miles around, so one more stranger in the midst of the sale would not be noticed. In the language of field research, "access" was not a problem. Unobtrusive observation would also not be a problem as it is easy to simply wander around an auction. Another advantage to this research site was the amount of talk occurring. A farm auction is a sprawling event, with one cluster of people following the auctioneer as he or she sells the farmer's possessions while other clusters of people are wandering all over the farm, examining equipment, vehicles, furniture, and the home. All the while, people are talking. Aside from collecting public talk, I imagined interviewing the farmer and his family, the auctioneer, as well as selected participants. A third reason this research scene attracted me was the drama of the event itself. In the mid-80s, the farm crisis was a significant public problem, and as Lindlof and Taylor point out, "[p]ublic problems in society can be rich sources of research ideas," and "[e]thnography, generally, is well-suited for digging deep into the lived experiences of the poor, disenfranchised, and outcast" (72). I was interested in how farmers' articulated their loss of home, in many cases their loss of identity. I was also interested in how others—neighborly farmers, for example—felt about participating in the dissolution of a family's home, farm, and livelihood. I assumed, then, that I was ready to conduct research at a farm foreclosure auction. I had access to a dramatic research scene where a significant amount of talk would occur. What I did not have was an acceptable role to perform in this research setting. The liability of engaging in nonparticipant observation became clear at the auction when I was looking over a green monster of a John Deere combine, and a young farmer asked whether this was a "four" or "five-head combine." I could not answer this apparently simple question, and as I mumbled something about being uncertain, the young farmer looked at me as if I had four heads. While I had been around rural communities all my life, I was no farmer. I felt out of place, like an imposter, like the post hole digger the Maranatha minister perceived me to be. The multitude of qualitative theories, the variety of data collection methods, and the array of data analytical tools now in my head could not help me perform in this rural setting. At that moment, I knew I needed a research role that would better integrate my academic persona with rural communities.

Finding an appropriate research role is critical when conducting field research (Emerson, Fretz, and Shaw 1-4; Lindlof and Taylor 143-52; Taylor and Bogdan 34-35). As Howard Schwartz and Jerry Jacobs, in their book, *Qualitative Sociology: A Method to the Madness*, point out, "The main question is, how does a social scientist mesh himself into [the] world so that he finds out the things he is interested in while simultaneously avoiding the danger that his 'enmeshment' will become a source of distorted information?" (52). The role a qualitative researcher assumes determines the types of questions that can be asked, the kinds of observations that are possible, the types of data that can be collected. I was neither comfortable with the "complete observer" role nor a student role.[7] I needed to assume a participant role that would merge my academic role with my interest in rural communities. During my first year at Kansas State University, the opportunity to carve out such a role presented itself.

The Kansas Center for Rural Initiatives: Growing into the Rural Ethnographer Role

Taylor and Bogdan argue that "The conditions of field research—what, when, and whom you observe—must be negotiated continually" (34) while Lindlof and Taylor write "a research perspective develops and flourishes as the researcher works into a role . . . that makes sense to the participants and satisfies the intent of the project" (111). Indeed, I believe that a field researcher's role does develop through an incremental and negotiated dialectic process emerging from the interaction of the ethnographer's character—her demographic characteristics, history, attitudes, and values—with the culture under investigation and with the readers of one's ethnographic work.

I have grown slowly into the role I use when studying rural culture. From Eldon to Olean to Spring Hill to Manhattan to Lincoln and finally back to Manhattan, my academic and personal growth has not always been smooth. There have been bumps along the way, instances where my academic training still separates me from participation in rural culture. My rural ethnographer role began to take shape during my first semester at Kansas State University (KSU). In October 1987, I read a university notice that a rural development center—The Kansas Center for Rural Initiatives (KCRI)—was being created by faculty in rural sociology, agriculture, and community planning. The agency's mission was to link the resources of KSU to rural Kansas. As part of the university notice, KCRI made an open call to faculty who might be interested in working on rural issues. I responded to their call. I let KCRI know that I was interested in assisting with rural communities. Given my status as a communication faculty member, I suggested my role might be to conduct "leadership development" or "communication" workshops. "Call me if you need someone for one of these types of jobs," I said. I heard nothing for over a year. Evidently, they perceived that a speech faculty member was an odd fit with this kind of work. Again, it seemed, my academic training had separated me from the study of rural community. Then, I received my first call. KCRI was conducting a one-day, strategic planning workshop in Colby, Kansas, and was looking for someone to help their assistant director to facilitate the project. "Was I interested?" they asked. I took the opportunity. As I look back on this initial project with KCRI, I think it was a test of some sort. They were interested, I believe, to see what a "speech guy" knew about rural Kansas and how I might act. After Colby, again I heard nothing for another six months.

Then, in 1989, KCRI was charged with facilitating a series of focus groups for

Kansas Economic Development Districts. Again, they asked if I would be interested, and again, I accepted. This was a two-day project and I worked with a number of KCRI staff members and other faculty involved in rural community and economic planning.

Following this meeting, KCRI told me that the State of Kansas was beginning a five-year program of countywide, strategic planning efforts in rural Kansas and that facilitators were needed for several of the projects. Over the next three years, I facilitated strategic planning meetings in Lincoln, Mitchell, McPherson, and Sherman counties.

At the same time, KCRI was beginning a community service program for Kansas State students. As part of this project, KCRI was enlisting faculty to serve as mentors for the student teams and liaisons between the university, student team, and rural communities. Again, KCRI asked if I would be interested, and I served as a faculty mentor for community student teams in the rural communities of Russell, Halstead, Glasco, Hutchinson, and Garden City.

In 1994, KCRI became involved with service learning. I used this opportunity to introduce service learning into my graduate field research methods course. My classes collected oral histories for rural heritage museums and assisted rural communities as they planned, organized, and performed community festivals.

Through my association with KCRI, I have expanded my contacts with rural citizens and communities. From a colloquium sponsored by KCRI, I made contact with the Kansas Sampler Foundation (see chapter 7), and from that connection, I started working with the Kansas Humanities Council. From this work with these professional rural associations, I have gained enough experiences and credibility that I have been able to network community development contacts on my own.

My association with KCRI has been crucial to my work in rural community development. Initially, KCRI serves as a sponsor for my research and rural community work. Lindlof and Taylor point out that "a sponsor . . . takes a very active interest" in the project. "In addition to granting access, a sponsor is someone who usually goes around to others and personally introduces the researcher, vouches for the project, and helps the researcher find informants or resources" (104). When I travel to a rural community to facilitate strategic planning or conduct a leadership workshop or mentor a student community service team, I arrive under the credibility umbrella of KCRI.

KCRI also provides me with a specific role for rural community work. I have a legitimate reason to be working with small towns and perform specific jobs while I am there. Whether I work as a strategic planning facilitator, a community service mentor, or a service learning fellow with rural communities, I perform important functions for community development. Robert Emerson, Rachel Fretz, and Linda Shaw explain:

> Many contemporary ethnographers advocate highly participatory roles in which the researcher actually performs activities that are central to the lives of those studied. In this view, assuming real responsibility for actually carrying out core

functions and tasks, as in service learning internships, provides special opportunities to get to, participate in, and experience life in previously unknown settings. Finally, close, continuing participation in the lives of others encourages appreciation of social life as constituted by ongoing, fluid processes. (4)

Further, the roles provided by KCRI have integrated with my professional persona. As an "expert in communication," I use my understanding of the general principles of communication when facilitating group dynamics in strategic planning or conducting a workshop in leadership communication or managing communication between student service learning teams and rural communities. My role has now evolved to the point where rural communities contact me for planning assistance, for rural grant application help, for presentations regarding communication processes.

By engaging in these highly participatory roles, I am in a position to listen to and better understand rural issues. Especially when I facilitate strategic planning meetings, I hear rural citizens talk about their community's strengths, weaknesses, opportunities, and threats. These issues are discussed in terms of youth flight, economic development, corporate farming versus family farming, community infrastructure, community pride, community negativism, and rural community health issues. My role places me in a position to understand, empathize, and question rural citizens. It allows me to view and hear power relations in these rural communities.

Bogdan and Taylor warn that a problem ethnographers often face "is being forced into a role incompatible with conducting research" (34). They go on to explain that often ethnographers are placed in roles where they neither effectively observe nor collect the data necessary for their research interests. In contrast, the roles I engage in facilitate observation and follow-up data collection. Because my roles are legitimate task roles, my presence and my need to ask questions are understood. Citizens do not appear to be self-conscious in my presence because we were all working on the same community project. I am easily able to move from my role as strategic planner, leadership consultant, community service mentor into my role as rural community researcher. In truth, these roles meld together. As I facilitate strategic planning, conduct leadership training, and mentor community service teams, I am always looking for the ways rural citizens work together to build community. I then use my knowledge of the community and my local contacts to follow up with more detailed descriptions, interviews, and analysis.

Still, role-taking in my ethnographic work remains a balancing act. When communicating with rural citizens, I think I am sometimes perceived as one of those overly educated professors from the state university while my scholarly readers (editors and reviewers) sometimes suggest that I am too closely aligned with rural citizens.

As I interact with rural citizens, they are cooperative, considerate, and polite as we talk about working on local issues and problems. Yet, there are times when they remind me in both subtle and not so subtle ways of our differences. At times,

I am referred to as "the knowledgeable professor from K-State" or "the good doctor." At nearly every meeting, someone asks how is it that a speech person is working in community development. Following its publication, I forwarded one of my rural ethnography essays to some key rural development people. The response to the essay was, "I tried reading it, but gave up. Kinda academic don't you think?" In a strategic planning meeting, I was listing the towns in the county that could be assisted by our work. I referred to one community as "Wisdom," rather than "Windom." Much of the remainder of the evening sounded something like this: "Dr. Procter (sung in a sing-song voice), could we visit Windom to get a little Wisdom?" and "Maybe the Professor could help us get a little Wisdom in Windom." At another meeting, in Lincoln, Kansas, we were finishing a strategic planning sessions when a local farmer made the following statement:

> Ya' know, it's up to us! We're the ones out here dealing with a lack of jobs, a lack of health care, our towns dryin' up and blowin' away. Tomorrow, these professors are going back to their teachin' jobs, worried about eighteen-year-old kids, not us. If any action is going to happen, we gotta' do it, not some professors from K-State.

These kinds of comments serve to remind me that no matter my early experiences with rural America, no matter my compassion for rural communities, and no matter how much I work to assist them, there exists a gulf between us. I don't live and work there. My financial, cultural, interpersonal, and familial existence do not, on a daily basis, depend on rural America. Instead, my education, occupation, and many of my attitudes separate me from the very rural people I wish to study, and at times, these folks remind me of that fact.

Ironically, just as some rural citizens have subtly, and not so subtly, reminded me of my physical and attitudinal distance from rural communities, some scholarly reviewers have criticized my work on the very grounds of being too close to the rural citizens and not academic enough. Reviewers and editors have questioned the "distance" my role offers, arguing my work is too "like-minded." Others have suggested my scholarship is "unreflective," offering a "somewhat complacent outlook" and thereby undermining "my own credibility." These reviewers have suggested that I need to consider taking a more "critical stance" in my ethnographic work.

Conclusions

John and Lyn Lofland argue that field studies require three tasks: (1) gathering and assembling data, (2) focusing data around social scientific questions, and (3) analyzing and presenting data (1-5). The first task in field research is gathering data. Part of this task is to select a research setting in which you have some experience, interest, understanding, and empathy. The Loflands refer to this stage as "starting where you are" and argue this research stance "provides the necessary linkages between the personal and emotional on the one hand, and the stringent intellectual operations to come on the other" (15). I believe it is important for field researchers to study settings in which they have some experience, interest, and understanding. Field research requires a long-term commitment, and one must have the experiential background to sustain such research. This chapter has detailed my long-term connection with rural communities. It has illustrated my continuing connection to rural America even as I have, at times, studied and worked in more metropolitan locales.

Beyond simply experiencing and empathizing with a research setting, however, field researchers also need to be able to ask and explore appropriate and important social scientific questions about the research scene. Lofland and Lofland refer to this stage as "focusing" one's research (1-2). Such focus can come from training, reading, and practice in the theoretical and methodological orientations of one's given field. This chapter has illustrated my efforts to engage, understand, and utilize social and rhetorical theories through my work at various universities.

Once equipped with the experience and education to explore a given research setting, field researchers must then grow into an appropriate research role. Such roles are incrementally and continually negotiated. An appropriate research role is one the researcher ultimately feels comfortable with and also is recognized as legitimate by those individuals in the research scene. Research roles are continually negotiated by the scholar and the research subjects. It is affected by the researcher's interests, needs, history, and political orientation. It is also affected by the interests, needs, and history of the context under examination.

The third task in field research, according to the Loflands, is analysis and presentation of data. The remainder of this text, then, is the presentation of analysis of the research I have conducted over the last ten years in rural communities. This research is presented in the form of a number of rural community case studies and is presented in part II of this text.

Field research challenges scholars to go "to the field" and study people in their natural settings. Cultural scholars interact with people as they go about their daily activities and talk about what is important to their everyday lives. Ethnographers then present their research findings in such a way to appropriately represent the culture under study. Yet these scholarly tasks omit an important part of the research equation—the evolutionary development of the research role and perspective taken by the field researcher. In this chapter, I have tried to address this missing research puzzle piece by relating the importance of developing cultural understanding, field research knowledge, and role acquisition. I have also tried to illustrate some of the struggles one faces in developing an ethnographic stance—highlighting the complexities and, at times, the contradictions in assuming ethnographic roles.

Notes

1. There is an increasing number of these types of studies. See for example, Lyall Crawford, "Personal Ethnography." *Communication Monographs* 63 (June 1996):158-70; H.L. Goodall, Jr., *Casing the Promised Land:The Autobiography of an Organizational Detective as Cultural Ethnographer* (Carbondale: Southern Illinois University Press, 1989); Tamar Katriel, *Performing the Past: A Study of Israeli Settlement Museums* (Mahwah, NJ: Lawrence Erlbaum Associates, 1997); Lisa Tillmann-Healy, "A Secret Life in a Culture of Thinness," in *Composing Ethnography*, eds. Carolyn Ellis and Art Bochner (Walnut Creek, CA: Alta Mira Press, 1996), 76-107; Nick Trujillo, "In Search of Naunny's Grave," *Text and Performance Quarterly* 18 (October 1998): 344-68; Nick Trujillo, "Interpreting November 22: A Critical Ethnography of an Assassination Site," *Quarterly Journal of Speech* 79 (November 1993): 447-66.

2. This chapter represents, in the words of John Van Maanen, a "confessional tale." As Van Maanen explains, "Confessions . . . appear with increasing frequency, as separate articles, chapters of books devoted to fieldwork practice, or lengthy appendixes attached to realist monographys" (75). See John Van Maanen, *Tales of the Field* (Chicago: University of Chicago Press, 1988), 73-100.

3. Kemmis writes of the tradition of citizens helping one another to accomplish fundamental civic and family goals. Kemmis recalls this tradition in his call for a renewal of "the culture of cooperation"—or civic communion. Kemmis uses the example of barn raising to illustrate the tradition of individuals working together for broader community goals. See Daniel Kemmis, *Community and the Politics of Place* (Norman: University of Oklahoma Press, 1990), 64-83.

4. Because there are few people concentrated in a localized area, access to services and activities like health care, recreation and entertainment, cultural diversity, diversity of trade, and governmental services is often restricted. See Kenneth Wilkinson, *Community in Rural America* (New York: Greenwood Press, 1991), 113-15.

5. Gary B. Melton argues that "Rural people are said to be (relative to urban people) conservative, religious, work-oriented, intolerant of diverse ideas, familistic, individualistic, fatalistic. . . . There is some evidence to support the contention that there are real mean differences in these values between urban and rural populations." See Gary B. Melton, "Ruralness as a Psychological Construct," in *Rural Psychology*, eds. Alan W. Childs and Gary B. Melton (New York: Plenum Press, 1983), 5.

6. I note, in a 1986 issue of *Speaker and Gavel*, that "The majority of the evidence cited in this study comes from nondirective interviewing and participation in Maranatha Campus Ministries revivals." For this study, I initially watched their public evangelizing outside the University of Nebraska-Lincoln student union. From this observation, I contacted some of the most active members and conducted interviews with them. I also conducted interviews with the leaders of the UN-L group. Finally, I attended several of their religious meetings and engaged in participant observation in that context. See David E. Procter, "The Metaphoric Worldview of Maranatha Ministries: Working God's Harvest on College Campuses," *Speaker and Gavel* 23 (1986): 80, footnote 2.

7. The "complete observer" is a research role in which the investigator does not reveal his or her research intentions and tries to simply blend into the scene, observing completely unobtrusively. Complete observers have no identity that is explicitly recognized by the social actors in the cultural scene. In this research stance, a field worker attempts to observe people in ways which make it unnecessary for them to take him into account, for they do not know

he is observing or that, in some sense, they are serving as his informants. See Raymond L. Gold, "Roles in Sociological Field Observations," *Social Forces* 36 (March 1958): 221

Part II

Civic Communion Case Studies

3

Performing Gender through Local Festival: Waterville's Victorian Days

My wife and I walk up the limestone stairs and into Waterville's historic Weaver Hotel. We are here for an English "high tea." Inside the hotel, built in 1905, I feel as though I've stepped back in time. I am surrounded by women in Victorian dress and the delicate sounds of stringed instruments. We are directed across worn oak floors to a table covered with a white lace cloth and set with Willow-Blue china. From our table, we notice the polished hard pine trim encasing the room and numerous paintings depicting frontier life. We gaze through a six-foot window onto Waterville's Front Street and notice a large crowd gathering. As we sit down, an elderly, genteel-looking woman serves us from a three-tiered cake plate brimming with tea sandwiches and pastries. We sip almond tea and taste blueberry scones with clotted cream. We notice the crowd on Front Street now seems agitated. People are running around, pointing, and talking excitedly. The sounds of cello and violin bring us back to our English tea. We sample quiche lorraine and tea sandwiches of smoked salmon and cucumber watercress. The tea culminates with desserts of chocolate petit fours, lemon curd tartlets, Madeira cake, four-cream chocolate drops, and English tea cakes. Several sharp blasts from a shotgun jar us from our casual conversation. Our hearts race as we notice men running down Front Street shooting pistols and shotguns. A cowboy lies face down on the dirt road. People along the street are laughing, cheering, and walking away. The "End of the Line" gang has just performed another street play depicting good and evil on the frontier.

The Victorian Days festival is in full swing.

Community Festivals as Civic Communion

Scholars from a variety of disciplines have argued that community festivals provide a special moment in civic life when a community reflects upon, celebrates, and ultimately presents an image of itself. Cultural theorist Frank E. Manning argues that community festivals represent a "text" or a vivid aesthetic event that depicts, interprets, informs, and celebrates social truths (6). Anthropologist Carole Farber argues that community festivals "provide ideal *entrees* into a community's symbolic, economic, social, and political life" (33). Robert H. Lavenda, a cultural anthropologist, argues festivals are "one of the few moments in the annual cycle when . . . a community publicly celebrates itself . . . and a public culture emerges" ("Festivals and the Creation of Public Culture" 77). Likewise, professor of English Michael Marsden suggests that "the community festival might provide a significant window into the culture of a community. It may well provide us with a narrative about the community's cultural essence" (157). And communication professor Raymond J. Schneider contends that by examining the way people play, the way they take time out to celebrate or to tell stories during festivals, we are able to determine much about the culture and even subcultures shared by communities (334). Each of these scholars, representing varied academic disciplines, argues that through civic festivals, communities celebrate, sanctify, and promote important local sociopolitical structures. In short, community festivals function as civic communion.

Initially, festivals are symbolically and behaviorally framed moments in the life of communities. They are generally annual events, organized around some significant community event, history, issue, or person. While festivals do occur repeatedly, they are not the normal state of community affairs. They are, as Roger Abrahams writes, "times out of the ordinary, . . . when gifts are given and ties are renewed, and community of spirit becomes more important than social structure" (163). During festivals, according to Alessandro Falassi, a community's "daily time is modified by a gradual or sudden interruption that introduces 'time out of time,' a special temporal dimension devoted to special activities" (4). Festival organizers take significant time out of their daily routine to produce the event. Likewise, festival goers take time out from their daily and practical affairs to participate in this performance of local social structures. As Falassi argues, "Festival time imposes itself as an autonomous duration, not so much to be perceived and measured in days or hours, but to be divided internally by what happens within from its beginning to its end, as in the 'movements' of mythical narratives" (4). Importantly, festivals are recognized as a special community moment of both celebration and pause, of reflection and performance of cultural truths. As Lavenda argues, through festivals, "municipalities create a *momentary*, if recurrent, . . . symbology of local significance" ("Festivals and the Creation of Public Culture" 77; emphasis mine). Festivals are therefore transitory, yet significant events, bracketed by months of planning and concluded with a time of celebration and festivity that ultimately performs a text of some community ideal.

These impermanent, yet significant community events provide a moment of common experience, a reference point for interaction and reflection through which a broad range of collective participation from local citizens is invited. Frank Manning, for example, argues that "celebration is participatory. . . . Celebration actively involves its constituency; it is not simply a show put on for disengaged spectators" (4). Festival participation is, according to Karp, "totalizing," "democratic and nonjudgmental" ("Festivals" 282). In other words, festival participation involves a broad constituency of the community and the entire person. Varieties of citizens work to prepare the festival—cleaning buildings, setting up booths, managing crowds, cooking food, etc. Festival performance enlists the efforts of many groups of people. From children reciting poems to historical reenactors, from speeches to community-wide parades, from dances to business leaders promoting the community to outside vendors selling wares at the festival, the shared goal is to attract and entertain a large and diverse group to the festival. Festival performance itself exhibits a broad a range of participation. Citizens listen to and watch parades and festival performers. Participants smell and taste foods distinct to the particular area and festival. They can touch crafts, festival performers, and community monuments. Citizens become part of the festival performance by joining in parades, dances, speech events, or community skits. Festival celebrations are also available to anyone wishing to attend. Certainly many centrifugal forces exist in the community, including religion, politics, patterns of kinship, class, friendship, mutual interests, and work (Lavenda et al., "Festivals and the Organization of Meaning" 49). Festivals provide a momentary opportunity to transcend these differences and come together as a collective body to produce, reflect on, and perform community ideals and identity. As Lavenda et al. conclude, festivals "provide a meeting place and a set of common experiences" for citizens ("Festivals and the Organization of Meaning" 34).

Ultimately, community festivals, as cultural texts, are organized to dramatically enact important civic values. As Carole Farber argues, "the small-town festival is precisely [a] key dramatic performance—a performance in which official town myths and ideology are presented and re-presented in parades, talent shows, costume judging, sports competitions, masquerades, and the like" (36). By highlighting, celebrating, and performing important community symbols, histories, events, or people, the festival is a transitory moment when citizens collectively participate in reflection, articulation, and promotion of civic truths.

Interestingly, however, many scholars argue that festivals remain a virtually unstudied context of civic life and cultural production. Michael Marsden and Ray Browne, for example, contend: "The community festival is one of the least understood areas of celebration" (6). Amitai Etzioni argues that this scholarly area has received "little consideration" (113) while Marsden calls the festival "one of the least studied areas of human celebration" (157).

Waterville's Victorian Days Festival

In 1999, I was teaching a course in research methods and was looking for a small-town event my graduate students could assist with while engaging in the qualitative methods of participant observation, interview techniques, and thick description. I became aware of Waterville's Victorian Days, and we began to explore the community as a research site. We learned that Waterville is a rural community of about 650 citizens located in north central Kansas. In 1990, a small group of Waterville women gathered together and brainstormed ways "to earn money for the historical preservation of the buildings in . . . town" (Victorian Days Committee Meeting 6/2/03). They decided to organize a community festival that would be highlighted by "hosting a tea party" in the town's historic hotel (Harding interview). Initially, "most people in town just didn't think much of the idea," according to Sandy Harding. "They kind of 'pooh-poohed' the idea. They thought we were silly, but we made it work, and that was thirteen years ago, and each year it has evolved into what it is today. It's a pretty big deal" (Victorian Day Meeting, 2/3/03). Victorian Days is now a festival that highlights Waterville's prairie Victorian past. In the late nineteenth century, Waterville briefly rivaled other cow towns like Abilene, Kansas; Kansas City, Missouri; and St. Joseph, Missouri, for commerce generated from the cattle industry. Because of railcar availability and good grazing land, cattle were herded to Waterville and then transported east. The railroad was a significant presence in Waterville, and while cattle were shipped east, the railroad brought settlers west (Fitzgerald 12). Capital flowed into the town. During this time, "The little town shed its rough image and took on a gracious air of gentility as the monied and professional people began building new homes" ("Waterville Celebrates" 1). The cattle boom, however, was short-lived, and the money, the railroad, and capitalists soon left Waterville. Still, today there are remnants of this bygone era. Victorian Days is a festival that performs and celebrates these former times. Through an English "high tea" in the historic Weaver Hotel, through Victorian home tours, through children's schoolhouse performances, through frontier reenactments of pioneer days gone by, through an 1880s church service, through quilt displays and tea shops created specifically to highlight a Victorian era, Waterville performs its prairie Victorian past. Now, the festival weekend sees the community double in size. Hundreds of people visit this tiny rural community to participate in the high tea, tour Victorian homes, watch children perform at a one-room schoolhouse, tour a frontier encampment, watch historical reenactors, buy fancy baked goods, participate in an 1880s church service, and tour local museums. From my initial contact with the organizers of Victorian Days, interviews with selected committee members, and interaction with festival goers, it also became clear the festival was organized by women who created attractions primarily for women.[1]

I thus viewed Victorian Days as a moment of civic communion to through which to examine gender roles as enacted through festival performances. As Beverly Stoeltje points out:

festivals are imbued throughout with the social representation of gender, because such events characteristically enact essential concepts which shape everyday life, and central to any society's social concept is the idea of gender. In festival, with its widespread performance and participation, persons embody concepts—become the signs of concepts—and thus representations of gender. (219)

Despite Stoeltje's assertion, both she and Etzioni argue the performance of gender in festival has received little attention consideration in scholarly research (Stoeltje 221; Etzioni 134). This chapter seeks to address the twin scholarly concerns represented by a lack of research on community festivals and specifically on gender displays in those community festivals.

Methodological Contexts

Data Collection

Research teams were created to examine gender performances and cultural constructions associated with this community festival. These research teams examined the Victorian Days festival in 1999, 2001, and 2003. The research teams were composed of students from my graduate research methods classes.[2] Following Douglas's admonition that research teams should be "constructed in accord with the demands of the concrete setting and research goals" (194) and Lindlof and Taylor's recognition that "studying people who share some of our own characteristics (e.g., women researching women about women's issues) has its advantages" (84), especially in establishing rapport early, I assigned primarily women to the Waterville research teams.[3]

Research teams engaged in participant observation and direct observation. They conducted both structured and ethnographic interviews, and examined relevant documents. Participant observation began by contacting festival organizers months before the weekend festival. Douglas argues it is important for the research team to be involved "during the early stages of research. . . . This way they learn the basic things at the same time, meet key people from the beginning, and pool their many ideas" (216). During initial meetings with festival organizers, research teams requested and were granted access to festival committee meetings. Over the course of examining three different festivals, the research teams attended and recorded fifteen meetings with each meeting lasting approximately ninety minutes. In exchange for this access, research team members offered to assist the committee as they produced the Victorian Days.[4] Research team members were subsequently assigned job tasks for assisting the festival. "One of the greatest advantages of team work," according to Douglas, "is that it allows [the research team] to use the specialized characteristics, interests, and specialized knowledge of the members for the multiplied benefit of the whole project" (210). Indeed, we capitalized on role specialization during participant observation. Specialized talents of graduate students were connected to tasks associated with the festival production. For example, one graduate student worked as a baker in an espresso shop during the school year. Consequently, she assisted the Victorian Days committee with baking high tea pastries. Another graduate student was proficient with computers and helped enhance the festival's web page. Additionally, team researchers conducted television and radio interviews promoting the festival, helped the committee clean downtown buildings, worked as tour docents in the Victorian home tours, and assisted as servers for the high tea.

In addition to engaging in participant observation, research team members conducted direct observation. Adler and Adler explain: "Qualitative observation is fundamentally naturalistic in essence; it occurs in the natural context of occurrence, among the actors who would naturally be participating in the interaction, and follows the natural stream of everyday life" (378). Whereas in participant observation we would observe communicative behavior from some participatory role, in direct observation we simply placed ourselves in locations where the festival was occurring around us. Research team members would unobtrusively watch and interact in the festival as would any other participant, looking for "community-building" communication and behaviors. We followed Carol Brooks Gardner's suggestion to look for "something of a sudden, though minor, epiphany as to the . . . importance of an event or phenomenon" (as quoted in Adler and Adler 378).

A variety of interviews were conducted, including twenty structured interviews. Thirteen of these interviews were with members of the Victorian Days organizing committee,[5] five were conducted with Waterville citizens not directly connected with organizing the festival,[6] and two with individuals visiting Victorian Days.[7] In addition, ethnographic, or informal, interviews were conducted with several festival participants.

The research team also collected a variety of public and rhetorical documents. Relevant books, locally produced publicity materials, newspaper articles and editorials from the *Waterville Telegraph*, the *Manhattan Mercury*, the *Topeka Capital Journal*, and the *Tour Kansas Guide* were collected and examined. Finally, demographic data regarding the Waterville community and Marshall county were collected.

In an effort to triangulate the analysis relevant to the civic communion function of this community festival, triangulation was employed by utilizing multiple sources of data over multiple years. Patricia and Peter Adler suggest this form of team research can, in fact, "enhance the validity of observations, as researchers can cross-check each other's findings" (381). The analysis was also triangulated by using multiple methods data collection—analysis from participant observation, direct observation, interviews, and rhetorical documents. From the data collected, gender statements and performances were identified and analyzed.

Women's Roles Performed during Victorian Days

Since the festival's genesis, which originated as a high tea and one home tour, the organizing committee has solicited, encouraged, and incorporated many voices, ideas, and events into the festival, all of which now function to materialize a mediated version of Waterville's Victorian and frontier past.[8] During Victorian Days, many festival events offer idealized displays of gender. I contend that while ostensibly enacting Victorian-era gender roles, festival event performances also say much about current gender role behaviors and attitudes. Thus, I believe Victorian Days now stands as a polyvocal, performative, cultural text, which not only materializes an idealized look at gender roles during the Victorian frontier era, but also informs our current understanding of community gender roles in rural America.

The following section explores the festival's three major events—high tea, the home tours, and the schoolhouse skit—and the gender performances enacted in each of those events.[9] I argue these events present a bifurcated image of women—on one level festival performances articulate a conservative and subordinate female role, and yet, on another level, those same performances present women as the shapers, molders, and builders of local community. For each gender performance, I examine the gender roles displayed, the gender ideology embedded within those performances, and, finally, how these Victorian Days performances give voice to female community-building efforts.

Woman as "Angel in the House"

Two major attractions for the Victorian Days festival are the English high tea held in Waterville's historic Weaver Hotel and tours of Waterville's Victorian-style homes. These attractions perform what the Waterville women argue is a "Victorian elegance . . . born out of a more rough-hewn time" ("Victorian Days").

The Victorian era refers to life in England, France, and America during the reign of Queen Victoria (1837-1901). During this time, there was "an extreme polarization of sex roles" (Hellerstein, Hume, and Offen 3). Victorian conceptions of the ideal woman were epitomized in Coventry Patmore's poem, "The Angel in the House" and Alfred Lord Tennyson's "The Princess." "In her most perfect form, the [Victorian] lady combined 'gentility' (Jorgensen-Earp 84), sexual innocence, conspicuous consumption, and the worship of the family hearth" (Vicinus ix). Waterville women enact Victorian gender roles most clearly through the high tea and the home tours.

The Gender Performance

The most important Victorian gender role for women was presiding over the domestic sphere. The home was to be a pastoral idyll, offering respite and refuge from the harsh turmoil and corruption of public, commercial life. "Victorian prescriptive literature celebrated women's work *in the home* and applauded the notion of good household management" (Hume and Offen 273; emphasis Hume and Offen). Waterville women enact the role of guardian of the domestic sphere through performance of the high tea at the Weaver Hotel and through local Victorian home tours. The once elegant Weaver Hotel stands as a reminder of Waterville's past. In 1906, the *Waterville Telegraph* called the Weaver Hotel "the pride of Waterville," and proclaimed: "We believe we can boast of having the finest hotel of any town of its size and even many times larger in the state" ("Welcome to Waterville's"). Today, the Weaver Hotel stands unused and vacant for much of the year. It is, in many ways, symbolic of the decline and abandonment of rural America. Still, the hotel remains an important civic symbol of Waterville's past prosperity. So, for Victorian Days, the hotel is identified as the space for the festival's most prominent event—the English high tea. Thus, Waterville women work to transform the hotel from a derelict building which stands empty fifty-one weekends of the year into the luxury hotel it once was. As former chair of the Victorian Days organizing committee, Pam White, argues, "[the Weaver Hotel] always looks beautiful when it's fixed up. The gals have a real nice touch on it, the way they do things" (White interview).

While some women clean the hotel, other women engage in domestic activities such as preparing elaborate desserts, gathering fine china, collecting lace tablecloths and handsewn napkins, and decorating the hotel. The weekend of the festival, with the hotel restored to its past elegance, genteel Waterville women dressed in opulent Victorian costumes serve delicate tea foods and speciality teas while soft stringed music soothes the numerous hotel guests.

The Victorian home tours are the second most celebrated attraction during Victorian Days. These Victorian homes are symbolically constructed as "a reminder of the Victorian era, the financial success and the 'Gay Nineties'" (Fitzgerald 48). The homes are described in terms of conspicuous consumption and the hallmark innocence associated with the Victorian era. Publicity materials proclaim: "Large, stately Victorian homes, replete with gables, gingerbread balconies, colonnades, turrets, and towers, . . . stand today along the tree-shaded streets of Waterville" ("Waterville Celebrates" 1).

Months prior to the festival weekend, local Victorian homes are cleaned, renovated, and elaborately decorated. These are times when Waterville women direct "renovations" and "major projects" (Walter interview) and complete home tasks that have long been postponed (Minge interview). During the festival weekend, home tourists "sign in" and don surgical booties to gain entrance into the homes. Once inside, tourists are greeted by the female of the house who is dressed in a magnificent Victorian costume. After a welcome by the home owner, festival participants are directed by volunteer docents through the stately homes restored to earlier elegance and adorned with objects of wealth. The docent explains the process of restoring the homes, emphasizing the intricacies, uniqueness, and elegance of each home. The description of the Powell/Minge home is representative:

> The current owner has lovingly and painstakingly restored the home to its former glory. Cherubs on the ceiling gaze blissfully around the room. Pocket doors divide

the parlor from the music room/ballroom. Elegant inlaid patterns enhance the hardwood floor that falls in perfect chevrons. Restoration revealed seven Tiffany stained glass windows, three fireplaces with imported woods and tiles, three large pocket doors, and the original portieres. Original motifs on the walls and ceilings of the homes reflected designs made popular by William Morris and the Pre-Raphaelities in England. The whole house was designed and built with refinement and elegance. ("Waterville Man" 3)

Both the Weaver Hotel and the Victorian homes are constructed as "[s]acred shrines [which are] solemnly displayed and become the destination of visitations from within the immediate boundaries of the festival, or of pilgrimages from faraway places" (Falassi 4).

The Gender Ideology

The genteel, idyllic repose constructed through the high tea and home tours offers idealized performances. While Waterville women publically enact the role of the *"Angel in the House,"* appearing to preside "comfortingly and protectively over [their] homes" (Yang 25), these performances mask an ideology of domesticity faced by rural women.

"If sentimentally envisaged as a haven, the Victorian home was in reality a workplace" (Hume and Offen 278). "The Victorian matron was rarely a lady of leisure" with "the survival of the family depending on the judicious management and hard work" (Hume and Offen 279). The many job tasks associated with these festival performances highlight a variety of domestic gender roles including cleaning, cooking, baking, and serving. One of the most difficult tasks in preparing for the festival is refurbishing the several building utilized during Victorian Days. Many downtown buildings used by the festival stand empty but for one weekend a year. Calling the cleaning and refurbishing process "hectic" (Stewart interview), "exhausting," (Irons interview), and an "intense amount of work" (Walter interview), Waterville women renovate, refurbish, clean, and decorate these buildings so they are usable and suitable for Victorian Days. LuAnn Roepke, former chair of the organizing committee, points out that because of the Victorian Days festival, local women have "cleaned up and fixed up" several downtown buildings. A one-time produce market, now a vacant building, is annually cleaned and converted into the "Front Street Saloon." The rarely used Masonic Hall is transformed into "Victoria's Tea Shop." Mary Irons, the organizer of the tea shop, and Pam White, the 2001 chair, explain the process:

Mary: It was a challenge to make the Masonic Hall entrance not look like the Masonic Hall entrance. We had to decorate bare walls, haul in furniture. We had to take the "man look" away.
Pam: Mary, your shop was darling. The lace curtains really helped
Everyone laughed. (Victorian Days Committee Meeting, 5/7/01)

Secretary Gay Stewart reported that "getting the buildings ready is hard to do.

It is absolutely one of the hardest things you can imagine (interview, 4/1/03). The biggest job, however, is cleaning the Weaver Hotel, which normally stands unused and unheated. Weeks prior to the festival, Waterville women gather and laboriously clean the hotel, "mopping the floors, wiping down the walls, cleaning and polishing the woodwork, puttin' a spit shine on that old hotel" (Pam White, Victorian Days Meeting, 2/03/03). In the following exchange during a March 2003 meeting, it is clear that cleaning the hotel is a difficult, but expected, task.

> *LuAnn*: I know we've got to clean the hotel. Whoa! That thing needs cleaning. It's bad.
> *Bevy*: But the weather is too cold.
> *LuAnn*: We may have to go in there with some kind of auxiliary heat. It's just cleanin,' that's all it is. It just takes work. But I always enjoy doin' it, cleanin' that ole' building. Don't ask me why. But I do enjoy cleaning that thing up. So, bring your rubber gloves. (Victorian Days Meeting, 3/03/03)

Linked to cleaning is food preparation. Margaret Williamson argues that during celebrations and festivals, most preparations are done by women. Decorating the house, fixing a lavish dinner, dressing up the house, and glorifying the hearth and home are all major tasks for women (235; see also Etzioni). Cooking especially has been associated with the gender ideology of domesticity. Part of maintaining the home is preparing and serving food to others. Susan Bordo argues the ideology of women preparing food for others is "as prescriptive in 1991 as in 1891" (119). Preparation of the festival food is a significant job. The festival chair indicated that "we've got that cookin' down to, I think, maybe three weeks" (Victorian Days Meeting, 3/3/03). Weeks prior to the festival, women gather at various homes to bake the thousands of pastries to be served and consumed at Victorian Days. At one meeting, Mary Irons, chair of the tea shop, reported, "we're a little behind schedule" in the effort to bake 1,200 cookies and 200 loaves of tea bread. The majority of the baking, however, is conducted at Ruth Ann Roepke's home. Everyone acknowledges Ruth Ann has the final word in terms of baking schedule and "quality control." Ruth Ann organizes groups of women to come to her home and bake desserts. As one committee member stated, "she just kind of makes up a schedule, 'today, we're going to do tart shells. Next week, we're going to make shortbread.' And it all gets done."

In addition to cleaning and baking, Waterville women engage in the domestic role of server as they serve festival guests at the high tea. Nick Trujillo argues that "serving food may be the quintessential traditional activity of . . . family women" ("In Search of" 354) while Etzioni argues that women disproportionately function as servers for special meals, including holidays and festivals (133). Bordo contends that serving food has been ideologically constructed as "woman's natural role" (124) and has been used as an activity through which women have been subordinated in our culture, especially when cooking and serving is "representationally 'reproduced' as a quintessentially and exclusively female activity" (125).

Woman as "Schoolmarm"

The most difficult event to attend is the Victorian Days schoolhouse performance. During the festival weekend, local children enact a frontier-era schoolhouse performance at Waterville's one-room schoolhouse. The schoolhouse seats forty people, and there are four performances during the festival weekend. It is difficult to find an available seat. At the 2003 wrap-up meeting, one of the organizing committee members stated what everyone knew to be true. The school performance was, according to LuAnn Roepke, "one of the favorite things. Honest to goodness, they just love that little schoolhouse. It's a favorite" (Victorian Days Meeting, 6/2/03).

The Gender Performance
Waterville's first schoolhouse was built in 1870 and was refurbished in 1904. Called the Game Fork schoolhouse, it served as Waterville's educational facility until 1952. Today this country schoolhouse sits in Waterville's community park and stands as an idealized symbol of frontier one-room schools. The A-frame, rectangular schoolhouse is painted white with three windows on each of the longer sides.[10] Inside the schoolhouse are forty desks, a slate blackboard, and a pot-bellied wood stove. The Game Fork school actually shows some improvements over more modest rural schools, boasting a vestibule for storing student coats, hats, overshoes, and lunches. Atop the vestibule sits an ornate belfry and bell.

For Victorian Days in 1999, the schoolhouse served as the performance site for children reciting and performing Emily Dickinson poems. In 2001, children recited the poems of Robert Louis Stevenson. In 2003, fifteen elementary-aged schoolchildren performed "A Patchwork Performance of Pieces and Plainsong," organized, produced, and narrated by local schoolteacher Jeannette Bergquist. Mrs. Bergquist's 2003 program was a series of poems and songs which depict what the "Last Day of School Celebration" might have been like at a country school around the turn of the century. Dressed in a plain white shirtwaist and modest black skirt and wearing a black hat, Mrs. Bergquist opened the program by ringing the school bell. A mostly elderly audience sat in the school's forty desks. Elementary-aged schoolchildren, dressed in costumes which evoke idealized images of rural schoolchildren—pinafores and gingham dresses for girls, bib overalls for boys, and shoes for a few—file in from outside and take their places at the front of the schoolhouse. Casting the program as more than simply a celebration of the school's last day, Mrs. Bergquist proclaims in her introduction:

> We're here to celebrate our closing day of school, but first we wish to show you how much we've learned. It is not just for school that we learn. It is for life that we learn, and it's what we do with our learning that is important. So, take a seat at the old desks and perhaps remember some of your past. ("Patchwork Performance")

For the next forty-five minutes, the schoolteacher and children sing songs, tell stories, read poems, and show artwork, all offering a nostalgic look at the frontier school, teacher, and students. At the same time, however, the program offers life lessons and admonitions on gender behavior and attitudes.

The Gender Ideology

It is appropriate that a schoolhouse performance is part of Waterville's Victorian Days festival and that the schoolhouse skit is led by a female schoolteacher. Although the household remained the most common workplace for women during the Victorian era, women were increasingly becoming wage earners outside the home. "Primary school teaching offered one of the . . . most important new job opportunities" during the Victorian era (Hume and Offen 283) and was "the most popular professional career for western women" (Peavy and Smith 120). According to Glenda Riley, "teaching . . . was considered a natural concomitant of women's domestic duties because of the inherent qualities that women supposedly possessed in the areas of child care and nurturing" (Riley 103). In fact, Hume and Offen argue: "Teaching was in effect an extension of a woman's traditional role as educator of the young and could be viewed as an apprenticeship for motherhood" (283). As "women began to dominate the [teaching] field, men had a tendency to regard schoolteaching as 'woman's work,' and to shun it for that reason" (Fuller, *The Old Country School* 160).

Further, females proved attractive as teachers because not only would they work for less than half the salary men commanded,[11] they would also more likely endure harsh and restrictive teaching conditions. The prim, white, A-framed schoolhouse sitting in Waterville's community park belies the stark and primitive nature of the early frontier schools. Built out of whatever materials were available—logs, sod, rocks—these schoolhouses often had dirt floors, greased paper windows, and poorly ventilated stoves. The schools were built by local farmers and teachers were not consulted. Schoolhouse sites were most often selected where land could be cheaply purchased, and consequently, schools were built on treeless, rocky hills or insect-infested swampy bottoms (Fuller, *The Old Country School* 61). Not only were women expected to teach in these conditions, they were often expected to maintain the building while constantly enforcing discipline among a wide-ranging age of children. Women also faced harsh psychological conditions, enduring the loneliness and isolation of a frontier schoolteacher. In the face of these harsh conditions, rural schoolteachers "were expected to be exemplary models of moral behavior" for the children and community. Mrs Bergquist's dress performed this moral code. Samuelson quotes a list of late nineteenth-century rules for Kansas's female teachers. Among other things, a female teacher was restricted from "dying her hair," "wearing face powder, mascara, or lip paint," or "dressing in bright colors" (79).

Besides the gender roles enacted by Mrs. Bergquist and embodied in the schoolhouse, the "Patchwork Performance" program offers admonitions of gender roles as well. The topics performed by girls and boys reinforced traditional gender roles, stereotypes, and behaviors. Girls performed poems and sang songs which featured females in domestic roles—quilting, sewing, gardening, and cleaning house. Boys, on the other hand, enacted performances which highlighted male role stereotypes—public speaking, fishing, chasing girls, eating too much, telling the truth, and achieving success.

Embedded in the text of the various songs and poems are explicit statements of appropriate gender attitudes and behaviors. The most overt statement of gender behaviors comes in a dialogue entitled "A Difference of Opinion," between a young girl and young boy:

Young Girl:	Young Boy:
I could have more to eat,	I could have a heap of clothes,
And make lots of noise,	And my hair in curls,
And not always be so tidy,	They wouldn't always hush me up,
If I were one of the boys.	If I were one of the girls.
But when it's dark at night,	But only dolls and kittens!
Close to mamma I can curl,	And no baseball! No sir!
And needn't make believe I'm brave,	I'd rather have two lickins'
Because I am a girl.	Than be a girl—like her!

Even the pieces that are not overtly about male and female behavior embody gender stereotypes. The program featured a patriotic section about George Washington and the U.S. flag. Embedded in the patriotic poems and songs were these admonitions about gender. A second-grade boy read the following poem about George Washington:

> I think I'll be like Washington,
> As dignified and wise;
> Folks always say a boy can be
> A great man if he tries.

In contrast, a third-grade girl read this poem:

> I cannot be a Washington,
> However hard I try.
> But into something I must grow
> As fast the days go by.
> The world needs women good and true,
> I'm glad I can be one.
> For that is even better than
> To be a Washington.

In the boy's poem, the hero identified is a military and political leader. The attitude inherent in the poem is that the boy *can* be dignified and wise like Washington (emphasis mine). Further, this poem inculcates the belief that boys can achieve greatness if they only try. Contrawise, the girl's poem explicitly tells her she *cannot* be like Washington. Further, the female poem's subtext reads that being a good woman—and thereby adhering to traditional female roles—is an important goal. These two poems would seem to reify very traditional gender roles.

Woman as Community Builder

Gender and Municipal Housekeeping

Cary DeWit contends that "a tradition of strong division between male and female roles persists today on the High Plains more so than it does in other contexts of American society" (31). Much of the gender ideology intact during the Victorian era remains in place today on the plains of rural America. Indeed, Lisa Bourke and A. E. Luloff argue that in the rural myth, "gender roles are more traditional, patriarchy more evident, and gender differentiations more profound" (238). DeWit continues her analysis by acknowledging that "Men typically attend to farm, ranch, or business, while women tend to domestic duties and work as teachers, nurses, clerks, or secretaries" (31). Linda Stoneall points out that "in addition to sharing responsibilities for the farm, all women are responsible for the home and cooking" (22). Additionally, women remain the dominant presence in the K-12 classroom. In a 2002-2003 profile of elementary and secondary Kansas teachers, it was reported that 74 percent of all public schoolteachers were female (Kansas State Department of Education).

Much of the literature on community building is oriented around a gender ideology. Community building and community development, for example, are often defined around male-dominated activities—creating economic development and opportunities, achieving and wielding political influence, holding formal leadership positions. Recently, research has argued, however, that the concept of community building and development should be reconceptualized and broadened because much of the work women engage in builds and develops community. This research argues and this study confirms that women engaging in traditional female roles have extended those roles to include work directed at building community. As Meghan Cope reports, "women [have] extended their role as women, as caretakers of the family and community, and as a source of moral authority to the broader political arena" and that they extended their "caretaking role in order to fix things they saw as wrong, a movement referred to as 'municipal housekeeping'" (60-61).

Victorian Days performances enact community maintenance, preservation, identification, and education roles, and when the women of Waterville discuss Victorian Days—the work, the goals, the benefits—their talk is cast in the gendered terminology of cleaning, protecting, educating, and preserving their community.

Initially, the Victorian Days committeewomen view the festival work as their job. These Waterville women express some frustration that they receive little help from males in the community. This frustration begins with the elected and paid male city officials. Ruth Ann Roepke argues that an impetus for Victorian Days was to help preserve the community, but "we got no support from the city, very little" for our ideas (Victorian Days Meeting, 6/2/03). Once the festival was organized and under way, Sandy Harding talks about the frustrations of getting the city to help.

> We need some crowd control. We need some cooperation from the town officials that we don't get. That's it in a nutshell. Doris actually called, and I don't know if she called Chuck or Larry. But she called and asked him to come and be on the streets Sunday. Because it was dangerous out there. I mean, [bicycles] in and out of the crowd. If we'd had a busy crowd, somebody would've been hurt. I think it is unfortunate that we don't have any cooperation from our city officials, which we don't have. (Victorian Days Committee Meeting, 5/7/01)

Committeewomen further point out that individual males work very little on Victorian Days. During one meeting, it was suggested that the committee ask men to volunteer some help, to which a woman sarcastically responded, "finding men helpers, that's like looking for hen's teeth" (Victorian Days Committee Meeting, 4/9/01). Local men do not disagree with these characterizations, noting that "male volunteers hadn't . . . been involved" (Terry Roepke interview). In fact, a Waterville police officer stated, "This [Victorian Days] is a woman's day and most of the men I know decide to head for the hills, or else you might get pushed into helping with this thing" (Tormondson interview). Males that do work tend to work "in the background" (Walter interview) and do the physical labor like hauling supplies (Whitesell interview), hauling and setting up furniture (Walter interview), and rearranging rooms (Walter interview).

The essential work of the festival—the planning, organizing, and performing—is conducted almost exclusively by women. Their festival work is cast in the language of traditional, domestic feminine roles. Certainly the festival performances—the high tea, home tours, and schoolhouse program—enact these female roles. But festival preparation is also discussed through the lens of feminine domestic roles. The organizing committee talks about cleaning, restoring, renovating, and preserving their community much as they would talk about cleaning and preserving their homes. As LuAnn Ropeke pointed out:

> That's one thing that happened from Victorian Days that you don't think about until you start thinking back, is what it did, not just in monetary terms. I don't know how many buildings we've cleaned uptown so that we could have something in 'em. Several of 'em. And uh, it's just kind of been an interesting thing what we've kind of cleaned up to put on Victorian Days. (Victorian Day Meeting, 3/3/03)

Indeed, committeewomen routinely offer a litany of cleaning and renovating projects associated with Victorian Days. Labor and proceeds from Victorian Days has "redone the chandelier in the Opera House" (Whitesell interview), "put on a new [museum] roof" (Harding interview) and "installed new linoleum flooring" (LuAnn Roepke interview, 17 April 2001) in the Thompson Museum, saved segments of the local Burlington Northern's railroad tracks (Genschorck interview), provided playground equipment for the community park (Victorian Days Meeting, 6/2/03), cleaned up the Masonic Hall (Irons interview), and cleaned an empty downtown building so it could be used for the festival "saloon." The most significant cleaning and renovating effort, however, is associated with the three-story Weaver Hotel. Each year the hotel, which sits empty 363 days a year, is cleaned, scrubbed, polished, vacuumed, dusted, and painted for the festival weekend. Curtains, tablecloths, china, and flatware are collected, cleaned, and brought to the hotel annually in preparation of the annual festival. Through local labor (most by Waterville women), Victorian Days receipt money, and historic preservation grants (applied for by Waterville women), the Weaver Hotel has gained a new porch, new exterior doors, and new windows (Scott, "Dressing Up" A10).

The immediate goal of cleaning and renovating the various Waterville buildings is to prepare them as suitable performance spaces for Victorian Days. The more overarching and important goal, however, is to preserve and sustain the Waterville community. The committeewomen are interested in creating a positive community through what they consider to be the purview of women. Just as they care for and preserve their own homes and families, these women see Victorian Days as an agency to care for and preserve Waterville (Irons interview; Victorian Days Meeting, 6/2/03; Stewart interview; Tormondson interview; Walter interview). By many accounts, their work has, in fact, saved several historic buildings. Waterville's male mayor acknowledges that their efforts have "kept the museum open" (Whitesell interview). Proceeds from Victorian Days constituted the third largest donation to the construction of the Waterville Community Center (Victorian Days Meeting, 3/3/03). Their funding has sustained the Waterville railroad depot (Walter interview). The committee has also contributed over $50,000 to restore and preserve the Weaver Hotel. From seed money provided by Victorian Days, the community received a $75,000 historical preservation grant in 2001 to work on the exterior of the hotel (Victorian Days Meeting, 3/3/03). The community received word in the summer of 2003 that they had been awarded a $1.4 million federal grant to renovate the interior of the Weaver Hotel (Scott, "Dressing Up" A1).

Besides historical preservation, other community-building goals have been identified by the Victorian Days' committee. The committeewomen argue that the Victorian Days festival provides the critical community-building function of bringing of communal bonding (Harding interview; Irons interview; Minge interview; Victorian Days Meeting, 5/7/01). This bonding manifests itself in several forms. Initially, there is the bonding that results from working to organize and produce the festival. There exists a special bond among the core organizing committee. As the Victorian Days secretary notes, "I really like the camaraderie and the social part of the experience" of producing the festival (Stewart interview). Indeed, Lavenda writes that "organization of [any] festival, since it takes several months of meetings and coordinated effort, creates a special sense of solidarity among organizers" ("Festivals and the Creation of Public Culture" 80). Sandy Harding notes similar communal benefits in regards to the larger community who working together for Victorian Days.

What can I say when you get over 100 people to show up [to help at the festival]. I thought this was a big tribute to this community. I said, no matter what we made or how many people bought tickets, I think Victorian Days does something for the Waterville community that is above and beyond any monetary value that we ever gain from it. You looked around the room and you had people from all walks of life in our community gathered for one cause, and to me, that was worth anything and everything. (Victorian Days Meeting, 5/7/01)

Not only does Victorian Days function as a bonding experience for those engaged in producing the festival, there is also a communal experience for all those who participate in the weekend festival. Many people, ranging from committee-women to local citizens to outside tourists, participate in a community-wide expression of fellowship. Victorian Days creates a common event, a moment of community reflection and celebration when a great variety of people come together, perform together, participate together, or just take the opportunity of the festival to get together and catch up on the latest Waterville news. Festival organizers and participants alike report the communal benefits of participating in Victorian Days (Irons interview; Minge interview; Whitesell interview). Finally, Victorian Days creates a communal bond as it functions as a source of community pride for those living in Waterville. Mary Irons suggests that Victorian Days is a vehicle to "put our community on display," while Sandy Harding argues that Victorian Days "sets us up to be an example and leader to all the surrounding towns and communities. . . . When you say Waterville, people sit up and take notice. We are a model to a lot of communities" (Irons interview; Harding interview). Ann Walter echoes this sentiment when she contends that Victorian Days "has been very successful and certainly brings a lot of people into our community and keeps our community . . . alive and well. And we have a reputation. Waterville is known for its beautiful homes and a clean environment and an active community" (Walter interview). Victorian Days ultimately becomes symbolic of Waterville's achievements and pride. It becomes a coalescing symbol of identification for local citizens.

Conclusions:
Festival as Gendered Community-Building Agency

Despite increasing evidence that suggests women are critical to sustaining local community, males continue to be "recognized as local leaders by rural residents more often than women" (Bourke and Luloff 239). Community-building scholars reinforce this perception according to Stoneall, as "community analysts have defined and studied communities with a singular focus on men" (25). Licuanan, Panjaitan, and van Es bluntly state that "there is a dearth of research on the importance of gender on community development efforts" (137).

The study of Victorian Days in Waterville, Kansas, addresses this paucity of research and suggests a symbolic and strategic means for women to assume greater influence in rural community affairs. The path centers around the creation, performance, and purpose of festival as civic communion. Indeed, Marilyn Aronoff argues that festivals "may stimulate innovation by helping participants to move beyond traditional models of behavior to develop new paradigms" (369) while Stoeltje argues that festivals can function to alter the social construction of women (221). I believe producing a civic communion moment such as the Victorian Days festival provides women with a strategic path for entree into local community power and development. There are several characteristics of festival as civic communion which make this type of event particularly effective for women to integrate into the community power hierarchy and receive acknowledgment for community development works, including: (1) festival communication is consistent with a feminine rhetorical style; (2) festivals allow women to symbolically invert the sociopolitical hierarchy; (3) festivals facilitate a metaphoric extension allowing women to be viewed as managers and protectors of community, and finally, (4) festivals connect women positively to important community symbols.

Initially, the rhetoric of festivals is consistent with a feminine rhetorical style, thus making festival symbolism an appropriate medium for social change. Ivan Karp argues that festivals are a "sensual, emotional" cultural text ("Festivals" 282) and a "participative, inclusive" celebration of local community (284). As contrasted with elite, male, rational discursive argument structures, festivals present "particularizing stories" by "non-elite and informal" community storytellers (Karp, "Festivals" 282-83).[12] Waterville women perform Victorian Days festival rhetoric to highlight a variety of stories of historic preservation and community development. They articulate these stories in a manner that is nonthreatening and noncompetitive and generally not possible in everyday life.

Many festival scholars agree that festival performances often function to invert the social order (Abrahams; Manning; Stoeltje). Festivals as celebratory play allow those with little sociopolitical power to dress in costumes of power, act in powerful ways, and change their social identity and status for the festival weekend. During Victorian Days, rural women are the organizers and the decision makers. These rural women dress in luxurious costumes; bake, display and serve splendid desserts; and offer performances of frontier women who survived the harsh conditions of the American prairie around the turn of the century. The festival performance and play thus allow these women to transcend and subvert the patriarchal systems of power so dominant in rural America.

Additionally, festivals are metaphoric. Frank Manning writes that festivals as celebrations have "a metaphoric structure and content," extending meaning, relating one form of comprehension to another. Manning continues by arguing that through metaphor, festivals "work to promote change" and "flourish among those who are relatively powerless, and whose pragmatic interests lie in changing the balance in their favor" (27). As discussed earlier, historically and still in many rural areas, women's expected work remains primarily identified with the managing and preserving the home. Through Victorian Days, Waterville women metaphorically extend the concept of the domestic sphere from the home to the community. Waterville citizens perceive a natural correlation in job tasks as Waterville women clean, refurbish, renovate, and ultimately protect and preserve local historic buildings just as they would perform these tasks in their homes. Consequently, women associated with Victorian Days logically become viewed as the managers and protectors of the local community. Metaphoric festival rhetoric and performance thus offer women a seemingly natural entrance into local development efforts.

Finally, the women associated with Victorian Days become symbolically connected with highly valued symbols of community. Festivals function to highlight and celebrate important community symbols. Festivals work to create and reify community identity through the celebration of local symbols. In the case of Waterville, the important community symbols are the very historic buildings the women have worked to preserve through the festival they created. Victorian Days has promoted and preserved Waterville's historic buildings, and now those very buildings give Waterville its community identity. Consequently, the Victorian Days committeewomen have achieved a level of influence not attained by many rural women.

This analysis of Victorian Days in Waterville, Kansas, offers information for several important but underresearched areas. Initially, this study illustrates how community festivals function as civic communion. As civic communion, community festivals enact important local, social, and political structures. One social structure festivals perform is local gender roles. Further, this analysis suggests that embedded within these festival performances are gender ideologies. These gender ideologies offer insight into the place and status of women in local community. Finally, this analysis has demonstrated how women might use festival as an agency to bridge perceptions of influence disparity in local community development.

Notes

1. Despite some who argue that Victorian Days attracts both men and women, a significant amount of evidence indicates that the festival is organized by women primarily for women. The major attractions—the high tea, home tours, and schoolhouse performance—are organized and produced by women. The entire organizing committee is female and over 80 percent of the participants are female. Interviews support the perspective this festival is heavily gendered. Interviews reported that no men serve on the organizing committee (Whitesell interview) and, further, that the women are not all that interested in men serving on the committee (Irons interview; Stewart interview). As the chair of the committee stated, the committee is "fine the way it is. It works. If it isn't broke, don't fix it. I mean, it's not that we wouldn't welcome them (men), but um, it's not a thing that we are upset about" (Harding interview). Additionally, both men and women agree the events are primarily oriented toward women (Genschorck interview; Harding interview; Tormondson interview).

2. Three different research teams of graduate students assisted with this field research project. In 1999, the research team included: Clayton Johnson, Andy Douglas, Michele Griffith, and Amanda Olsen. In 2001, the graduate research team included: Wendy Zeitz, Kittie Grace, and Christy Meller. In 2003, the research team included: Barbara Marshall,

Amanda Buoy, Kristi Garber, Misty Cooper, and Greg Watt. All graduate students were part of a Field Methods in Speech Communication course and studying community festivals became the basis of the semester research project.

3. Over the three research periods, graduate student research teams worked with other rural community projects including: The Tulip Festival in Wamego; the Peabody Heritage Museum; the Halstead Heritage Museum and Depot, and the Goessel Mennonite Museum. In Waterville, I was very conscious about the gender mix of the research team and consequently used more women than men on the research teams. Specifically, nine women and three men served on the Victorian Days festival research teams.

4. We entered the research site with the openly acknowledged goal of conducting research on the community-building function of small town festivals. In this way, everyone knew that the research teams were collecting data. Our research teams functioned as "participant as observer." Our research role and observations pivoted from the perspective of participation. For a discussion of this field method research stance, see Raymond L. Gold, "Roles in Sociological Field Observation," *Social Forces* 36 (March 1958): 220-21.

5. Victorian Days committee members interviewed included: Pam White (chair, 2001), LueAnn Roepke (founder, English Tea chair, interviewed 1999, 2001), Ruth Ann Roepke (founder), Mary Lou Roepke (Victorian Home Tour chair), Gay Stewart (secretary), Paulette Wassenberg (Group Tour chair, 1999), Sandy Harding (chair, 2003), Mary Irons (Bake Shop chair, 2001, 2003), Yvonne Larson (Street Entertainment chair), Ann Walter (committee member), and Cindy Genschorck (committee member).

6. Those Waterville citizens interviewed who were not intimately involved in organizing Victorian Days included: Terry Roepke (newspaper), Alan Minge (Victorian homeowner), Jerri Dorn (librarian), Scott Tormondson (police officer), and David Whitesell (mayor).

7. Etta Ann and Joel Grace were visiting the Waterville area from Salt Lake City, Utah, and consented to be interviewed regarding the Victorian Days festival.

8. The major events for Waterville's Victorian Days include: an English high tea, local Victorian home tours, a one-room schoolhouse performance, a frontier church service, a display of quilts from the Civil War-era, tours of Waterville's railroad depot, gunfights at the Front Street Saloon, a frontier encampment, tours of the Waterville historical museum, displays and demonstrations of turn-of-the-century bicycles, performances by a cowboy humorist, performances by a female palm reader, and tours of local churches. In addition, many downtown businesses and buildings were converted to a Victorian Days theme specifically for this April weekend.

9. I selected these three events as they have traditionally been: (1) the most popular attractions at the festival—people had to sign up for specific times to attend the schoolhouse performances, and (2) they are the events people must pay to attend.

10. Wayne Fuller writes that, "At first glance, these little [school] buildings—almost invariably painted white—seemed so much alike that they appear to have been constructed from the same set of architectural plans." See Wayne E. Fuller, *One-Room Schools of the Middle West* (Lawrence: University Press of Kansas, 1994), 14.

11. Nearly every source examining rural, frontier schools made the argument that one reason women were attractive as teachers was that they would work for less money than would male teachers. See, for example, Wayne E. Fuller, *One-Room Schools of the Middle West* (Lawrence: University Press of Kansas, 1994), 59; Leslie Parker Hume and Karen M. Offen, "The Adult Woman: Work," in *Victorian Women,* eds. Erna Olafson Hellerstein, Leslie Parker Hume, and Karen M. Offen (Stanford, CA: Stanford University Press, 1981), 284; Glenda Riley, *The Female Frontier* (Lawrence: University Press of Kansas, 1988), 105; and Bill Samuelson, *One Room Country Scools of Kansas* (Emporia, KS: Chester Press, 2000),

62. The first teacher at the Game Fork Creek School was Emma Cooley and she was paid $22 a month. During its existence, there were sixty-five different teachers at the schoolhouse. Of these sixty-five teachers, fifty-three were women ("Welcome to Waterville's Tenth Annual Celebration," 2000).

12. Jane Blankenship and Deborah Robson detail the characteristics of a feminine rhetorical style. They argue women are essentially storytellers who use concrete, particular examples to personalize issues. They also contend that women's speech values "inclusivity" and "seeks ways to empower others." See Jane Blankenship and Deborah Robson, "A 'Feminine Style' in Women's Political Discourse," *Communication Quarterly* 43 (Summer 1995): 359-62.

4

Building Community
through Strategic Planning

The two-story stone farmhouse now stands abandoned. Its glass windows and wooden roof gone, its thick cream-colored, Greenhorn limestone walls in ruins. Weeds weave in and around the foundation, extending through vacant windows. Where there were once interior walls, beds, tables, and chairs, now only elm trees reside. These volunteers stretch up and beyond where a roof once existed. Like a stone relic, this farmhouse now sits in the middle of a sprawling, productive wheat field. The fenced farmyard has long since given way to this cultivated cash crop. In the southern distance meanders the narrow Saline river. This watercourse, which once supported the homestead and many others like it, now feeds the recreation class at Wilson Lake some fifty miles away. I believe this Lincoln County, Kansas, stone farmhouse, wheat field, and river stand as organizing images for this rural culture. They embody both the culture's strengths and weaknesses, and are symbolic of rural Kansas's physical, cultural, sociopolitical, and rhetorical place.

Space, Place, and Community

Many scholars contend that physical environment is fundamentally linked to cultural and community persona.[1] Researchers describe this connection as "a medium, milieu or context in which personal relationships are embedded" (Altman 31), as "a vast repository out of which symbols of order and social relationship can be fashioned" (Duncan, "The House as Symbol" 136), and as "part of the weave of a sense of the context that lives alongside of us, influencing our perceptions of meaning, our judgments of persons, places, and things" (Goodall, *Living in the Rock N Roll Mystery* 70).

It is clear that an understanding of community is, in part, constructed through the symbolic responses natives have to their surrounding environment. This symbolic response begins when humans first encounter the environment. This interaction is direct perception of the physical, empirical experience (Allison and Allison). At this experiential moment, the environment exists as undifferentiated space (Allison and Allison; Tuan). Philipsen, for example, notes that when he first encountered "Teamsterville," "the community appeared . . . as merely a series of unconnected streets, buildings, people, and activities" (*Speaking Culturally* 4). When first confronting an environment, space "has no fixed pattern of established human meanings; it is like a blank sheet on which meaning may be imposed" (Tuan 54).

As humans interact within the physical environment, they begin to name the environment and attach symbols to the surrounding space. Low argues, "there is a transformation of the experience of a space or piece of land into a culturally meaningful and shared symbol, that is, place" (166). Such a transformation of the environment creates shared memories, contexts, and cultural models, which, in turn, give birth to a sense of place (Allison and Allison 632). Within this communication process of assigning meaning and value to the physical environment, humans convert space to place. As Tuan argues, "When space feels thoroughly familiar to us, it has become place" (73). Again, Philipsen explains this process through his Teamsterville study: "By the time I left [Teamsterville], it was, for me, not just a setting, but a scene, a place suffused with activity, with meaning, with significance . . . for those who had grown up there and those who lived there permanently" (*Speaking Culturally* 4). Indeed, Philipsen found "a sense of place—at once both hierarchical and physical—is a 'major unifying perception' in [Teamsterville's] cultural worldview" ("Places for Speaking" 16).

Constructing symbolic place creates identity, social relationships, value structures, and appropriate ways of acting.[2] As individuals symbolize place, their constructions cluster with others, creating community boundaries and cultural images. Differing communities emerge when groups respond differently to the physical environment. For example, in his critical ethnography of John F. Kennedy's assassination site, Trujillo argues that the "Dealey Plaza is a 'cultural site in which multiple voices vie for critical space and cultural definition'" (449). These cultural definitions come from different rhetorical communities communicating differing values, social relationships, and actions in response to the same landscape. By examining reaction to the physical environment, it is possible to sketch the boundaries of community.

This chapter is an analysis of how citizens in Lincoln and Mitchell counties in north central Kansas carved community identity from their surrounding landscape. It is an examination of the physical space these counties occupy, the symbolic response citizens have to this physical environ, and how the interplay of the symbolic and material landscape works to construct community identity. After a discussion of strategic planning as civic communion and the methodological context of the current study, this chapter moves to a specific examination of responses to this place. From this examination, it is possible to place the physical, cultural, sociopolitical, and rhetorical boundaries of this rural culture.

Strategic Planning as Civic Communion

Urban and regional planning has a long and rich history that is deeply rooted in both the physical design arts and the social sciences (Throgmorton 7). For purposes of this study, however, I am more interested in the history of the communicative relationship existing between planners and their audiences or clients. Planners have historically been guided by the foundational principle that *scientific planning should guide societal change* (Throgmorton 8; emphasis Throgmorton). Planners have traditionally taken the perspective that by collecting and analyzing data scientifically and organizing that data into accepted city designs, urban development can be properly and efficiently managed. This modernist view of planning, however, has located the planner on a "central plateau" from which an ideal, objective observer can discern what is best for society (Throgmorton 3).

Increasingly, planners have rejected this elitist model of planning and have argued that community planning is more properly conceived of as *"persuasive and constitutive storytelling about the future"* (Throgmorton 5; emphasis Throgmorton). In this perspective, planners facilitate meetings where the planning audiences articulate competing stories about their local identity and future. The community then selects those narratives which most persuasively constitute the image the community wishes to project. In short, planners are increasingly taking the perspective of this chapter, namely that communities can best be understood as social constructions.

One popular form of community planning in the 1990s was strategic planning. Originally developed in the private sector in the 1960s, strategic planning is a "disciplined effort to produce fundamental decisions and actions that shape and guide what an organization is, what it does, and why it does it" (Bryson, *Strategic Planning* 4-5). During last moments of the twentieth century, rural communities confronted an uncertain and chaotic future by turning to this business planning model as an avenue to strengthen their own regional and global positioning. As "local leaders discovered that their communities were being influenced by outside factors, they felt a need to anticipate change and move their communities in new directions" (Tatarko et al. 23). Fundamental to community strategic planning was working through a decision-making framework that articulated a vision of community, highlighted community strengths, weaknesses, opportunities, and threats, and identified goals for future development based on appropriate allocation of existing resources. In the early 1990s, the Kansas State Legislature did indeed adopt a three-year program of community strategic planning grants that provided funds to county-wide and multicounty economic development entities (Ott and Tatarko). Legislators believed it was important for Kansas counties to assume responsibility for planning and development so as to strategically position themselves within the rural, state, national, and international economies. The goal of these strategic plans was to strengthen and expand local and regional economic development efforts, thereby maximizing chances for county stability, growth, and long-term survival.[3]

Interestingly, however, the planning sessions conceived to strategically position the counties and communities economically also became moments in which these rural communities reflected upon themselves. During strategic planning meetings, participants talked about the vision they held of their county's image. They highlighted their counties' strengths and opportunities. They identified weaknesses and threats in the counties. In short, the strategic planning meetings evolved into moments of civic communion.

Organizationally, civic communions are collective moments of intense, yet transitory praise for community. The Kansas strategic planning sessions were, in fact, segmented moments of reflection about local communities and counties. The strategic planning grants were temporally bounded so that community discussion would be more intensely focused by recognition that a strategic plan had to be written by a certain date. Further, a fundamental goal of strategic planning is to involve as many community groups and citizens as possible. As Daniels, Keller, and Lapping argue, in the planning process there is a general phase of participation in which "neighborhoods, community groups, individuals, and special interest groups are all brought together as a public to offer opinions and suggest goals and objectives" (18). Likewise, Bryson contends that "planning on behalf of a community almost always involves substantial citizen participation" (*Strategic Planning* 43). The strategic planning process in Lincoln and Mitchell counties occurred over the course of eight months and seven meetings. While levels of participation varied with each meeting, an average of forty people attended each planning session. Individuals attending included farmers, city and county commissioners, homemakers, lawyers, ministers, business owners, teachers, librarians, county extension agents and other state employees, state legislators, and community college teachers (Cyr).

Rhetorically, civic communions are moments of enthusiastic praise for local community structures. The Kansas strategic planning process offered structured moments to reflect on and praise counties and local communities. For example, strategic planning models ask citizens to articulate the vision they have for their community. As Bryson points out, a vision statement includes the community's mission, its basic philosophy, and core values. The vision statement emphasizes the community's social purposes and its ethical perspective (*Strategic Planning* 165). This planning process also asks citizens to identify their community's strengths, weaknesses, opportunities, and threats. Again, according to Bryson, identification of these issues can lead to a community's "distinctive or core competencies and resources" (*Strategic Planning* 30). During these moments in the strategic planning model, citizens are, in fact, working through a process in which they identity and celebrate their community. Rural Kansans told of their history and dreams, their needs and goals. While the explicit goal of Kansas's strategic planning process was to strategically "place" counties and communities economically, communities likewise articulated powerful narratives of community identity. As James Throgmorton explained, planning narratives are not simply factual and persuasive, but rather are also constitutive as they "write and shape community, character, and culture" (51).

Methodological Contexts

Throgmorton argues that planning is "an enacted, future-oriented, narrative in which the participants are the actors and joint authors, and we can think of storytelling as being an appropriate style for conveying the truth of planning action" (48). I thus decided to conduct an analysis of constitutive narratives told by the strategic planning participants in Lincoln and Mitchell counties. To collect data, field research was conducted over a three-year period. Data collection was initiated during the eight-month strategic planning process and continued during several subsequent research trips into Lincoln and Mitchell counties over the following two years.

During the strategic planning sessions, I served in the role of facilitator.[4] During the strategic planning meetings, my role involved providing an agenda of planning issues and sustaining and organizing conversation among the county participants. Normally, I simply listened and only interjected my voice into the flow of discourse when some issue seemed unclear, when someone was dominating the discussion, or to draw in additional voices to the conversation. While I was physically present at all meetings, most conversation occurred between the citizens of Lincoln and Mitchell counties. Thus, I could easily jot down brief narratives occurring among county citizens. I would also write notes on topics I wanted to pursue during subsequent interviews. This type of participative role afforded me the chance to both witness and participate in their cultural enactment.

Within the strategic planning meetings, citizens of Lincoln and Mitchell counties imagined, articulated, and enacted their cultural vision and worked to locate the uniqueness of their region. I noticed there were constant references to "place." I began to believe that not only did the county citizens construct an interpretation of the place they occupied, but their interpretations of place worked to constitute their cultural identity as well. I pursued this focus during subsequent trips into the counties by conducting follow-up interviews and researching in their libraries, historical societies, newspaper, and law offices. From disparate bits of data coming from: (1) strategic planning narratives; (2) narratives from interviews; (3) narratives found in newspaper features, editorials, and letters to the editor; as well as (4) descriptions of the land, the communities, the people, and their economic conditions, I attempted to piece together a composite identity of this rural culture.

Placing Lincoln and Mitchell Counties

The Physical and Cultural Boundaries

Viewed from a distant perspective, the boundaries of Lincoln and Mitchell counties physically form a rectangle measuring forty-six miles north to south and twenty-nine miles east to west. This quadrangular block is situated halfway between Missouri and Colorado, in the northern half of Kansas, just thirteen miles southeast of the geographic center of the United States. The land, situated in the Smoky Hills, is a vast and broken landscape of high plateau-like uplands, isolated buttes, hills, limestone escarpments, and rolling lowland plains (Ball et al.).

There are, however, three specific environmental features of this area that give it shape both physically and culturally. First, this mass of Kansas is on the eastern edge of a vast expanse of prairie that extends west for three hundred miles. Second, Lincoln and Mitchell counties are situated in the heart of "post rock country" (Muilenburg and Swineford). Finally, two rivers—the Saline in the southern Lincoln County and the Solomon in the northern Mitchell County—run through this bicounty rectangle and empty into two lakes—the Saline into Wilson and the Solomon into Waconda—that anchor the southwest and northwest corners of the counties, respectively. County citizens use these physical sites as touchstones for their sense of identity and to identify both the strengths they possess and the threats they face.

The Prairie

The 98th meridian—considered by many as the gateway to the great American West—slices through the heart of Lincoln and Mitchell counties. While a few cottonwood, elm, ash, and willow trees are clustered near creeks, rivers, and lakes, it is cropland and a variety of native grasses that cover the floor of these two counties. The land is given a checkerboard effect by fields of wheat, milo, and sunflowers mixing with natural bluestem, buffalo, and Indian grasses. Fields of crops and grasses easily grow waist high and stretch out for miles in all directions.

To area residents, these expansive vistas of rolling hills, cultivated fields, and native grasses symbolize a region which is beautiful, peaceful, safe, clean, and rich in opportunity. A Mitchell County commissioner relates the following story during a strategic planning meeting:

> Ya'know, I was out by myself doing chores the other night. No big deal, that's just what I do. But I looked off to the west and there was a beautiful sunset. That's what it's all about here. The pure air, the pure land, and beautiful view. We have a quality of life that's really superior to life in the cities.

During another strategic planning meeting, a tremendous thunderstorm moved into Lincoln and Mitchell counties. As the thunderhead clouds billowed and rolled eastward across the prairie toward us and fingers of lighting crisscrossed the sky, a young farmer observed, "these clouds are my Rocky Mountains. They're so majestic and ever-changing. I watch these clouds and feel in awe of their beauty, their power, their vastness." An entrepreneur and recent immigrant to this area tells a similar tale of the good life connected to the natural environment through his story of entering the region:

> Two years ago, I moved out here from southern California—Newport Beach—and restored the old Woody house into a bed and breakfast. This is a wonderful life out here. There's no crime, my kids can play wherever they want, there's no smog, I'm not driving two hours to work and back every day, and the country's beautiful.

Finally, an economic developer echoes the previous stories with his narrative which includes a business spin:

> People out here don't realize what a desirable place we now live in. People in Chicago, Los Angeles, Houston all drive two hours into work. And it's all through bumper to bumper traffic. What's the difference between that and driving from here to Salina, Manhattan, even Wichita through beautiful, peaceful country. I think if people knew about this place, with its quality of life, we could get some business-people out here.

Lincoln and Mitchell county residents consistently describe the land positively. It is symbolized as beautiful, pure, safe, and peaceful. But the land is also con-structed as a scene for opportunity. It is portrayed as vast enough, private enough, and bountiful enough to accommodate whatever one wishes to do for enjoyment and/or employment. County citizens construct the land as free of barriers—freedom from crime, freedom from crowding, freedom from constraining traffic, freedom from burdensome government—allowing them and others to act and work as they desire. As a Lincoln lawyer and consultant argues, "The resettlement of rural America is facilitated by technology, justified by economics and because they think that rural life is better for their kids, peace of mind, and sense of place" (Crangle, "Resettling of Rural America").

The Post Rock

Inches below the prairie sod in Lincoln and Mitchell counties are thick layers of a cream-colored Greenhorn limestone. The rock, also known as "fencepost limestone" or "post rock," is unique to this region. When quarried from the earth, this rock breaks evenly in dimensions suitable for building. When split from ravine ledges or dug from just beneath the topsoil, the chalky limestone slabs are "seldom less than eight inches or more than twelve inches thick. . . . It [is also] soft enough to shape with chisel or other tools when freshly quarried but would harden after being exposed to the air" (Muilenburg and Swineford 39). This band of Greenhorn limestone stretches about two hundred miles southwest from north central Kansas to just a few miles north of Dodge City, Kansas. "East to west, the boundaries of the area so zigzag that its width ranges from less than ten to forty miles. Roughly it covers five thousand square miles, or more than three million acres" (Muilenburg and Swineford 5). This geologic unit of rock and prairie has come to be known as "Post Rock Country."

References to post rock and stone are part of the narratives told and written by citizens in these counties. Whereas general descriptions of the land provide a sense of the physical boundaries, county rhetors use post rock narratives to construct the cultural and value boundaries of this region.

Post rock is used by rhetors to symbolize ingenuity, progress, strength, persever-ance, defiance, and compassion. A strategic planning participant remarked, "As I look at what's left of these old [stone] houses and walls of eighty and ninety years ago, the thought comes to my mind, those people loved this land and did the best they could with what they had." A reference in a Mitchell County Historical Society newsletter echoes the value of ingenuity. Post rocks, it claimed, are "monuments to ingenuity of Kansas pioneers. Trees were scarce, lumber hard to get. So the settlers did the best they could with what they had."

Post rock is a symbol of progress. Post rock was sledged out of the ground by hand and shaped with stone hammers and chisels. From this rock, stonemasons shaped and set thousands of fenceposts stretching over forty thousand miles (Trus-sell). The limestone symbolized hard work, perseverance, and ultimately progress as county settlers were able to carve homes, towns, and businesses out of the rock below the prairie. Pioneers used post rock to build banks, barns, bridges, homes, schools, churches, courthouses, libraries, sidewalks, and tombstones (Muilenburg and Swineford), literally carving civilization out of the ground.

Post rock also symbolizes strength, perseverance, and defiance, for these rural citizens have used it to withstand, harness, and transform the wildness of the Kansas prairie. Bill Bryson, a Kansas geologist, writes that just like the post rock, citizens "out here" are "indestructible and gaining strength as time goes on" ("Why Post Rock" 30); they "weather as the seasons go by, but their sturdy character battles the Kansas winds and natural adversities with strong indifference" ("Why Post Rock" 3). A *Seattle Times* article likewise wrote: "The two-tone, light tan, rusty-brown streaked limestone is the heritage of north central Kansas. Like the people, [post rock] has resisted storms, droughts, grasshopper plagues, and time" ("The Story of Post Rock" A6).

Finally, citizens use the stone to symbolize their fundamental compassion. Greenhorn limestone is "soft enough to shape with a chisel or other tools when freshly quarried" (Muilenburg and Swineford 39), but hardens when it comes in contact with the air, thus protecting the inner portions of the rock. The core of the rock, in fact, remains soft. The rock thus provides context when a gruff county supervisor told me: "ya' know, people are basically good out here." Thus, while rural citizens may outwardly appear gruff and intolerant, at their core, they perceive themselves as understanding and compassionate.

Whereas the Lincoln/Mitchell county landscapes are used to depict the physical scene, post rock constructs a value touchstone, highlighting values of ingenuity, perseverance, defiance, strength, compassion, and progress. Narratives referencing this unique stone create a value hierarchy which functions to weave together the texture of this culture.

The Water

Lincoln and Mitchell counties are framed on the southwest and northwest by a physical resource very important to middle America—water. County residents talked about water contamination issues and flooding issues, but most often and intensely talked about water supply issues. While this area is semiarid, receiving only about sixteen inches of rain a year, the counties have access to adequate supplies of water due to availability of water from two large reservoirs—Lake Wilson and Lake Waconda. County citizens realize that this water is literally their life and economic fluid. As a Kansas state representative wrote in the *Lincoln Sentinel Republican,* "any threat to the water supply in Waconda Lake is a real threat to the economic survival of the area . . . for the communities that rest their water supply hopes on it and for the communities immediately adjacent to Waconda Lake" (McClure 3).

The importance and intensity of the water supply issues became salient through two political proposals by state politicians. The first was a state legislative proposal to alter control of the state's water sources, essentially moving away from very local control of water supply to metropolitan centers of water control. Lincoln and Mitchell county citizens were vehemently opposed to this change in political control of their water. Citizens believed they had always been responsible for water usage while others had been irresponsible. They did not want "the urban interest," "the big city boys" telling them how to manage their water supply. On a hot and humid August night, a Lincoln County extension agent argued, "We've been conserving, taking care of our water for years and years. It's helping us live. I was in Kansas City the other day and those sprinklers were going everywhere. They want that water just to make sure they keep their lawns green."

The second proposal which illustrated the importance of water to the region was a political suggestion to provide water from sources in Lincoln and Mitchell counties to the community of Hays, a town about 100 miles to the west. A Mitchell County commissioner told the strategic planning audience:

> Well, I heard they had helluva meeting down at Hays the other night on this water issue. It didn't come to blows, but it was headed there, I guess. Hays has got too many folks for their water. Rein in your development, I say. Why should we let them stick a pipe in our lake and suck it dry just to keep 'em going for another ten, twenty years?

These bicounty residents use the land to locate themselves physically and culturally. According to their interactions, they reside in the scenic Smoky Hills, in a vast and beautiful shortgrass prairie, in small, safe communities, in a clean and pure environment that allows them to pursue employment and enjoyment as they desire. County citizens also use environmental touchstones to organize their value structure. Citizens reference post rock to symbolize ingenuity, perseverance, defiance, strength, compassion, and progress. Water narratives likewise highlight values of responsibility, local control, and self-reliance. Talk about water also constructs a sense of protectionism and a view that only the strong survive rural Kansas.

The Sociopolitical Boundaries

Characteristics of this rural region invite outside responses to the land. From the reaction of others to their place, county citizens articulate their relationship with outsiders. Outside reaction is often negative and harsh, invoking local perceptions of outsiders as uninformed and exploitive.

Deborah and Frank Popper of the urban studies department at Rutgers University argue: "The brute fact is that most Plains land is simply not competitive with land elsewhere. The only people who want it are already on it, and most of them are increasingly unable to make a living from it" ("The Great Plains" 16). They point to the large number of bank collapses, farm foreclosures, and business failures and note that "many small towns are emptying and aging at an all-time high rate, and some are dying" ("The Great Plains" 14). The Poppers conclude that while American culture has traditionally "stood on three legs—land, water and timber, in the Plains, not one but two of these legs were withdrawn—water and timber—and civilization was left on one leg—land. It is a small wonder that it toppled over" ("The Fate of the Plains" 112-13).

Since the plains are not perceived as acceptably profitable or populated, the Poppers suggest an alternative use for the land. These academics suggest using one hundred sparsely populated counties spread throughout the plains to create a pre-white environment hospitable to native grasses and buffalo: "a Buffalo Commons." According to the Poppers:

> The Plains run from the curling east wall of the Rockies to roughly the ninety-eight meridian. . . . The Great Plains are America's steppes. They have the nation's hottest summers and coldest winters . . . worst hail and locusts and range fires, fiercest droughts and blizzards. We believe that over the next generation the Plains will . . . become almost totally depopulated. At that point, a new use for the region will emerge, one that is in fact so old that it predates the American presence. We are suggesting that the region be returned to its original pre-white state. ("The Fate of the Plains" 99)

Not surprisingly, local response to the Buffalo Commons has been resoundingly negative. A former Kansas governor responded that the "Great Plains do not equal the Sahara. Why not seal off declining urban areas as well, and preserve them as museums of twentieth-century architecture" (Matthews 3). A Mitchell County resident also proclaimed: "Another strength we have here is we take care of ourselves. It's like those Poppers from New Jersey sayin' they're gonna give this area back to the buffalo. They're nuts. To say we're goin' down the tubes is pure bull.

Buffalo bull."

But the Poppers are not the only ones suggesting alternative uses for the land in Lincoln and Mitchell counties. In 1990 and 1991, Fort Riley, Kansas—an Army installation about eighty miles east of the counties—proposed appropriating eighty-two thousand acres of Lincoln County land to expand its training facilities. The military contended "sophisticated weapons need more space to maneuver," and the increased space would "permit more realistic battalion-size exercises." (Satchell 32, 34). A government study likewise argued "to minimize losses and to win on the modern battlefield, Army soldiers must have realistic peacetime training. Greater mobility and enhanced capabilities of modern weapons systems . . . have heightened concerns within the Army about the adequacy of its training space" (GAO 2).

County citizens responded that the Army targeted their rural land because they "see the area as a vast wasteland, nothing but rock and grass" (Ernst 8). County rhetoric opposing the base expansion was framed, not from a defense or strategic perspective, but from a land perspective. A brochure from the Kansas Coalition to Preserve Kansas argued, "The land is a precious, fragile, and finite resource. How much more can we stand to lose?" while another position paper proclaimed: "We don't live here by accident or because of a chance job offer. Our property holdings are not investments and we aren't land speculators. The Flint Hills and Smoky Hills are our ancestral home. These lands are our lives, and our children's heritage."

These outside proposals for Lincoln and Mitchell county land and the resultant local reaction work to reveal sociopolitical relationships. This interaction creates fissures between county residents and out-groups. The physical and symbolic boundaries between county residents and the outside world are cast in sharp relief. County residents argue their communities and people are neglected and/or exploited by the outside world. According to the owner of a local rock quarry:

> We're really the old grizzlies out here. Down at the Post Rock factory, they cut and shape the rock. Pieces of the rock get busted off, they're too small or just plain destroyed somehow. They get filtered out. They're the old grizzlies. We've been cut out filtered out of the economic boom that went on in the 1980s. We're the old grizzlies of this country.

Other residents argue the problem is not simply neglect, but malicious exploitation. A Lincoln County developer describes the relationship in a vocabulary of geo-political colonialism:

> We are literally the third world of the United States. Third world nations export their products at an obscenely low price to a powerful nations who transform those products into value, making huge profits. Corporate and government interests come in here and take our products out of the land, manufacture it, market it, sell it making huge profits. We don't see any of that money. Farmers don't see any of that money. Also, just like a third world nation, our government doesn't care about us.

Because county citizens perceive they are neglected and exploited by outsiders, responsibility and personal effort become the avenue for both local progress and combating threats. This is the case whether the issue is strategic planning, economic development, or protecting their land from military expansion. During an evaluation of the strategic planning sessions, one participant argued: "The state could've done a lot better job of being sensitive to local needs. They came out here and painted everybody out here with the same brush, trying to get everybody to follow the same model. Hey, some of us have been doing strategic planning for thirty years and we'll still be doing it whether we get [state] grant money or not." In economic development, editorials remind readers that "small businesses in Rural America have been failing in great numbers" and encourage residents to "try local merchants first" and "buy at home" ("Shopping Season"). Another Lincoln County resident told this story of bringing business into the community:

> A year ago, a bunch of us each put up several thousand dollars to get a decent restaurant in Lincoln. This is money that we'll probably never see again. We used this money to underwrite the renovation of Collenders [a restaurant] and bring in a good chef. Today, it's still going—mainly because a bunch of local citizens wanted to see it happen and were willing to put their money on the line. The bank sure wasn't going to do anything to take a risk. It had to be us.

The effort to combat Fort Riley's land expansion was also very localized. Nine different grassroots organizations such as The Heartland Alliance, Preserve Rural America, and Save the Heartland organized in or near Lincoln and Mitchell counties. Lincoln County officials even employed a group of Kansas State University students to "document historical and culturally significant antiquities to prevent expansion of Fort Riley into the county" (Ball et al. 46). Lincoln and Mitchell county citizens contrasted their grassroots effort with the efforts of Manhattan and Junction City (communities closest to Ft. Riley) who supported expansion by spending hundreds of thousands of dollars on professional lobbyists in Washington, D.C.

The Rhetorical Boundaries

Finally, the way Lincoln and Mitchell citizens interact with the land places them rhetorically. I believe their symbolic responses to place ultimately cohere around the ideograph "freedom" and constructs a local culture of individualism.[5] The freedom articulated by residents of Lincoln and Mitchell counties is a freedom "from," referring to the absence of constraint, being left alone by others, not having other people's values, ideas, or styles of life forced upon one, standing unencumbered by government, thus allowing one's talents to take one as far as possible (Bellah et al.; Flathman).

The citizens' individualistic rhetoric begins with the physical characteristics of the land. The vastness of the plains suggests freedom. As Tuan argues, "Spaciousness is closely associated with the sense of being free. Freedom implies space; it means having the power and enough room to act. . . . Space lies open; it suggests the future and invites action" (52, 54). Indeed, county citizens construct their physical place as a vast scene of opportunity, free of barriers, where life can be "designed to meet individual needs for information, entertainment, friendship, religion, and education" (Crangle, "Designer Community").

County citizens also convert significant environmental touchstones into a value hierarchy consistent with individualist freedom. Their responses to the prairie, rock, and water highlight values of self-reliance, responsibility, defiance, ingenuity, and perseverance. Kemmis contends that individualism has always been particularly noticeable in the American West because it is, almost by definition, a hard place to live. People do not venture lightly into it. The frontier "selected people who were willing to accept a substantial amount of hardship for the sake of being left alone" (*Community and the Politics of Place* 44). The values constructed from the citizens' response to the environment are the values necessary to live and succeed in such an environment.

Conclusions

This chapter has explored the relationship of place to community and culture by examining the way a group of rural Kansas citizens respond to their physical environment. Conclusions about both strategic planning as civic communion, place theory, and this rural culture can be drawn from this research.

Initially, even though strategic planning came from the world of business, and communities used this planning model to position themselves economically, this chapter illustrates that embedded in the economic discussion, strategic planning narratives also construct community identity. Visioning exercises and identification of a community's strengths, weaknesses, opportunities, and threats are especially valuable as moments of community reflection. These moments in strategic planning are clear examples of times when citizens articulate "constitutive narratives" of their community and cultural identity.

Further, this chapter has contributed to scholarship exploring the symbolic process of converting space to place. Physical environment exists initially as a vast repository of undifferentiated space. It is through the selection of certain elements of the physical landscape and symbolic process of naming and symbolizing physical environment that individuals and groups attach meaning and value to space, thereby creating place. This study has demonstrated how two counties in rural Kansas transformed their space to locate themselves physically, culturally, sociopolitically, and rhetorically. It has also illustrated how dissimilar groups construct the same land in significantly different ways. Transforming space into rhetorical form provides descriptions of the land, structures values, and guides appropriate action for each of these groups.

This chapter also argues that this transforming process worked through "the telling of stories . . . that people's linkage to the land is through the vehicle of the story and identified through place naming and language" (Low 173-74). It has affirmed Fisher's contention that "[c]ommunities are co-constituted through communication transactions in which participants coauthor a story that has coherence and fidelity for the life that one would lead" (214). In interviews and editorials, residents told of the importance of place. But the narrative-building process was perhaps most dramatic in the strategic planning sessions. During these meetings, participants would tell narratives about place to each other and to the entire group. One narrative about place would often lead to another similar narrative. Stories told during the strategic planning meetings wove together to create a master narrative regarding the environment/culture connection. These place stories not only provided reaction to the physical landscape, but also invited the participants to join in the cultural perspective articulated.

Upon completing the strategic planning process, county participants summarized their discussions and policy initiatives in a strategic plan. The importance of place is prominent in this written document. When describing an image of themselves, they wrote: "There is a strong devotion to the land which is not taken lightly regardless of where one might live within the two counties," and "Residents firmly believe their living environment is one of the best" (Cyr 2). When describing their strengths, they listed: "landscape with natural beauty," "access to both quality and quantity of water in Waconda and Wilson Lakes," and "The rural nature of the area is attractive to those tired of the urban lifestyle" (Cyr 19-20). Importantly, this plan became a public and cultural document for Lincoln and Mitchell counties. It was constructed and approved by the county strategic planning participants. The plan was then presented and approved by the Lincoln and Mitchell county commissions and then forwarded to the State of Kansas Department of Economic Development. Thus, this community-building process and the narratives of place are likely to be referenced in future county discussions. In this way, the strategic planning process became a moment of cultural enactment.

Conclusions can also be drawn about the individualist rhetoric that characterizes Lincoln and Mitchell counties. The rhetoric of individualism that propels citizens in Lincoln and Mitchell counties to take local initiative and persevere against outside threats also leaves them vulnerable to each other and to outsiders. In their strategic plan, the citizens identified perceived threats to their counties: "We seldom depend on one another"; "There is a rural attitude of keeping to oneself" "Communities are not used to cooperating with or helping one another"; "We are isolated from one another"; and "We live single-mindedly" (Cyr 22). This individualist rhetoric translates into other problems for the counties including: lack of sufficient start-up capital, little political clout, and a lack of organized efforts to secure social and medical services. As one Lincoln County citizen wrote, because "money usually flows from empty acres to crowds, [seeping] out of farm houses . . . to big urban centers" (Crangle, "Money Maps"), Lincoln and Mitchell counties "urgently need new wealth in our towns. . . . Without new wealth a town stagnates" (Crangle, "Small Towns") and lacks financial and political clout. Writing on the Ft. Riley expansion issue, a rural resident recognized the tension between rural individualism and political power. "It will have to be the grassroots which stops Fort Riley," he wrote, "but time and tradition sadly favor the Army" (Knight 4). As Bellah et al. conclude, individualism "is an ideal of freedom that leaves Americans with a stubborn fear of acknowledging structures of power . . . leaving "community ties so fragile" (24-25).

The same freedom that rewards talent and effort also entices the young of the counties to leave for a better life. The Lincoln County Strategic Plan expressed "a strong concern over the loss of job opportunities for young people" while a letter to the editor of the *Lincoln Sentinel Republican* argued:

> We have instilled [in our children] the idea that indeed the world is there for the taking; obstacles can be mastered, and they can succeed at whatever they do, wherever they do it. . . . [Now] they move on to other towns, to other industry, to other cities and jobs which fit their education and career goals. I mourn for our town in that it loses many talented and creative individuals. (Peters 3)

I first met the citizens of Lincoln and Mitchell counties at the strategic planning orientation session at the Farmway Cooperative in Beloit, Kansas. At the end of the evening's meeting, a farmer from Sylvan Grove, dressed in blue jeans, work shirt, and boots, approached me and talked about his hopes and fears for the upcoming process. As we ended our conversation, he looked at me closely and said deliberately, "Out here, it's like Thoreau wrote, 'we're living lives of quiet desperation.'" During the last strategic planning meeting in Lincoln and Mitchell counties, we met in the Mitchell County courthouse—built of post rock in 1901. A road crew supervisor for Lincoln County summed up the sessions this way: "We've gotta remember that we've been planning for thirty years or more out here. If anything's going to happen, we gotta keep going whether these guys [the facilitators] are here or not. I truly believe things are getting better. But it's up to us."

These two statements, while seemingly contradictory, highlight the rhetoric of individualism in this rural land. Citizens believe that if progress is to occur—land protected, business developed, community centers built, tourism established—the effort must come from them. At the same time, this individualism leaves the people and the land vulnerable to neglect and exploitation.

Finally, studying the way a community constructs its place provides a tool in community building for scholars and/or practitioners. Talking about the local environment heightens a community's sense of place. It brings communities together by crystallizing community values and identifying appropriate forms of action. By examining the way communities respond to place, scholars and practitioners can demonstrate the positive and negative consequences of citizens' place construction. This analysis of local place talk can enable citizens to better understand their community and help them recognize and deal with the opportunities and threats they could confront. Ultimately, communication about place very likely intensifies commitment to community and dedication to preservation of that culture.

Notes

1. See Eric W. Allison and Mary Ann Allison, "Using Culture and Communications Theory in Postmodern Urban Planning: A Cybernetic Approach," *Communication Research* 22 (December 1995): 627-45; Irwin Altman, "Dialectics, Physical Environments, and Personal Relationships," *Communication Monographs* 60 (March 1993): 26-34; J. S. Duncan, "The House as Symbol of Social Structure," in *Home Environment. Vol. 8. Human Behavior and Environment: Advances in Theory and Research,* eds. Irwin Altman and Carol M. Werner (New York: Plenum Press, 1985), 133-55; Daniel Kemmis, *Community and the Politics of Place* (Norman: University of Oklahoma Press, 1990); Setha M. Low; "Symbolic Ties That Bind: Place Attachment in the Plaza," in *Place Attachment. Vol. 12. Human Behavior and Environment: Advances in Theory and Research,* eds. Irwin Altman and Setha M. Low (New York: Plenum Press, 1992), 165-85; Tarla Rai Peterson and Cristi Choat Horton, "Rooted in the Soil: Understanding the Perspectives of Landowners Can Enhance the Management of Environmental Disputes," *Quarterly Journal of Speech* 81 (May 1995): 139-66; Gerry Philipsen, "Places for Speaking in Teamsterville," *Quarterly Journal of Speech* 62 (February 1976): 15-25; Yi-Fu Tuan, *Space and Place: The Perspective of Experience* (Minneapolis: University of Minnesota Press, 1977).

2. See Tarla Rai Peterson and Cristi Choat Horton, "Rooted in the Soil: Understanding the Perspectives of Landowners Can Enhance the Management of Environmental Disputes," *Quarterly Journal of Speech* 81 (May 1995): 139-66; Gerry Philipsen, "Places for Speaking in Teamsterville," *Quarterly Journal of Speech* 62 (February 1976): 15-25; Gerry Philipsen, *Speaking Culturally: Explorations in Social Communication* (Albany: SUNY Press, 1992).

3. According to Section 3 of the official version of House Bill 2603—The Community Strategic Planning Assistance Act—the purpose of this legislation was to: (a) build and enhance economic development capacity at the local and regional levels; (b) develop and sustain long-term commitments for local development efforts; (c) encourage broad-based local and multi-county development strategies that build on local strengths and complement and reinforce statewide economic development strategy; and (d) maximize state investments in economic development through more efficient implementation of limited resources.

4. The characteristics and roles of facilitators are explored and detailed in community development and adult learning literature. The characteristics were a useful guide in my role as participant observer. For example, Brookfield offers several principles of facilitating including: facilitation respects participants' self-worth, facilitation is collaborative, facilitation fosters critical reflection, facilitation involves the continuous process of exploration and reflection of ideas, and facilitation is nurturing self-directed and empowered others. Ewert, Yaccino, and Yaccino identified effective interpersonal skills, listening skills, group management skills, the ability to ask effective questions, and the ability to assess the group situation as the skills important for community development facilitation. See Stephen D. Brookfield, *Understanding and Facilitating Adult Learning* (San Francisco: Jossey-Bass, 1986), 9-20; D. Merrill Ewert, Thomas G. Yaccino, and Delores M. Yaccino. "Cultural Diversity and Self-Sustaining Development: The Effective Facilitator," *Journal of the Community Development Society* 25 (1994): 27-31.

5. Ideographs are abstract value terms that serve as powerful, normative warrants for public behavior. These warranting terms emerge from their historical, discursive interactions with one another and from their standing as "the moral of the story." These language units function as agents of political consciousness. See Celeste M. Condit, "Democracy and Civil Rights: The Universalizing Influence of Public Argumentation," *Communication Mono-*

graphs 54 (March 1987): 1-18; Michael Calvin McGee, "The 'Ideograph': A Link Between Rhetoric and Ideology," *Quarterly Journal of Speech* 66 (February 1980): 1-16.

5

Constructing Community from Conflict: Manhattan and the Ten Commandments

6:30 a.m., December 7, 1999

Three cars emerge out of the dark and pull into the parking lot of the UMB bank. Stretching and yawning, three election officials enter the bank and slowly begin to transform the bank's break room into Manhattan's Ward 4, Precinct 6 polling station.[1] A metal sign on an iron tripod, announcing "Vote Here," is positioned outside the bank near the glass double-door entrance. A cardboard "Vote Here" sign is taped just inside the bank, giving citizens directions to the break room. Inside the break room, five red, white, and blue voting booths are set up side by side next to the neon Pepsi machine. Number 2 pencils are placed inside each booth. The bank's round lunch tables are taken down and replaced with a long, rectangular table. On one end of the table, voter registration books are laid out. Ballots are spread out across the middle of the table, and a gray, steel, pad-locked ballot box is placed at the far end of the table. A small American flag sits in the middle of the table.

7:00 p.m., April 27, 1999

"I pledge allegiance to the flag of the United States of America and to the republic for which it stands, one nation under God, indivisible, with liberty and justice for all." With this oath, Mayor Roger Reitz opens a special Manhattan City

*Commission meeting to discuss and decide whether a four-foot granite replica of
the Ten Commandments, given to the city by the Fraternal Order of Eagles in 1958,
will remain in front of City Hall or be moved to private property. City Hall is
packed. Over two hundred and fifty citizens have jammed into the City Commission
chambers to express their views on this issue. After listening to four hours of
emotional debate, City Commissioners Karen McCulloh, Carol Peak, and Bruce
Snead form a majority coalition and vote three to two to remove the monolith from
city property. The majority reasons that this decision will be the "less divisive
course of action for our community."[2]*

The Event

The 1999 Manhattan, Kansas, Ten Commandments controversy really began in
1943. A Minnesota juvenile court judge, who was also a member of the Fraternal
Order of Eagles, proposed the idea of posting a copy of the Ten Commandments in
state juvenile courts across the country to give young people a clear statement of
proper ways to act. Movie producer Cecil B. DeMille, who was producing the film
The Ten Commandments at the time, contacted the judge, suggesting the Eagles send
out bronze plaques inscribed with the Ten Commandments concurrent with the
release of the movie. The Minnesota judge suggested and DeMille agreed to create
stone or granite tablets featuring the engraved Ten Commandments. Several Eagles
chapters, including the chapter in Manhattan, Kansas, purchased the stone monuments and then donated them to local and state governments (Miller "City's Attorney").

Manhattan's Ten Commandments sat inconspicuously on the side of City Hall
from 1958 until the public building was renovated in 1998. At that time, the monolith was reset by the front door so that all visitors entering the building would pass
by it. Almost immediately, questions and concerns were raised about possible
violations of separation of church and state. Informal polls were taken; petitions were
signed. Overwhelmingly, the vocal public wanted to leave the monument where it
stood. Yet, on April 7, 1999, the American Civil Liberties Union and Americans
United for Separation of Church and State filed suit against the City of Manhattan
claiming the monument violated the "establishment clause" of the First Amendment
to the Constitution, which forbids creating an official state religion. The City
Commission scheduled a special session for April 27, 1999, to collect public input
and decide the issue. After several hours of public discussion, two newly elected
commissioners and a commissioner in her second term voted as a majority to remove
the monolith. The day following the vote to move the Ten Commandments off city
property, the monolith was unceremoniously dumped behind the local Eagles' lodge.
A group of citizens promptly formed a recall petition committee and, after five
months' work, secured enough signatures on that petition to force a recall election
of two-term Commissioner Karen McCulloh.[3] The special election was called for

December 7, 1999. Despite the commissioners' assertion that their vote was the "less divisive course of action for our community," the special commission meeting and monolith vote marked the public beginning of a most divisive community conflict.

Public conflicts, such as the Ten Commandments controversy, and resolution of those conflicts powerfully function to build local community and establish or reaffirm a locale's public identity. Indeed, public conflict and the resolution of that conflict is one variant of the community-building rhetorical form "civic communion."

In this chapter, I initially explore conflict as civic communion using the Manhattan, Kansas, Ten Commandments controversy and subsequent recall election as my case study. I then explore the competing community visions surrounding the controversy and finally offer some community-building lessons learned through this conflict.

Methodological Contexts

I first became interested in this event following the special City Commission meeting on April 27, 1999. The meeting seemed a special moment in the community when divergent groups were persuasively and intensely promoting their particular view of Manhattan's identity. For days following the special meeting, citizens used the radio and newspapers to publically express their opinions about their community through the Ten Commandments controversy. I decided to seize this rhetorical moment and explore how groups were using it as a time to promote their desired community image.

Given the public and rhetorical nature of the controversy, it seemed quite appropriate to utilize a method of study which would allow me to trace and track public discourse surrounding this conflict. Data for this chapter, then, included the public and rhetorical documents associated with this conflict. By "public documents," I refer to discourse recorded in some public way and is available to the viewing, listening, or reading public. Data does not include, for example, the internal messages of the executive sessions of the City Commission or private interviews of City Commissioners or leaders of the recall effort.

Specifically, data included a videotape of the April 27, 1999, special City Commission meeting, thirty-nine news stories, ten newspaper editorials, and 196 letters to the editor printed in three local newspapers—the *Manhattan Mercury*, the *Manhattan Free Press*, and the *Kansas State Collegian*. From references made in news stories, I determined the controversy really began before the April 27 meeting, and so I collected all rhetorical, public documents on this issue beginning with a *Manhattan Mercury* story on October 20, 1998, in which the newspaper reports the Ten Commandments monolith was displayed prominently in front of City Hall and speculated that this display might place Manhattan in legal jeopardy (Miller, "Command Performance" A1). I collected rhetorical artifacts until December 14,

1999 (one week following the recall election). Therefore, the data set for this chapter includes all rhetorical, public documents surrounding the Ten Commandments controversy from October 20, 1998, to December 14, 1999.[4]

From this body of public discourse, I selected language units to be examined. I wanted rhetorical data units which would allow me to track and examine the community-building efforts of the various sides in this controversy. I decided to connect the works of Richard Weaver, Walter Fisher, and Celeste Condit ("Democracy and Civic Rights"; *Decoding Abortion Rhetoric*) in order to chart each community's value hierarchy, narratives, and the images they held of each other.[5]

In his chapter, "Ultimate Terms in Contemporary Rhetoric," Richard Weaver describes units of value discourse he labels, "god" and "devil" terms (211-32). According to Weaver, "god terms" refer to "that expression about which all other expressions are ranked as subordinate and serving dominations and powers" (212) while "devil terms" are "terms of repulsion," representing the counterpart of the "god terms" (222). As Weaver explains, communities and cultures manage "to achieve some system of relationship among the attractive and among the repulsive terms" (212). Weaver's notion of ultimate terms provides a language and a heuristic to chart the value hierarchies of the various communities in the Ten Commandments controversy.

In his essay, "Narration, Reason, and Community," Walter Fisher argues that "community depends on particular forms of communication" (199). The particular communication form Fisher identifies is the story or narrative. According to Fisher, "[c]ommunities are co-constituted through communication transactions in which participants coauthor a story that has coherence and fidelity for the life that one would lead" (214). For Fisher, "Stories . . . are not isolated utterances or gestures but symbolic actions—words and/or deeds—that have sequence and meaning for those who live, create, or interpret them" (205-6). In narratives told, communities routinely provide a moral and value-laden justification for actions taken (Fisher 206).

Fisher also points out, "Central to all stories is character" (207). Following Fisher, Celeste Condit argues that "narratives are constructed of characterizations—universalized depictions of important agents, acts, scenes, purposes, or methods" (*Decoding Abortion Rhetoric* 14). These characterizations are either positive or negative, complete or incomplete, and are powerful units of discourse when persuasively connected to value-laden narratives.

Examining these three discourse units makes it possible to track the march of public argument and the shift of social lineament in this public controversy. Both rhetorical argument and community grouping evolved throughout the yearlong contrariety, moving from a debate about the wisdom of relocating the Ten Commandments monolith to a campaign over the recall of Commissioner Karen McCulloh. In the end, the results of the recall election functioned to affirm a symbolic stamp of legitimation on Manhattan's overall community identity.

7:00 a.m., December 7, 1999

The polls officially open. There is already a crowd waiting to vote. A line forms in the UMB break room. As citizens wait to vote, they engage in small talk seemingly about any topic except the election. "Are you headed to work?" "After I finish here, I'm off to the hairdresser." "I just jogged over. My route's half done." "Looks like it's going to be a nice day." The act of voting seems quite social. The voting line continues to grow, as the line extends outside the break room and into the lobby of the bank. It seems everyone wants to add their vote to the recall issue.

3:00 p.m., April 28, 1999

The Manhattan Mercury *arrives. The paper is full of news stories, editorials, and letters to the editor commenting on last night's special City Commission meeting. It seems everyone wants to add their voice to the monolith issue. The letters to the editor are frenzied. Josie Kleiner proclaims that the decision to move the monolith is "a slap in our Savior's face." Barbara Tate tells the voting majority they have "brought about disgrace to our once fair city before the nation." J.D. Shea laments that "we as a society have stood by as our courts stripped prayer and the Christian God from our schools" and argues that it is this attitude that has led to the school shootings at Columbine high school in Colorado. In one of the* Mercury's *news stories, there is talk of organizing a recall campaign.*

Conflict as Civic Communion

Organized community conflict—those community disputes over economic issues, issues involving power and authority, or from differences over cultural values and beliefs (Coleman 5-6) that are public and enjoined by a significant number of citizens—is one form of social drama that functions as civic communion. These conflicts exhibit the characteristics of civic communion as illustrated in the Manhattan Ten Commandments controversy. Indeed, this public conflict was a transitory event that functioned to: (1) organize divergent rhetorical communities; (2) generate very emotional responses to community structures; and (3) highlight diverse community views of Manhattan, Kansas.

When an organization or community faces some form of conflict, divergent rhetorical communities emerge through their differing response to the conflictive issues and through their differing visions of local community. Using the idea of "social drama," Kirk Fuoss describes this process:

When a social drama occurs, certain of the externally articulated communities or internally articulated positions within a community are highlighted by the crisis and imbued with a heightened intensity. Participants in a social drama tend to distinguish between "us" and "them," "inside" and "outside," "ally" and "opposition" on the basis of the particular external articulation of community or internal articulation of a position within a community that has been highlighted by the conflict that ushered in the social drama. (82)

The Ten Commandments monolith and the decision whether or not to move it off city property certainly functioned as a catalyst of community organizing. Following the news story about the city displaying the monolith in front of City Hall, a group of seven Manhattan citizens organized and filed suit against the city. In response, a group of Manhattan citizens immediately mobilized to persuade commissioners to leave the monolith in place (Cayton, "Ten Commandment Backers Mobilize"). After the decision to move the monolith was made, supporters of that decision aligned themselves with and accepted help from the American Civil Liberties Union and the Manhattan Alliance for Peace and Justice, and formed their own political action committee called Citizens for Sensible Government. Opponents of the decision urged citizens to organize against those commissioners who voted to move the monolith. "What I saw Tuesday evening," Anne Larson opined, "was the solidification of much of the Bible-believing Christian community" (Letter). Ken Ebert proclaimed that "a sleeping giant has been awakened" (Letter), while Don Rose urged "there be a meeting to organize a recall election" (May 6, 1999 Letter). Indeed, opponents of the decision did organize a recall committee and a local political action group called Concerned Citizen's Recall Committee. They also aligned with and accepted help from statewide political action groups—Kansans For Life and the Family Action Network.

In the understatement of the year, Gregg Potter noted, "Emotions have certainly been stirred" (Letter). In fact, the monolith controversy raged intensely over the next eight months with each side passionately articulating their position. The dispute generated a crush of emotional rhetoric. Opponents of the move announced that the City Commissioners "were worthless" (Marshall), "cowering dogs," (Blair), and told them that "the day will come, on the other side of the grave, when your names will be removed from the Book of Life." (Mullin). Proponents of the move shot back that the efforts of the local "Bible thumpers" (Felber, "Voting by Petition") were a "clear effort at theological cleansing" (Shoop) and sarcastically suggested the proponents of the move invite "Slobodan Milosovic to come to the Little Apple to plan a program of ethnic cleansing" (Ossar).

The controversy was picked up by regional and national press. Editorialists writing for the *Denver Post, Omaha World Herald*, and *Kansas City Star* weighed in linking the conflict to national debates over the public display of religious symbols. Court TV traveled to Manhattan and filmed an episode on the controversy, and the issue was also parodied on *Saturday Night Live*'s "Weekend Update." Hostility, harassment, and vandalism associated with the conflict were routinely reported. This controversy came to be, in the words of Richard Harris, "about the future viability of our city government" (Letter).

Embedded within each group's emotional public discourse lies the contours of their rhetorical community. Community analysts can examine the various rhetorical communities as each subgroup praises their vision of community, celebrates their value hierarchy, pays tribute to their particular heroes, and rebukes their villainous foes.

But importantly for those interested in community-building efforts, conflict serves not only to highlight community, but also functions to alter the social organization of those communities (Poplin 196). Coleman points out that "as controversy develops, associations flourish *within* each group, but wither *between* persons on opposing sides" (11; emphasis Coleman). Conflictive rhetoric provides, in stark relief, material evidence of divergent attitudes, value hierarchies, and policy agendas of local rhetorical communities. Through conflict, rhetorical communities not only become more clear, but their positions harden, and many citizens more intensely identify themselves with one position or another. Community-building scholars, then, may fruitfully examine this conflictive rhetoric to identify local communities and their rhetorical positioning relative to the issue in controversy.

In addition, public conflict among divergent local communities also has status implications. These conflicts ultimately, and quite often only temporarily, come to some form of resolution. As the conflict is resolved in some public manner (e.g., a public election or administrative decision), the winner of that election or decision achieves legal, civic, and symbolic status in the local power hierarchy. Through the outcome of an election, local government is publically committed to supporting the winning position. The winning coalition's position is, therefore, legitimized through the election results (Trent and Friedenberg 4). The conflict and subsequent election also becomes a symbolic structure of legitimacy that the locale may then use to highlight policies, attitudes, values, or lifestyles to outside communities and interest groups. As Joseph Gusfield writes, "Victory in issues of status is the symbolic conferral of respect upon the norms of the victor and disrespect upon the norms of the vanquished" ("A Dramatic Theory" 248).

The next section explores the worldview each community constructed in this conflict.

10:00 a.m., December 7, 1999

Officially, there is to be no talk concerning the election by election officials or those waiting to vote. Still, there are times when folks just blurt out their feelings. An elderly man walks into the UMB break room, now converted into an official polling station, and slowly reads the recall petition. As he finishes, he looks deliberately at the three election workers and announces, "These City Commissioners are just damn near worthless!" "Now, listen here," the senior election official admonishes, "we can't talk about the commissioners or the election in this polling sta-

tion." "I know that," the old man concedes, "but these people are idiots." "I'm going to have to ask you to quit talking like that." The election judge is more stern now. "We want you to vote, but you can't make speeches in here."

10:00 a.m., May 10, 1999

In a speech before local media and flanked by the two City Commissioners who voted to retain the monolith in front of City Hall, Manhattan Christian College President Kenneth Cable proclaims, "I strongly believe this monument belongs to the citizens of Manhattan, and we will make it very visible to everyone who drives by our campus." The speech marks the public announcement that the Ten Commandments would be on "permanent loan" from the Eagles to the Christian College and that the College would prominently display the monolith on a major thoroughfare that runs adjacent to the College. A Mercury editorial lauds the decision and wonders whether this "reasonable resolution will help mend the lingering wounds this controversy has caused."

Shortly following President Cable's speech, a recall petition charging Commissioner Karen McCulloh with misconduct is filed with the county clerk's office. The recall committee begins moving door-to-door through local neighborhoods securing signatures to force a recall election. Several businesses around town erect signs announcing citizens can "Live the Ten Commandments, Sign the Recall Petition Here." RC Motors, the Manhattan Christian Bookstore, and the Knopp law firm all take a public stand in favor of the recall election. A "recall booth" at the Riley County fair offers "travel mugs" which proclaim "Trust God" as a gift for signing the petition.

Constructed Communities
in the Ten Commandments Conflict

The Debate Phase: October 1998 to September 1999

From the time the local newspaper highlighted the monolith's presence in front of City Hall and wondered if this put the city in legal jeopardy, rhetorical communities began to materialize. The contours of the divergent communities initially organized around a debate over the wisdom and consequences of moving the stone Ten Commandments from city property. Examination of the discourse units in this conflictive phase revealed two general communities: one opposed to and one supportive of the monolith move.[6]

Community in Opposition to the Monolith Move
      This community began to materialize almost immediately following the October

1998 *Manhattan Mercury* story and became even more clearly defined following the City Commission's vote in April 1999. This community was organized around an overarching narrative which was a dark and vengeful mix of religious and politically conservative rhetoric. The community's constitutive narrative characterized Manhattan as a "fallen" community sinking into the abyss of secular humanism, governed by a City Commission violating its sworn duty, and controlled by liberal university faculty conspiring to dictate local values and policies. Moving the monolith was taken as evidence of Manhattan's fall away from both God and effective government. The logical step emerging from this narrative was to replace those City Commissioners who voted to remove the Ten Commandments from City Hall.

This rhetorical community's worldview was organized around two god terms—the "Ten Commandments" and "majority rule." This rhetorical community articulated a narrative in which City Commissioners violated both god terms.

Initially, the Ten Commandments were constructed as a coherent statement of axiomatic and infallible truths. Local ministers explained that "the Ten Commandments are still God's standards for our daily life" (Aldrich) and that "the Ten Commandments do not always tell us what we want to hear. They do tell us the truth, the whole truth, and nothing but the truth. They clearly define life's boundaries. They give a distinct and definite division between right and wrong" (Weston).

The message of the Ten Commandments was constructed as especially crucial in today's world as Americans are living in "desperate days" (Weston). Rhetors in this community surveyed the American political and social scene, identified problems in society, and concluded that we are confronted by difficulties precisely because we have lost our connection to the transcendental truths espoused by the Ten Commandments. Carmen Eichman compared the troubles of this millennium to the Roman Empire's troubles a millennium ago when she wrote that the Romans "allowed so many forms of religions to guide their thinking that it soon grew to be too much, too confusing [and] we know the rest of the story" (C9). J. D. Shea made the link specific to America's societal woes:

> We watch the TV, read the printed news and discover that many people seem confused and surprised at the school massacre in Colorado. We witness expert after expert explain or attempt to explain the "whys" of the event. I have not heard one of the experts mention a very real set of circumstances that may have greatly influenced those who appear to have been involved.
>
> We should not be surprised when incidents such as this happen. We as a society stood by as our courts stripped prayer and the Christian God from our schools. We accepted the fact that "killing babies" is a constitutional right of each citizen. Our children are raised by educators who in many situations are more willing to make sure that "political correctness" is taught. We have not challenged our schools as they rewrote our history books to ensure that any references to the Christian God are downplayed. (Letter)

Community rhetors made the link specific to Manhattan. Darren Emery, for example, noted, "I do not think it coincidence that the Ten Commandments were removed from our City Hall within the same two-week period that . . . our local youth asked for recognition of a list of communistic ideals presented as rights" (Letter) while Linda Morgan urged "the person or persons who started this whole confrontation [to] redirect their time and energy toward the situation at Manhattan High School and the existing and potential problems there" (Letter). Morgan goes on to identify "alcohol, drugs, teenage pregnancy, and violence" as significant problems confronting local youth.

Removal of the monolith, however, was not simply the removal of a positive life message for Manhattan. The vote to move the monolith was, according to this rhetorical community, "an attempt to remove God from our lives and our community" (Weston) and a strike in favor of secular humanism. According to Dale Herspring, "The state cannot be neutral. By being neutral, the government is in fact favoring one side over the other—in this case secular humanism" ("Neutrality Tilts Scales"). In fact, this rhetorical community argued that the commission vote "further established 'secular humanism' as the official policy of the city" (Miller, "Secular Humanism"). Secular humanism functioned as a powerful devil term in this community's lexicon. Secular humanism seeks to "elevate man to the role of God" (Miller, "Secular Humanism") and is the root of a host of societal evils. Dale Herspring explained, "Proponents of complete separation of church and state are arguing in favor of secular humanism [and that] usually takes the form of diversity, radical environmentalism, and political correctness" ("Neutrality Tilts Scales"). Commissioners who voted for the monolith removal were cast as "gods of political correctness and new tolerance" (Larson). Community rhetors characterized the removal vote as based on "the great tea cup of political correctness" (Eichman), leading to "situational ethics" (Campbell), and moving the community toward the "slippery slope of a valueless society where 'tolerance' and 'acceptance' are the battle cries of every minority opinion" (Emery).

At a time when society in general and Manhattan in particular are faced with significant problems, it is folly, these rhetors argued, to remove God's influence from city government. As Todd Weston asked, "Are we fully prepared to commit an act that is tantamount to telling God He is no longer welcome at City Hall and then go it alone into the new millennium?" The obvious answer for this community is "no," and the solution is to oust those commissioners who removed God from City Hall.

Not only did these City Commissioners violate the sacred laws that govern the soul, according to this community, the commissioners also violated the secular law of "majority rule." This community argued strongly that the majority of Manhattan citizens supported displaying the monolith on city property. They argued that the winning coalition on the City Commission put personal agendas ahead of the wishes of the majority of Manhattan citizens and had, therefore, violated the foundational concept of representative government.[7] Because the city commissioners violated this civic responsibility, this community reasoned they should be removed from office.

Following the vote, this community wondered rhetorically and sarcastically if we still lived in a democracy. Steven Neal reflected, "I thought that in a democracy, the will of the majority overruled the minority and dissenting opinions. Am I confused?" (Letter). Likewise, Barbara Tate asked, "The bigger question is, what kind of government do we have when the minority wins? It certainly is not 'of the people, by the people, and for the people'" (Letter).

Clearly, this community supported a view of democracy in which elected officials act "as an agent, deputy, substitute, or delegate" (Crubel) and uphold the will of the majority (Eichman). Thus, those commissioners who voted to move the monolith were characterized as "uncaring," "untrustworthy," "ignoring the will of the people," "pursuing personal agendas," "simply appearing to listen," "pandering to the minority," and "caving into the American Civil Liberties Union." The special commission meeting itself was characterized as a "sham," merely a "vehicle to appease Christians," "simply a formality," and "a show."

After violating both sacred and secular law, the obvious action was to remove those City Commissioners who voted to move the monolith. Some community rhetors suggested that the commissioners simply resign (Herspring, "Monolith Vote"; Marshall; Shamburger). But recognizing "that will not happen [because] the lust for power and influence is too great" (Herspring, "Monolith Vote"), rhetors suggested turning democracy back on the untrustworthy commissioners and voting them out of office. A few rhetors noted they would remember these commissioners and vote against them during the next scheduled city elections in 2001 (Potter; Sills; Sisco). Still others were less patient, calling on concerned citizens to join a recall effort to oust the offending commissioners (Rose, May 6, 1999 Letter; Scott, "Recall Inquiries Surface").

Community in Support of the Monolith Move

This general community was organized around a hopeful and affirmative story in which citizens value and respect one another. It was a story of celebrating the diversity in others—other traditions, other customs, other religious beliefs. This community narrative told of a wise and just, but protective, local government that courageously works to ensure all rights, but is especially mindful of minority rights. The constitutive narrative warned of the danger of brute majority rule and religious intolerance, and exhorted all to remain vigilant to groups that would seek to impose a narrow set of religious beliefs onto an entire community.

This community's worldview was fundamentally organized by two interrelated god terms—"protection of minority rights" and "tolerance." Each of these ultimate terms highlighted slightly different subgroups, both supportive of the monolith move.

Using "protection of minority rights" as their preeminent ultimate term, one subgroup materialized through a constitutional and historical narrative. Rhetors in this community recalled our country's rich history of protecting minority rights, arguing this value has been fundamental in creating our national identity. Examples of this argument included: "I sincerely hope this alleged 92% majority will turn back to their third-grade history books and read again about the Massachusetts

Pilgrims, the Pennsylvania Quakers, the Maryland Catholics, the Kansas Menno-nites and all the other religious minorities who found in America freedom from tyrannical and self-righteous religious majorities" (Rintoul); "this country was built by a succession of oppressed minorities . . . and is stronger for the protection it afforded them" ("City's Decision"); "One only has to study the Federalist Papers to see that the effort all along has been to guarantee the rights of the minority" (Tummala); and "Although majority rule is a bedrock principle of our democracy, equally important is the principle that the majority should not be allowed to trample the rights of people who don't have enough votes to oppose the will of majority" (Vogel).

Community rhetors reasoned that the only way for local government to protect all citizens' religious freedom was for the government to remain completely neutral, invoking another historical and constitutional principle—separation of church and state. As Krishna Tummala argued:

> The monolith at City Hall raised the issue of separation of church and state in an avowedly secular state. A secular state is not an irreligious state; it only has no religion of its own. But it does respect all religions, and citizens are guaranteed the fundamental right to practice their own religion. It also means that no one should impose his or her religion on others.

Likewise, Linda Johnson averred that "Separation of church and state is a vital principle that was understood by our founding fathers and is necessary to maintain our essential right to freedom of religion" (Letter).

This subgroup characterized the vote to move the monolith and all those supportive of that decision positively. The commission vote was characterized as "a principled decision," a decision that was "sensible," illustrating "good judg-ment." The particular commissioners who voted in favor of moving the Ten Commandments and private citizens who stood and spoke in favor of the move were labeled "brave," "courageous," "vigilant," and "wise." Those who spoke against the move and who had written letters in opposition of the monolith move were characterized as "the log-rolling majority," "bullies," and desirous of "a theocracy."

A second, related rhetorical community was organized around the god term, "tolerance." Instead of offering historical and constitutional evidence for the protection of minority groups, this rhetorical community used secular anecdotes as well as biblical evidence to urge citizens to reflect on and celebrate local diver-sity.

Tolerating, indeed celebrating, diversity was fundamental to this group's worldview. David Sauer urged "all in this community to think beyond the frame-work of their own religious beliefs and realize that there are many other equally valid views of life's big mysteries" (Letter). Shawn Bunch continued by pointing out, "There are many fine, moral contributing citizens who do not hold traditional Christian or Jewish beliefs in our community; their differences and individuality should be celebrated, not vilified" (Letter) because, as Hillary Glasgow explained, when "we live in a community, every citizen should feel like he or she belongs" (Letter).

This community reshaped "tolerance" into "love thy neighbor," arguing in the religious terminology of the opposition that the commandment of loving others was actually the preeminent law set down by God. This narrative thread functioned to provide Christians justification for the Ten Commandments move. For example, Tummala's column both connected love to tolerance and divided her community from the opposition when she wrote, "It is strange and profoundly disturbing that good Christians who defend the Ten Commandments tend to ignore another commandment—Love thy neighbor. Where is tolerance?" Linda Johnson likewise distinguished her community's worldview from the opposition when she contended that love is the more recent commandment. "How sad that so many, in their defense of the Ten Commandments, seem to be violating the spirit of those Commandments and certainly going against the newer commandment given by Jesus, that we love one another" (Letter). Dianne Urban made the explicit argument, through biblical reference, that love is the preeminent commandment while subverting the local community focused solely on the Ten Commandments. She wrote:

> According to the New Testament, Jesus said that he came not to set aside the Law, but to fulfill it. Then he said, "The first and greatest commandment is this: You shall love the Lord your God with all your heart, with all your soul and with all your mind. This is the first and great commandment. The second commandment is like it. You shall love your neighbor as yourself." (Matthew 22:37-39)
>
> Also in the New Testament are these words, "Love, hope and charity, but the greatest of these is love. . . . And now abide faith, hope, love, these three; but the greatest of these is love." (1st Corinthians 13:13)
>
> For Christians, those stone-cold commandments leave out the most important part of their faith, namely love. Without love and forgiveness, the commandments are meaningless.

The action necessary, according to this subgroup, was not government protection, but private citizen tolerance and love. Citizens were reminded that "The power of the Ten Commandments isn't in their geographic placement; rather it's in their placement in people's hearts" ("City's Decision") and were urged to direct their daily lives to restore the spirit of the Ten Commandments in our culture. This rhetorical community characterized the opposition as "intolerant," "judgmental," and "self-righteous."

5:30 p.m., December 7, 1999

The "after work" voting rush has hit. Once again there are long lines waiting to vote on the recall issue. Through the grapevine, we've heard voting is heavy at all polling stations. At 5:45 p.m., Commissioner Carol Peak walks in. She looks tired, I think. Quietly, she waits in line for her turn to vote. She disappears behind the red, white, and blue curtain that gives the voting booth its privacy. Moments later she reappears and places her ballot in the gray, steel ballot box. "I hope," she whispers softly, "today's election finishes this recall business."

3:00 p.m., September 3, 1999

Standing on the steps of the Riley County courthouse, Don Rose proclaims, "Our business is far from finished." A small group of recall petitioners listen as Rose continues, "Now the real campaign for recalling Karen McCulloh begins! If we're successful in this fight, we will go after Carol Peak and Bruce Snead and restore God to our city government." The petitioners walk to the County Election Office and hand over their box of signed recall petitions—boldly wrapped with a large red bow—to the county clerk.

Three weeks later, the county clerk verifies that the petitioners have gathered enough valid signatures and schedules a special recall election for December 7, 1999, to determine if Karen McCulloh will be removed for misconduct in office.

The Campaign Phase: September 1999 to December 1999

Once the county clerk verified that the recall petitions contained the legal number of valid signatures, the campaign for and against recall immediately began. The communities that had formed in response to the decision to move the monolith evolved into campaign communities. Again, contours of divergent communities appeared through campaign rhetoric. Indeed, the lines between the various communities became more distinct and divisive. Several people echoed the sentiments of the citizen who wrote, "I went to a friend's house and saw the opposition's sign in their yard and felt as if a barrier was then formed between us" (Felber, "Among Jurors"). Examination of god terms, narratives, and characterizations in the campaign phase again revealed two broad communities: one in favor of recall and a second opposed to the recall effort.

"Just Because"—Community in Support of Recall
The community that originally opposed the monolith move evolved into a generalized community which cast the recall election as an opportunity to voice dissatisfaction about the direction Manhattan was headed. The recall was articulated as not only a moment to strike a vote for a Christian community, but also as a referendum on the popularity of Commissioner McCulloh and the policies of the entire Manhattan City Commission.

This community organized itself around two god terms—"representative government" and "freedom of religion." Just as in the debate phase, one subgroup of this community argued that Ms. McCulloh and the coalition of commissioners who voted to move the monolith had violated the concept of "representative government" by ignoring the principle of majority rule. Rhetors in this community were not so concerned about the religious aspect of the controversy as they were about the abuse of power Commissioner McCulloh and "the gang of three" exhibited by their vote to move the monolith. Asking whether "we still have a democracy, or is it an oligarchy?" Arlin Sarff declared, "governing must reflect the will of the majority, not the minority" (Letter). Ancel Sapp added that "[This recall] is not about church and state. It is about representative government. Karen McCulloh did not care about the views expressed by the overwhelming majority of Manhattan citizens. It is our right in a democratic government—when our leaders no longer represent the majority, when our leaders do not use good judgment in discharging their duties—to remove them from office" (Letter). This community lamented "that all three City Commissioners could not have been recalled at one time" (Deena Johnson), but argued it necessary to remove Ms. McCulloh because she was "a loose cannon," and her attitude of "disregarding the majority" represented a "dangerous trend" (Rose, October 10, 1999 Letter). She tried, according to Roger Seymour, "to stifle public opinion and the opposing viewpoint. That alone should be enough to scare everyone to vote 'Yes' [on the recall]" (Letter). Griffith G. Gates concluded that the recall was necessary because "our city is now controlled by three commissioners" and wondered "what other votes they may have cast" that we don't know about (Letter).

This community asserted that, far from adhering to the concept of representative government, city government is controlled by "the privileged," the "special interests," and a "very well organized group of liberal faculty." Instead of pursuing the agenda of the majority of Manhattan citizens, this community argued that "Mrs. McCulloh is furthering the personal agendas of a small but influential group of radical left-wing liberals who wish to gradually void America's government of any God-fearing principles" (Williams).

The subgroup organized around "representative government" moved to expand the constituency of this community by arguing "this election is not just about the Ten Commandments, although this was the catalyst. This is a referendum on representative government" (David Johnson). They called on the "silent majority" (Gates; David Johnson; Williams) in Manhattan to use the recall "as a unique opportunity to send our elected officials a message" (David Johnson) and voice our displeasure of city government policies. In fact, the pro-recall campaign theme became "Vote Yes, Just Because . . ." Pro-recall ads proclaimed:

"Vote Yes, Just Because . . ."

This commissioner fails to protect the poor and disadvantaged because of her vote on the Wal-Mart Superstore issue.

This commissioner places animals over people by voting to spend $1 million dollars just to build a new animal shelter.

We need a commissioner who will represent us all. Commissioner McCulloh votes "no" to expand the retail sales tax, "no" to increase our property tax base and "no" to employment opportunities.

Letter writers in this community worked to tap into a generalized citizen discontent. David Johnson articulated the community lines this way: "If you feel your best interests are being represented, that your money is wisely spent and your voice is being heard; then sit back and do nothing and nothing will change. But, if you're tired of not being listened to, having your tax dollars wasted and see representation only for privileged and special interest groups; then stand up and be counted" (Letter). This community identified nearly every controversial issue McCulloh had addressed. They complained about her votes on economic incentives and taxes. They resented her for her support of Habitat for Humanity, the ACLU, and a new animal shelter. They blamed her for higher than desired poverty rates, city government cost overruns, and a living wage amendment to the local minimum wage. As John Garwick explained, "'Just because . . .' is a fitting slogan for the recall election. I'll bet if you asked the 2,800 plus who signed the recall petition why, they would give you just as many reasons" (Letter). In a radio debate just prior to the election, recall organizer Stan Hoerman concluded, "We will stick to the issue of whether McCulloh is guilty of misconduct. However, we don't mind voters opposing McCulloh for any reason. Vote yes, just because" (Cayton, "Recall Face-Off").

Another subgroup of the pro-recall community organized around the god term "freedom of religion." This group articulated a four-step proposition concluding that Commissioner McCulloh violated citizens' freedom of religion. Rhetors in this community initially argued that "our country needs strength and guidance from above" (Heaton) and that "the Ten Commandments are key to the direction this nation will go" (Roffler). Second, they asserted that while the First Amendment prohibits establishing an official state religion, it "does not require a complete separation of church and state" (Hampton; Zentz). As evidence of this position, this subgroup provided historical examples ranging from "The Mayflower Compact," "The First Thanksgiving Proclamation," and the "Declaration of Independence" where earlier Americans invoked God's favor during significant moments in U.S. history (Heaton; Zentz). In fact, they contended, while the Constitution prohibits a "national religion," it "affirmatively mandates accommodation of all religions, and forbids hostility toward any" (Hampton). Third, this community declared that no governmental action can be value-neutral and that "any decision the City Commission made [on the monolith issue] would have been a religious choice" (Ukena). Therefore, by removing God's laws from city property, Commissioner McCulloh and the voting coalition were actually advocating a state religion—secular humanism. As Kent Hampton argued, "Cleansing our public of all religious expression inevitably results in the 'establishment' of disbelief—atheism as the State's religion. . . . Karen McCulloh failed in her sworn duty to uphold the Constitution [by not affirmatively accommodating the Christian religion] and that her action did intentionally and illegally advance the religion of Secular Humanism."

The logical choice for citizens who believed in this version of freedom of religion was to vote to recall Commissioner McCulloh.

"Reject This Vengeful Recall!" Community in Opposition to Recall

Fundamentally, this general community came out of the rhetorical community in favor of moving the monolith off city property. However, during the campaign phase of this conflict, this community's message transformed from a positive and hopeful discourse that celebrated diversity in others to a warning rhetoric predictive of dire circumstances if the recall election was successful. The constitutive narrative for this community warned of a disintegration of local government and a rise of a theocracy if the recall prevailed. To prevent this civic calamity, citizens were implored to make a powerful statement through their vote by rejecting the recall effort.

This community centered its message around two god terms—"rule of law" and "religious tolerance." The subgroup organized around "rule of law" articulated a narrative that contended a legitimate and regularly scheduled election had been conducted three weeks prior to the special monolith meeting. This regularly scheduled City Commission election functioned to validate the wishes of the Manhattan citizens on many issues including the location of the monolith. Further, this narrative asserted that Ms. McCulloh was legitimately performing her job as City Commissioner when she cast her vote to remove the monolith from city property. Thus, any subsequent attempt to overturn that election—unless evidence existed of significant and genuine commissioner misconduct—violated the fundamental rule of law.

Rhetors in this community validated the election process by calling it "the system we have chosen for our community" (Hayter), the "existing structures of the laws of our land" (McFarland), and by pointing out that "if voters are dissatisfied with their elected officials, their recourse is to vote them out of office when they run again" (Crane). Commissioner McCulloh, they argued, "has done nothing illegal, nothing unethical, nothing that can be construed as misconduct in office" (Fliter) and that she was simply "carrying out her duties" (McFarland). Commissioner McCulloh was further characterized as an "outstanding," "careful," "dedicated," "competent," and "conscientious public servant" (Thomas) who took a "principled stand on behalf of her fellow citizens." In other words, Ms. McCulloh was selected by rule of law and was abiding by law when she voted to remove the monolith from city property.

Conversely, this community characterized the charges of misconduct presented by recall supporters as "secular garbage" ("Reject This Vengeful Recall"), those creating the charges of misconduct as playing "fast and loose with the Ten Commandments" and "bearing false witness" (Richter). The recall effort was, therefore, characterized as "a witch hunt" and "a miscarriage of democracy" ("Chance to Vote") that sought "to abort an election" (Richter). The recall was cast as "a political lynching" that "jeopardizes our system of government" and "mocks our precious right to recall elected officials for genuine misconduct" ("Political Lynching"). Not only would the recall effort violate the rule of law of legitimate elections, this community argued, a successful recall would have a chilling effect on recruiting other competent and dedicated people to serve Manhattan.

The appeal to "rule of law" was a very robust argument. Not only did it organize and solidify those citizens who originally believed the monolith should be moved, it also attracted a significant group of citizens who disagreed with Commissioner McCulloh's original monolith vote. Several citizens articulated the position that: (1) they disagreed with the original monolith vote; (2) Commissioner McCulloh had the legal authority to cast such a vote; and (3) recall was an illegitimate response to dissatisfaction with the vote. Ron Sampson's letter clearly articulates this position. He writes:

> I stand with a possible majority in our community who disagreed with the decisions of the City Commission regarding the removal of the Ten Commandments monument.
>
> However, we voters empowered only five citizens to decide such issues, and I was not one of them.
>
> Regardless of how we feel about the Ten Commandments issue, we now must recognize what the recall election truly means. It either: (1) reflects a disturbing lack of understanding among many in our community about what a representative democracy is and how it works; or (2) is a subtle attack on the form of government that has served our nation so well over the last two centuries.

This position, articulated by several citizens, is crucial, I believe, to the results of the recall election and to Manhattan's community image. It effectively expanded the community opposed to recall by attracting community members originally opposed to the monolith vote. I believe at least some of the citizens who were opposed to the monolith move on the secular grounds of majority rule assimilated into this rhetorical community through the broader, more encompassing secular ultimate term, "rule of law."

Just as during the debate phase of this conflict, a significant community of citizens remained organized around the god term, "religious tolerance." As with the "rule of law" subcommunity, this rhetorical community argued that religious tolerance is historically the rule of the land (Butler). As James Hamilton explained,

"For us, the practice of religious tolerance at the political level has come to be the enforcement of a principle of governmental neutrality" ("Neutrality on Religion"). Bob Shoop asserted that "our government must be neutral in its protection of citizens regardless of religion. Our community has a history of tolerance" and this tolerance is "critical to a democratic society" (Letter). Community rhetors further contended that "to mix religion and politics endangers the health of our community" (Sanders) and that promoting a certain variant of Christianity "gives license to abuse power in order to control religion" (Mrozek). They also warned against returning "to the American Colonial days when public officials had to undergo a religious test to hold public office" (Butler).

This community cast Commissioner McCulloh as a "dedicated," "temperate," and "effective City Commissioner" (Mrozek) who served as a protector of "our values and our common political heritage" by practicing religious tolerance and remaining neutral on the issue of a state religion (Hamilton). Rhetors argued she "cast her vote for many reasons. Among them were religious reasons" (Sanders). Recall supporters, on the other hand, were characterized as "bullies" (Bennett) who were "cruel promoters of religion" (Mrozek) and their attempt to recall Commissioner McCulloh a "desire to re-establish a political-church bond" (Bidwell) and "a clear effort at theological cleansing" (Shoop).

Thus, for political, moral, and religious reasons, this community exhorted Manhattan citizens to vote in opposition of the recall.

7:00 p.m., December 7, 1999

The polls close. Voting to recall Karen McCulloh is now officially finished. Slowly, methodically, and quietly, the election officials count the ballots, not to determine who won, but to confirm there has been no voter fraud. The number of ballots marked equals the number of voters who signed the voter logs. There are sighs of relief all around. The ballots are placed into a heavy denim mail bag, the bag is loaded into a car, and two election officials drive the ballots downtown to the Riley County courthouse and Election Office.

The Election Office is ominously quiet. The only sound is that of marked ballots rushing through the automatic counter. A group of reporters and interested citizens are waiting for results, but saying nothing. In the back of the room, Don Rose and some recall supporters are talking quietly and looking anxious. Ironically, Karen McCulloh is attending a regularly scheduled City Commission meeting.

3:00 p.m., December 5, 1999

In their last interview before the election, neither side of the recall predicts victory, yet both sides still work to stake out their community's position and urge supporters to turn out and vote. "I took an oath to uphold the Constitution," Karen McCulloh points out. "The Constitution is quite clear. It was in the best interest of Manhattan to find a more appropriate place for the Ten Commandments. I think if the moderates come out, I'll be fine." Don Rose proclaims, "This election is going to show that this issue is fundamental to American society. A pro-recall decision will tell us that we have a community that will honor God and will honor the basic building blocks our country was founded on, including the original Ten Commandments. I hope the common folks of our town will come out and support those ideas."

9:00 p.m., December 7, 1999

County Clerk Rich Vargo announces to the press and all those gathered that the recall fails. An overwhelming 62 percent of the Manhattan electorate voted to support Ms. McCulloh and reject the recall effort. Across town at a regularly scheduled City Commission meeting, a teary-eyed Karen McCulloh asks the mayor for a five-minute break. She stands up from her seat, breathes deeply, and then rushes to hug her husband John, who declares, "This vote is a victory for the principle of representative government and a victory for moderation!" Back at the election office, Don Rose acknowledges that "the voters have spoken. We accept that. I continue to extend my hand to Karen in a friendly way."

Conclusions and Implications

A significant number of citizens rejected the recall effort and reaffirmed their support of Commissioner McCulloh. This type of analysis offers several rhetorical reasons why the recall ultimately failed.

In civic communions organized around public controversy, the conflicting sides essentially engage in a campaign to promote their vision of the ideal community. In the Ten Commandments controversy, two general communities articulated, constructed, and celebrated divergent symbolic structures of Manhattan. I believe the community that supported the monolith move and opposed the McCulloh recall were ultimately successful for several reasons. Initially, this community articulated a reaffirmative rhetoric. In this argumentative form, according to Fisher, citizens essentially reassert the validity of the community's fundamental creed (210). This rhetorical position cast the community opposed to the recall as incumbents in a political campaign. Their rhetoric defended the status quo in Manhattan. This community argued they were supporting traditional and historic symbolic structures. This allowed the community to speak positively about Manhattan's history. For example, as the site of a major university, this community recalled that Manhattan has been home to a diverse population for years. This community reminded citizens that faculty, students, and their families had come to Manhattan from countries literally spanning the globe, representing diverse belief systems. This community argued that Manhattan was a richer place because of this history of diversity. Because of this history, the appeal to "tolerance" and "love thy neighbor" likely resonated with Manhattan citizens. The supporters of the recall, in contrast, were forced to argue for change in the community social and symbolic structures. They urged citizens to "get right with God," and the necessity to "change the direction of the City Commission." Unfortunately for this community, this rhetorical position cast them as insurgents or challengers to the status quo and burdened them with a significant rhetorical challenge. To be successful, this community needed to both undermine the traditional community structures and offer alternatives attractive enough to convince a significant number of voters to essentially overturn the results of city election. The community of recall supporters was not able to muster sufficient rhetorical power to accomplish this task.

Additionally, during the recall campaign, recall opponents reminded Manhattan citizens that a regularly scheduled city election had put Commissioner McCulloh in office and that the appropriate time to remove a commissioner was at the next regularly scheduled City Commission election. To recall a City Commissioner without significant evidence of misconduct, this community contended, was violating America's fundamental "rule of law." The appeal to this god term was quite powerful and many citizens who originally opposed the monolith decision reported they would not support the recall effort based on this argument. Appeal to "rule of law" functioned as "universalization," subsuming public arguments by the community in support of the recall. According to Celeste Condit ("Democracy and Civil Rights"), "there is a tendency of public argument, *because of its very nature*, to favor those very values, stories, and descriptions directed at the most universal audience" (1, emphasis Condit). This analysis suggests that the appeal to "rule of law," materialized in the support of regularly scheduled elections, provided the most broad-based appeal in the recall campaign and ultimately persuaded a number of citizens who were initially opposed to the monolith move.

I believe a third reason the community opposed to recall was successful was because their message remained specific and consistent. Just as politicians try to "remain on message," this community articulated and celebrated a very defined message. Recall opponents essentially stuck to a consistent narrative which argued that Commissioner McCulloh had the legal right to cast her desired monolith vote, that her vote did not constitute misconduct, and that the only reason for violating the "rule of law" of a regularly scheduled election and removing Ms. McCulloh from office through recall was misconduct in office. In contrast, the community in support of recall allowed their message to become diffuse. Their campaign strategy of "Just Because . . ." sought to tap into Manhattan discontent about a variety of city policies. Unfortunately, for this community, citizen discontent over specific City Commission policies did not rise to the level of "misconduct" and therefore did not demand overturning the rule of law imposed by the regularly scheduled election. Further, "Just Because . . ." as a rhetorical strategy became a source of ridicule. This slogan was belittled as a strategy used "when [their] whole argument is based on untruths" (Richter), as evidence that there is a "lack of any real issue in their cause" (Wisdom), and as "an argument used to pacify children when good reasons don't exist" (Garton).

Finally, the community opposing the recall encountered a bit of luck. Independent of the City Commission, the Fraternal Order of Eagles and the Manhattan Christian College worked together and decided to display to Ten Commandments on a very busy and public thoroughfare. For citizens whose primary concern was display of the commandments, this move functioned to siphon some support and intensity away from the recall move. Recall supporter Bill Von Elling, for example, noted that "The Eagles Lodge and Manhattan Christian College are working hard to build a new and better home for the Ten Commandments" (Letter) while recall opponent Lindsey Roth argued that "The monolith has a fine new home at Manhattan Christian College, which is a much more appropriate spot" (Letter). So, as the recall campaign inched forward during the fall of 1999, the monolith memorial likewise inched toward public display.

Ultimately, then, the conflict over the Ten Commandments functioned as "civic communion." The controversy worked to construct, celebrate, and sanctify a particular community image for Manhattan, Kansas. This intense, yet impermanent, controversy generated an extravagance of praise and condemnation of community symbols, histories, values, people, and experiences which caused citizens to feel a kinship or identification with some local communities and division from others. The conflict functioned not only to both highlight and organize divergent communities in Manhattan, but the recall election functioned to imprint, at least momentarily, a community identity relative to religious tolerance and representative government.

Notes

1. I volunteered to assist with the December 7 recall election. I served as an election judge for the recall election of Commissioner Karen McCulloh. I helped set up the polling station at 6:30 a.m. and worked the polls until 8:30 p.m. when we turned in our precinct's ballots. I then stayed at the election office and watched the returns come in. To provide a sense of the events of unfolding on election day and also the events leading up to the recall, I divide each section of the chapter with narratives, based in news reporting, from these two colliding trajectories.

2. Commissioners voting to move the monolith reasoned that a quick decision putting the issue behind them was the best solution. Commissioner Carol Peak indicated she voted as she did because she "felt the community was being divided by the [monolith issue]. Karen McCulloh argued that, "I did not want to see our city become a ping-pong ball between two extremist organizations, the American Civil Liberties Union and the American Center for Law and Justice, which have lined up alongside the plaintiffs and the city respectively." See Rodd Cayton, "Living Wage Looms as Issue," *Manhattan Mercury,* 2 May 1999.

3. The recall was targeted against Karen McCulloh because, according to Kansas law,

elected officials cannot be recalled in their first 120 days of office. A regularly scheduled local election had just been conducted two weeks before the special Ten Commandments meeting. Commissioners Peak and Snead were elected at that time. Because Commissioner McCulloh was already on the commission, she was the only one eligible for recall.

4. Immediately after the special City Commission meeting, I started collecting data; I collected all news stories, editorials, and letters to the editor from the *Manhattan Mercury*, the *Manhattan Free Press*, and the *Kansas State University Collegian*. I probably have not gathered everything written, but I do know that I have collected nearly everything. I further believe that any piece of discourse I am missing would not significantly alter the findings I report in this study.

5. Using these three units of discourse is consistent with previous work charting conflicting communities. In both her works, Condit uses ideographs—a form of ultimate terms—narratives, and characterizations for her discourse units of analysis. See Celeste Michelle Condit, "Democracy and Civil Rights: The Universalizing Influence of Public Argumentation," *Communication Monographs* 54 (March 1987): 1-18 and *Decoding Abortion Rhetoric: Communicating Social Change* (Urbana: University of Illinois Press, 1990). In his essay, Fisher talks about analysis of narratives, good reasons (value terms), and characters for community building examination. See Walter R. Fisher. "Narration, Reason, and Community," in *Writing the Social Text: Poetics and Politics in Social Science Discourse,* ed. Richard Harvey Brown (New York: Aldine de Gruyter, 1992), 199-217.

6. There was a third general community that emerged in the debate phase and continued through the campaign phase of this controversy. This community—smallest of the communities—appealed to the god term "civility." Their master narrative argued that no matter one's position on the monolith move and no matter the results of the recall, the primary goal was to respect the democratic process and one another. This community called on all citizens to allow reason, good will, and logic to prevail. This rhetorical community praised both the City Commission and the individual citizens who spoke out and participated in special City Commission meeting. They likewise condemned those citizens on both sides of the controversy who spoke hatefully and divisively. This community took no position on the recall except to urge everyone to participate and vote. See Linda Hall, Letter, *Manhattan Mercury,* 3 May 1999; Dave Huddleston, Letter, *Manhattan Mercury,* 9 June 1999; Roger Reitz, Letter, *Manhattan Mercury,* 1 December 1999; Rose Simmons, Letter, *Manhattan Mercury,* 20 October 1999.

7. While attacked as fallacious by supporters of the monolith move, this rhetorical community relied on three fundamental pieces of evidence to argue the majority of Manhattan citizens desired the monolith to remain in front of city hall. Initially, once this monolith issue became public, the city manager asked for phone calls to gauge public opinion. Over 90 percent of phone calls received were supportive of keeping the monument in front of city hall. See Carrie Miller, "City's Attorney Says Monument May Stand Legal Test," *Manhattan Mercury,* 2 November 1998. Second, prior to the special commission meeting, those citizens in favor of keeping the monolith in front of City Hall circulated a petition in support of their position. They collected nearly 4,000 signatures on that petition. See Bill Felber, "Voting by Petition: Most Ten Commandments Petition Signers Sat Out the April 6 Election," *Manhattan Mercury,* 7 May 1999. Finally, at the special commission meeting, over fifty people spoke to the monolith issue and the vast majority of the speakers spoke in favor of leaving the monolith on city property. See Rodd Cayton, "Majority Returns Plaque as 'Less Divisive' Course," *Manhattan Mercury,* 28 April 1999.

6

Exhibiting Collective Memory: Halstead's Heritage Museum

Highway 50, one of Kansas's east-west highways, slices a southwesterly path from Kansas City, Missouri, to the Colorado border. About one hundred twenty miles southwest of Kansas City and thirty miles north of Wichita, this blue highway pushes into the Arkansas Lowlands, a physiographic region formed by the Arkansas river and the sand and gravel deposited in its meandering wake. The land, prairie-flat and nearly treeless, forms the eastern edge of the high plains. Farms and vast fields of milo and wheat checkerboard their way between small towns. As Highway 50 pokes into the eastern edge of the Arkansas Lowlands, it intersects with Highway 89, a brief stretch of a north-south roadway, also known as the Hertzler Memorial Highway, which concludes itself in Halstead, Kansas.

As Highway 89 empties into Halstead, you cross the Little Arkansas river, and the black asphalt of Highway 89 gives way to the red brick of Halstead's main street. Trundling slowly over the uneven bricks, you notice the tallest structure in town—a white grain elevator that announces Halstead, through faded blue lettering, as, "The Biggest Little City in Kansas." Sitting next to a solitary set of railroad tracks is the Halstead Heritage Museum and Depot. The depot, built in 1917, once transferred people and commerce to and from Halstead, but now transmits the community story to its patrons and visitors, providing citizens a sense of community and collective memory. The red-brick, former Santa Fe rail station is fronted by a worn, gravel parking lot. A small sign tells all who are interested that the museum is open Saturdays and Sundays from 2:00 to 5:00 p.m. You park, walk to the heavy front door, swing the door open, and enter Halstead's preserved past.

The Kansas Museum Association estimates that "there are well over 300 museums in the state" (Keckeisen).[1] It is my argument that these repositories of historical artifacts function to construct collective memory and that this collective memory works to instill not only a sense of local community, but also to reify national ideology. Indeed, I believe the local collective memory inscribed via Halstead's Heritage Museum integrates and reinforces the received national mythos. This chapter begins with an examination of the concept of collective memory and how museums function to construct that memory. The chapter then moves to a discussion of how museums work as civic communion, followed by a brief explanation of method. I then specifically explore how the Halstead Heritage Museum symbolically constructs local identity while concomitantly reinforcing the national mythos of the self-made man.

Collective Memory and Museum Civic Communion

People remember together as much as they remember individually. While some memories might be specific to an individual, most memories are socially constructed, "instantiated beyond the individual by and for the collective" (Zelizer 214). Remembering together, or collective memory, is defined by Browne as "a shared sense of the past, fashioned from the symbolic resources of the community and subject to its particular history, hierarchies, and aspirations (248). Collective memory is constructed by the cooperative symbolic efforts of sociopolitical groups, interests, or classes who form a shared sense of the past. This shared sense of the past is constructed from past communal histories, traditions, and experiences. Political speeches, history classes, and Hollywood films are a few of the ways collective memory is organized and articulated. An additional and powerful repository for these histories, traditions, and experiences is the local heritage museum.

Museums were once thought of as elitist storehouses of the dispassionate and objectively presented historical record of a community or culture. Likewise, they were viewed as repositories where patrons passively absorbed the received interpretation of a culture's artifacts. Museums today, however, are widely recognized as active purveyors of community memory. Further, the community memory articulated in heritage museums functions to offer meaning to the present through the past, promote a particular culture, construct identity, and assert a specific ideology (Armada; Duncan, "Art Museums"; Karp, "Introduction"; Katriel, "Studying Heritage Museums"; Katriel, *Performing the Past*). Museums are not mausoleums harboring *the one and only* recorded history of a community. Museums are, instead, sites of contested visions of a local civil society. As Carol Duncan writes, "a museum is not the neutral and transparent sheltering space that it is often claimed to be," but rather a "powerful identity-defining machine" (90). Bernard Armada offers a symbolic explanation. "Because of the limitations of symbol-use," Armada writes, "museum exhibits can only cue us in to segments of history—they can never represent 'the' past in all of its social, cultural, and political complexity" (236).

It is literally impossible for a museum to entirely represent a locale's history and culture. Instead, a political elite or group of citizens select a "finite segment of meaningless infinity out of the world process" and then confer it with meaning and significance (Luke 221). Object displays are created, strategically highlighting specific histories and cultures and thereby promoting specific identities and ideologies. As Bodnar explains, "The shaping of a past . . . in the present is contested and involves the struggle for supremacy between advocates of various political ideas and sentiments" (15).

Moments of museum civic communion are thus important when initially articulating the museum's message and then instantiating that message within the community. Creation/dedication ceremonies, museum celebration activities, debate over artifactual displays, and patron/museum interaction are all civic communion moments that construct the collective memory articulated by the heritage museum. Establishing the mission and the artifactual direction of the museum offers initial moments of civic communion. Museum dedication ceremonies and debate over museum displays function to communally establish the museum's message.[2] Duncan argues that "To control a museum means precisely to control the representation of a community and some of its highest, most authoritative truths" (102). Armada explains:

> [M]useums are powerful rhetorical sites in which the past is selectively presented.
> . . . Thus, history museums invite us to see ourselves and others in particular ways
> by virtue of the narratives told and the evidence selected as "important." By privileging certain narratives over others, museums implicitly communicate who/what
> is central and who/what is peripheral. (236)

Once the museum's message is defined, additional moments of civic communion work to instantiate that message within the local community. Museum fundraisers, volunteer appreciation days, and audience/museum interactions via object displays are all examples of museum civic communions that draw broad groups of citizenry together to celebrate the collective memory and ideology articulated by the heritage museum.[3]

Methodological Contexts

Stephen Browne directs rhetorical scholars interested in collective memory to "study at the intersection of text and the interpretation of public sites." He urges critics to "explore tensions between form and content; text and context; coherence and fragmentation" (248-49). Data collection and analysis focused on rhetorical dimensions of the visual and written narratives embedded in the individual displays at the Halstead Heritage Museum. Each display was then examined in a broader context, exploring how each contributed to an overarching museum narrative. Katriel explains this methodological move:

The museum story is constructed in such a way as to combine two very different layers of narrative construction: the first is the "master-narrative" that grounds the musuem's ideological message and frames its display, and the second is localized "object-narratives" that . . . concretize its message. . . . Each "object-narrative" stands in metonymic relation to the master-narrative and the ideological world associated with it. ("Sites of Memory" 10)

I explored each of the museum's displays as individual "object-narratives," initially examining the visual discourse of the display. Katriel argues that "visual signs provide the narrative backbone for the [museum's] storytelling" (*Performing the Past* 145). After examining the display's visual, I explored the display's accompanying written exposition. I then examined the overarching narrative emerging from the culmination of all object narratives.

Specifically, I examined the Charles Basore Gallery of the Halstead Heritage Museum. This gallery provides visitors with a visual and verbal description of the received Halstead history. Through objects, photos, and short narratives, the dominant and constitutive story of Halstead is told. By examining objects and photos gathered from auctions, fields, basements, businesses, and attics and examining each display's accompanying narrative, it is possible to reconstruct a history of Halstead and infer those people, events, issues, and values important to Halstead. The Basore Gallery displays are organized by topics to tell the received Halstead story, to celebrate the central values and attitudes of Halstead. Katriel explains this museological move is "decontextualization"—or the process of removing objects (and their stories) from their natural life contexts of production, consumption, and use, and then "recontextualizing" them in a museum setting (*Performing the Past* 22). The recontextualization of the historical artifacts occurs as the artifacts in each display are organized into a seemingly coherent historical and value narrative that focuses one's perception on those values, attitudes, and people constitutive of the community of Halstead. Written narratives are then added to each topical display to reinforce that display's significance and relevance to the Halstead community. As Luke argues, "Museum exhibitions are bolted together out of rhetorical fragments taken from specific discourses and practices. . . . Objects on display in museums are disembedded from their social contexts" (219) and then reconstituted into a display which subsequently narrativizes some social practice or identity construction.

Halstead's constitutive narrative, as articulated in the artifactual and narrative displays of the Basore Gallery, can be summarized as follows: Halstead is a community founded in the history of this country's westward expansion by Russian Mennonite immigrants looking for religious, political, and economic freedom. These immigrants persevered and thrived in the face of harsh and difficult conditions to carve a community out of the prairie. Today, Halstead remains an agrarian and deeply religious community defined primarily by the values of perseverance and innovation materialized in contexts of agriculture, health care, and sports. The Halstead story and values are given form through famous citizens who have transformed economic, social, and recreation contexts.

Further, however, I believe each individual object-display functions as metonymy, that each display is a symbolic piece of the much larger, national myth of individual success. Cumulatively, the specific displays function to not only construct local collective memory, but reify the American success myth as well. This reification of national myth is accomplished by focusing on individuals rather than place, highlighting success through perseverance, and focusing on success achieved through movement and mobility. In the following section, I examine each of the object displays and then illustrate how they function to achieve these three overarching rhetorical goals.

Rhetorical Functions of Halstead's Museum Discourse

Displaying Collective Memory

Susan Crane writes, "Museums, like memories, 'exist' on several levels. We encounter them first as spaces, buildings in the physical landscape of architecture, and then as their spaces of exhibition" (2). As one drives into the gravel parking lot, it is clear the red-brick Halstead Heritage Museum is a former rail station. The fact that the museum is in an old railroad depot is symbolic. Halstead was founded, in part, by westward-moving railroads looking for stations spaced approximately ten miles apart (In fact, Halstead sits on the Santa Fe rail line ten miles west of Newton and eight miles east of Burrton). Trains were symbolic of economic power, affluence, and mobility. In the nineteenth century, trains were the preeminent mode of transportation, shipping commerce and transporting citizens as the nation expanded both economically and in population. As a stop on the Santa Fe, Halstead was accorded economic power and became a natural place for people to settle. When the station was first constructed in 1917, the local newspaper celebrated it as a "modern station" and boasted it was "capable of assisting a town ten times our size."

As you swing open the heavy entry door, you literally enter Halstead's collective memory. "The defining dimension of museum encounters" writes Katriel, "is the setting itself, which combines the edifying and imaginative thrust of verbal expositions and narrations with the concreteness, authenticity, and authority associated with the material display" (*Performing the Past* 22). As the single entrance hallway separates into a "T" hallway, the depot transforms from railway station to heritage museum. A turn to the left and you move into the Lehman-Dreese Gallery—a former passenger waiting area, now a gallery exhibiting displays which rotate every four months and which tell unique, narrowly focused, and secondary Halstead narratives. Some of the displays that have rotated through this gallery include: Halstead hobbies, the ever-changing face of Halstead's Main Street, Halstead citizens and war. A turn to your right and you move into the Charles Basore Gallery—a former waiting room, and now the museum's gallery of permanent displays. The displays featured in the Basore Gallery articulate the central, constitutive elements of the Halstead story and provide the data for my analysis.

The Basore Gallery measures a 21-by-27-foot rectangle. Six general exhibits are displayed on the outside wall of the gallery much as numbers might ring a rectangular clock face. Three exhibits constitute a freestanding center display in the middle of the gallery. This center display case stands like a clock stem for the invisible hands of this gallery clock.

As you enter the gallery and begin a clockwise tour, the first exhibit—at about one o'clock—is a celebration of Bernard Warkentin and the Russian Mennonite history in and around Halstead. Visually, the photos highlight Warkentin and Mennonite farmers working a wheat harvest. Primitive agrarian tools—a wooden rake, scythe, pitchfork, and wheat seed sack—are displayed on the wall. An oxen yoke, small horse-drawn plow, a bread bowl, and knife sit in front of the wall display. The visual rhetoric communicates the hard work of wheat harvest in a field carved out of a vast and uncompromising prairie. The images illustrate the difficulty of surviving the prairie frontier. The images all depict work. There appears to be no leisure, and no one is smiling. The accompanying written narrative tells the earliest Halstead history. In the early 1870s, Russian law was revoking self-government, religious freedom, educational autonomy, and exemption from military service for Russian Mennonites. This religious sect began emigrating to the United States looking for greater freedom than was available in Russia. A leader of the Russian Mennonites, Bernard Warkentin, toured the United States in the early 1870s and found the Arkansas River Lowlands a suitable land for the agriculture interests of his religious sect. Halstead celebrates this moment as the birth of its community.

But the display points out that Bernard Warkentin and the Mennonites brought more than their religious ideas to the Great Plains. They brought gold in the form of Turkey Red wheat seed. The Mennonites and other Kansas farmers found this strain of wheat suited to the plains's climate. This particular variety of wheat remained the dominant form of Kansas wheat for over fifty years. "Turkey Red Wheat, without a doubt, established the wheat industry in Kansas and became the standard for judging all other varieties" and is considered the most successful event in Kansas economic history (Paulsen). Thus, by determination, perseverance, and hard work, Warkentin and the Mennonites transformed American agriculture in a very real way.

This display also highlights the Mennonites' interest in community building. From Russia, they brought money that they directed into economic, civic, educational, and religious ventures. They financed grist mills, founded the Halstead Bank, and donated land for the Halstead Cemetery. In 1883, a group of Halstead Mennonites formed the Halstead College Association. From this association, the Halstead Seminary opened to train church workers and prepare missionaries for foreign service. These buildings were eventually moved from Halstead to Newton and became Bethel College, which still runs today. In 1884, another Mennonite, S. S. Haury, formed the Indian Industrial Mission School and brought displaced Arapaho children to Halstead from Oklahoma. The school was organized in an area outside of Halstead known as Krehbieltown. Krehbieltown was actually a Mennonite farm where these Native American children received social, civic, and religious instruction during the fall and spring and then worked the farm during the summer. The Indian Industrial Mission School operated for twelve years, ceasing operation in 1896.

As you move clockwise to about four o'clock on the clock face of the Basore Gallery, the second display you come to specifically celebrates Halstead's religion. This display recognizes the varieties of religions in Halstead, thus highlighting the importance of religion to the community. The display features a stained-glass window from the First Methodist Church, photographs of the early churches in Halstead, and a chronology of when the first church of each denomination appeared in Halstead. Despite the incredible influence of the Mennonites in Halstead, ironically, the first organized church service was conducted by an itinerant Methodist minister by the name of John Harris in 1874. He conducted services in a local hotel until he organized the First Methodist Church later that year (Mayfield 45). Shortly thereafter, the First Mennonite Church was founded in 1875, the Catholic Church in 1877, the Presbyterian Church in 1877, and the Zion Evangelical Church in 1885. Today, the influence of the Mennonite church remains powerful. Nearly half the churches in Halstead (three of seven) represent the Mennonite faith.

The Basore Gallery six o'clock display celebrates "the most important man who ever lived in Halstead"—Dr. Arthur Hertzler (Mayfield 61). Dr. Hertzler, a German Mennonite born in West Point, Iowa, in 1870, became affectionately known as the "Horse and Buggy Doctor."[4] Dr. Hertzler transformed medicine on the Kansas plains. Through the values of perseverance and education, Dr. Hertzler established himself and Halstead as leaders in health care, and subsequently, health care became a constitutive piece of the Halstead story. The Basore Gallery displays communicate Hertzler's importance by the amount of space given to him and by the health care artifacts that make up the display. Initially, visitors to this display are confronted by a life-size bust of Dr. Hertzler. Beyond the bust, the display highlights the importance of Dr. Hertzler's life through a multitude of photographs chronicling his many private and professional achievements. Dr. Hertzler's life story materializes the values of perseverance and education. He grew up poor and supported his undergraduate college education by working as a blacksmith. He received his M.D. from Northwestern University. Following his father's death, he used his inheritance to study surgical procedures in Berlin.

Hertzler came to Halstead in 1894 after a failed medical practice in Moundridge—a Kansas community fifteen miles north of Halstead. He came to Halstead with "no practice, few friends, certainly no money. . . . But he had unlimited ambition, faith in his own ability, and incredibly skilled hands. Those hands made him a wonderful surgeon" (Mayfield 61). Jerrad J. Hertzler also wrote that Dr. Hertzler came to Halstead "armed only with his medical bag and a great deal of determination" (426). The Basore Gallery display reports that even after Dr. Hertzler moved to Halstead, he continued to face adversity. He was married three times and divorced twice. He was nearly bankrupt several times as he worked to build his practice and enhance health care in Halstead. Despite these difficulties, Dr. Hertzler persevered, becoming one of the best-educated people in Kansas, and building a strong health care system in Halstead that remains today.

The display celebrates Dr. Hertzler's surgical work—"one of the finest surgeons of our time"—as well as his accomplishments in the field of health care. Dr. Hertzler raised funds and built the Halstead Hospital—"the little mayo" (Prairie People 4)—in 1902, a school of nursing in 1905, and the Hertzler Clinic in 1926. Both the Halstead Hospital and the Hertzler Clinic remain today. The school of nursing closed in 1966. Dr. Hertzler's work in health care carved a lasting community image. Today, Halstead continues to be identified as a regional health care center. In addition to the hospital and clinic, Halstead boasts the Kansas Learning Center for Health Museum, which includes a medical research wing; Halstead Place, which is an assisted living center; and Via Christi Hospice. Today, the visual image of Dr. Hertzler's horse-drawn buggy remains an important symbol in Halstead. It is the corporate symbol for the Hertzler Clinic and is used as an advertisement for many Halstead events including its annual Old Settlers community festival.

At the eight o'clock position on the clock face of the Basore Gallery, Halstead celebrates its brush with Hollywood greatness. In 1955, Hollywood brought William Holden, Kim Novak, Cliff Robertson, and others to the Kansas plains to film the academy-award winning *Picnic*. This museum's visual display features photos of local citizens with William Holden and Rosalind Russell and a framed poster advertising the movie. But the most prominent artifact in this display features a large white swan float. The swan has become symbolic of the connection of the film to Halstead. In the movie, Kim Novak is crowned queen of the annual Neewollah festival (Halloween spelled backwards) as part of the festivities. She floats down the Little Arkansas River—which frames Halstead's northern border—on the swan. She floats under a white swinging walk-bridge that spans the river on her way to find romance with William Holden. The movie's most famous scene then occurs when the characters, played by Novak and Holden, sensually dance in Halstead's Riverside Park (Ebert, "Picnic") and then ultimately decide to leave Halstead for a chance at a better life. Halstead's Riverside Park is now revered. Both the park and the swinging walk-bridge are highlighted in connection with *Picnic* in Halstead's publicity materials. The walk-bridge has been maintained and upgraded. There is now a community walking trail accessed by the bridge. The bridge continues to be a place of local romance. Significant portions of Halstead's annual festival—Old Settlers—takes place in Riverside Park where a free "picnic" is held each year. Fine and Speer call this a process of "sight sacralization." Communities name a sight, frame it as physically and socially separate from the rest of its environment, elevate and enshrine the sight as worthy of cultural attention, and reproduce it through mechanical and social means. The white swan float in the museum becomes a cue for the *Picnic* narrative.

At the nine o'clock position on the gallery clock face, Halstead celebrates its battles and perseverance against nature's force. The display features photos of a devastating tornado in 1910 as well as photos and news stories of flooding by the Little Arkansas River, which overran the town in 1904, 1951, 1973, 1979, and 1993. One photo shows water as far as you can see. The only things emerging out of the water are a few treetops and the tops of three mailboxes. In another photo, men are shown stacking sandbags trying to restrain the water from flooding downtown businesses. In 1998, the City of Halstead built a levee along the Little Arkansas River to prevent future flooding. By contrasting these natural disasters against the overall museum message of community achievement and progress, one emerges with image that Halstead has persevered and overcome these violent acts of nature.

At the eleven o'clock position, Halstead celebrates its public schools. Artifactually, the display highlights a brick from the original Halstead grade school, vintage band uniforms, photos from each of the high schools the community has built, and an early Halstead all-school photo.

Three displays of the Basore Gallery clock-stem center celebrate Halstead's creation story and the community values of education and perseverance. Just as every individual is born with an essence and then given a name, Halstead was likewise imbued with both soul and moniker. Warkentin and the Mennonites provided Halstead's soul. Religion, hard work, perseverance, and innovation characterize the being of Halstead. Yet, at the time of Warkentin, there was no "official" town, no name providing identity to the cluster of Russian Mennonite immigrants who had settled in the Arkansas Lowlands. The name given to that place and group of people honored Murat Halstead. Mr. Halstead was a highly educated journalist, who, during his life in the nineteenth century, became the chief owner of the *Cincinnati Commercial-Gazette*, then editor of the *Brooklyn Standard-Union*, and served as a special news correspondent during both the U.S. Civil War and the Spanish American War. Evidently, Mr. Halstead traveled extensively and in the early 1870s, passed through the Arkansas Lowlands. The Basore Gallery display explains that the people Mr. Halstead met with were so impressed by him, they said if they ever incorporated the town, they would name it after him. They were, it seems, men of their word. It is often said that a child's name influences his or her being. In fact, it does seem Halstead's name has made an impression on the essence of the town as education has been an important value throughout the community's history.

Education is also celebrated through a display highlighting the Halstead nursing school. The school was founded in 1905 by Dr. Hertzler who wanted properly trained nurses working with him and in other health care facilities. This display, in fact, highlights the nurses' training. Artifacts include books the nurses used in their education, including *Human Anatomy*, the U.S. Constitution, a reference handbook for nurses, and a book of *Medical Solutions*. Also, to convey the importance of nurses in health care, the display presents their "tools," including surgical clamps, syringe packs, surgical needles, and mannequins wearing the nursing uniform.

Halstead's value of perseverance is most celebrated in the final center display honoring Halstead native Adolph Rupp—the long-time basketball coach at the University of Kentucky. The Basore Gallery display of Rupp features a photo of "The Baron of Basketball" in his distinctive brown suit, a copy of a *Sports Illustrated* issue highlighting Rupp and Kentucky basketball, and a University of Kentucky basketball inscribed with the years they won the National Collegiate

Athletic Association's national championship—1948, 1949, 1951, and 1958, and a citation reading, "Coach Rupp set the standard for winning basketball." The display's written narrative explains that Rupp's parents were German Mennonites who settled near Halstead. Adolph Rupp grew up in Halstead, attended and graduated from Halstead High School, played basketball at the University of Kansas under Dr. James Naismith—basketball's inventor—and went on to bounce from coaching jobs in Kansas, Illinois, and Iowa high schools. Ultimately, he moved to the University of Kentucky where he became the winningest basketball coach in America. During his time at the University of Kentucky, Coach Rupp won a record 876 basketball games, won twenty-seven Southeastern Conference titles, one National Invitational Tournament title, and four NCAA titles, was selected National Coach of the Year four times, was selected the Southeastern Conference Coach of the Year seven times, and coached the 1948 U.S. Olympic team. In 1967, he was honored as "Coach of the Century" (Padwe 126).

Through a clear philosophy and unwavering perseverance, Coach Rupp transformed college basketball. Known as "The Baron," Adolph Rupp ran his program as a "fiefdom." "'Nobody,' Adolph Rupp once stated, 'talks back to me.' That was his philosophy, and it made him the winningest college basketball coach of all time" (Padwe 125). His practices were legendary. They were long, hard, repetitive, and silent. Sandy Padwe quotes Coach Rupp as saying, "Basketball is a game of rhythm. The only way you're going to get that rhythm is by repetition. You do a thing thousands of times and pretty soon you do it easily and gracefully" (128). Perseverance came not only from his repetitive practice routine, but from his dogged pursuit of winning basketball games. After forty-two years of coaching, he retired as the winningest coach in college basketball. Adolph Rupp transformed college basketball. He is credited with introducing the "fast break" and with bringing "big-time" basketball to the South and to all of America. The *Orlando News and Observer* argued that Rupp "should be credited with basketball's growth, not just in the South, but all over the country in 1940s and '50s. Every time you see a basketball goal on a barn or kids in a playground, you have to credit Coach Rupp. His presence will last forever, in Kentucky and nationally" (Alexander).

Reifying the National Myth of Success

From the individual object displays, one gains a sense of the collective memory of Halstead. The museum's discrete displays articulate Halstead's history, highlighting Halstead's most famous citizens, institutions, and events, and revealing important local values. By examining and participating in the individual displays, it is clear that Halstead's collective memory is centered around the individual accomplishments of Bernard Warkentin, Dr. Arthur Hertzler, Adolf Rupp, and S. S. Haury within the contexts of education, health care, sport, and religion. Museum displays do feature the natural landscape, highlighting wheat fields and the Arkansas River, but those features function as a background for the accomplishments and successes of Halstead's famous individuals. I contend, in fact, that by examining the over-arching form of these discrete object displays, the Halstead Heritage Museum and Depot message ultimately functions to instantiate the national myth of success. The success myth or "idea that ours is an open society, where birth, family, and class do not significantly circumscribe individual possibilities, has a strong hold on the popular imagination" (Weiss 3). Martha Solomon summarizes the success myth "in simple dramatic terms. The protagonist is a strong individualist, confident, and op-timistic. With hard work, perseverance, and competitiveness, this individual can overcome barriers to achieve financial success and recognition" (174). From the writings of Weiss, Solomon, and Robertson, it is clear that the American success myth has several fundamental elements. To improve one's position, an individual moves beyond his or her place and station of origin, perseveres and overcomes hardship, and transforms him or herself and some aspect of the world. In the trans-formation, the community/society progresses.

Clearly, the Halstead Heritage Museum and Depot articulates a rhetoric of individualism. According to James Robertson, "the first requisite of individualism [is] the wish to change your lot," and "the significant outward sign of the process of changing one's lot, increasingly its most powerful symbol, [is] to move beyond one's native spot" (148-49). Fundamental to the American myth of success is mi-gration and mobility to a better place. Through museum visual and verbal narra-tives, visitors understand that Warkentin moved from the oppression of Russia to the unlimited opportunity of the Kansas plains. Dr. Hertzler moved from the per-sonal and professional limitations and failures of Iowa and Moundridge to the medical opportunities afforded by Halstead, and Adolph Rupp moved from Hal-stead through small-time basketball stops in Kansas, Iowa, and Illinois to opportu-nities offered by big-time basketball at the University of Kentucky. Even the movie *Picnic* articulates the power of mobility within this rhetoric of individualism and achievement. Film critics Roger Ebert of the *Chicago Sun-Times* and Mick LaSalle of the *San Francisco Chronicle* both argue that a central theme of the film is "ex-posing the limited options of a pretty girl [Kim Novak's character] in '50s small-town America" (LaSalle) and depicting "the utter irrelevance of women in that place [small towns] and that time" (Ebert, "Picnic"). Both Ebert and LaSalle, then, articulate the inconsistency of achievement and success with staying put—in this instance small-town Kansas. Likewise, William Holden's character in *Picnic* des-perately wants to be successful; he wants to be somebody. At a critical point in the movie, he forlornly proclaims to Kim Novak, "I gotta get somewhere in this world. I just gotta." Implied in his pronouncement is the notion that success means mobil-ity and movement to another place—both physically and economically. Both Holden and Novak's characters are seeking a better place and need to move from where they are. Holden's character needs to move spiritually and economically, while Novak's character feels she needs to move physically. As Robertson con-cludes:

> The importance of mobility to individualism has long been striking. . . . Physical mobility and social mobility are closely related. . . . Going West, seeking greener

pastures, leaving home, and moving on are not only physical moves which demonstrate and guarantee independence; they also carry the implication that they lead to better, higher social and economic status. (150)

Simply moving from one's place of origin to a place of more opportunity, however, does not equate with immediate success. This is because there are inevitably barriers and hardships that must be overcome. Those individuals who succeed must first conquer and transform some metaphorical or physical wildernesses. This element of the success myth materializes the value of perseverance. As Solomon points out, Americans have uniquely "embraced the notion that in this country a person of energy and initiative would inevitably achieve success through individual effort" (174). The Halstead museum narratives, in fact, highlight their famous citizens achieving success in the face of numerous barriers. The most significantly articulated hardship is the physical environment. In the display about Bernhard Warkentin, a photo depicts six Mennonite farmers loading wheat onto a large wooden wagon drawn by two horses. The task looks overwhelming. An everextending sea of wheat appears to go forever across a featureless field with only a few spare trees so far in the distance, they appear beyond reach. There are no clouds in the sky so one can easily imagine this difficult work on a brutally hot Kansas summer day. Offering further visual evidence of the environmental hardship, the photo is framed around one man drinking from a wooden water jug. All the other men are struggling with the wheat. The visual rhetoric is evocative of the physical strains of intense manual labor.

In another powerful image of the unforgiving prairie environment, Dr. Arthur Hertzler is depicted as "the horse and buggy doctor." In fact, this is the name of his autobiography (Hertzler, *Horse and Buggy Doctor*), and the horse and buggy is Halstead's most identifiable image. On the jacket of Hertzler's book, however, the horse and buggy are standing outside a solitary farmhouse on a winter's night. Except for a single pair of footprints leading to the home from the buggy, snow covers the ground, and smoke blows from the chimney, indicating a prairie wind. The photo articulates an individualist rhetoric in which the doctor working alone, in the middle of prairie, is battling the elements to bring medicine to rural families. Finally, as mentioned earlier, there is a permanent display featuring Halstead's battles against nature—the floods and tornadoes. From this visual rhetoric, Halstead's environment is cast as inhospitable, presenting a formidable challenge. By implication, only rugged individuals could exist in such a wilderness. But wilderness can also be metaphorical as in the wilderness of the unchurched or the wilderness of primitive health care.

The final element of the individual success myth is transformation of some wilderness into something of value so that progress might occur. Robertson offers a summary of this essential piece of individual success mythic rhetoric: "Wilderness shaped our national character as our forefathers met and conquered its early challenge" (113). Warkentin, Hertzler, Rupp, and S. S. Haury are identified as the forefathers of Halstead. Warkentin and the Mennonites moved to the Kansas plains, endured the physical hardships of this physiographic wilderness, but ultimately transformed agriculture by introducing Turkey Red Wheat—a strain of wheat suited to the harsh prairie winters. Progress, however, is not only recorded in environmental terms. Instead, it is often cast in metaphorical terms of "civilization" or "improvement." "Progress," Lowenthal argues, "was social as well as material" ("Pioneer Museums" 118). Thus, Dr. Arthur Hertzler moved from Iowa, to Moundridge, Kansas, to Halstead, floundering in the economic wilderness of bankruptcy. After attempting and failing to establish a medical practice three times in Moundridge, Hertzler finally made his way to Halstead. Following years of working as a circuit-riding doctor, symbolized by the horse and buggy, Hertzler ultimately transformed rural health care by bringing modern medical methods and facilities to Halstead and the surrounding rural areas. Benefits of transforming the wilderness also transcended economic gains. Conquering the wilderness of the unchurched brought civilization to the savage life (Lowenthal, "The Pioneer Landscape" 10). S. S. Haury, an early Halstead Mennonite missionary, worked to transform the unchurched Native Americans. In the late nineteenth century, Haury brought over one hundred Arapaho Native American children to Halstead from the Indian Territory (now Oklahoma). An Indian Industrial Mission School— known locally as Krehbieltown—was created at a local Mennonite farm. At this school, the children received civilizing instruction in agriculture, housework, schoolwork, and Christian living during the academic year. In the summer, these children worked on the Mennonite farm.

Halstead's museum rhetoric ultimately tells stories of individuals moving toward opportunities, battling wilderness, and ultimately transforming self and some institution. According to the museum's narratives, Halstead's citizens transformed the Kansas plains into the world's breadbasket, primitive rural health care into modern medicine, the destructiveness of the unrestrained flooding into a controlled river, savage Native Americans into Christians, and the neophyte game of basketball into a big-time sport.

Conclusions

The Halstead Heritage Museum and Depot functions as civic communion, building a sense of community in Halstead by constructing local collective memory. The museum functions as community symbol, community builder, and ultimately a transmitter of national myth. The museum itself is a symbol of America's westward progression and economic power. It now stands as a symbol of perseverance and stability as it has endured nearly an entire century, having been rebuilt three different times and sold two different times, and emerged as community symbol from the brink of demolition. The depot as museum now resides as a symbol of community.

The Halstead Heritage Museum and Depot also functions as community builder. Through the various moments of civic communion—creation/dedication ceremonies, local events that celebrate the museum, debates over the museum displays, and the interaction of visitors with the museum displays—the organizational, social, and rhetorical structures of Halstead are highlighted and celebrated. These moments of civic communion function to help confirm Halstead's identity, purifying and sanctifying its sense of civic order.

Ultimately, however, I contend the museum and depot functions rhetorically as an ideological transmitter reifying the national myth of individualism and the pursuit of success. Katriel acknowledges that museums are "increasingly important arenas for cultural production and ideological assertion" (1) while Lowenthal specifically argues that "pioneer museums are felt, and many deliberately seek to purvey, an American founding myth" ("Pioneer Museums" 120). Through local artifactual displays, the Halstead museum tells America's story of struggle and conquest, transforming the physical, economic, and religious wildernesses into progress and civilization. The organization and display of the museum exhibits transmit both a particular history that binds the local citizenry around a collective memory and articulates a national mythology which reifies an American individualist ideology.

Notes

1. It is difficult to know exactly how many functioning history museums are in Kansas. As Robert Keckeisen writes, the Kansas Museums Association "has set no criteria for what might constitute a 'rural museum' and when the issue is discussed, "it unfortunately bogs down in terms of how one defines a museum" (Letter to author). Katriel recognizes this same problem in her museum work in Israel as she writes: "There is some ambiguity in terms of what counts as a museum because some of them are outgrowths of temporary exhibits and some are attached to local archives. There is also some ambiguity as to which heritage museums count as settlement museums in this context." See Tamar Katriel, *Performing the Past: A Study of Israeli Settlement Museums* (Mahwah, NJ: Lawrence Erlbaum Associates, 1997), 13.

2. Decisions about which museum narratives to privilege often come from the crucible of debate and persuasive speech among interested community members and groups. The president of the Hastead Historical Society acknowledged that "the Museum Committee, made up of volunteer members, makes all the decisions concerning the displays" (Murray interview), and society member, Carolyn Williams, explained that "some people wanted the museum to be a site for genealogy study, others wanted it to be a place to store historical artifacts, and still others saw the museum as a place to tell Halstead's story" (Williams interview).

3. Museum/patron interactions function as a civic communion moment in the rhetoric of museums. In our society, museums are often regarded as sacred places housing important historical, political, and cultural truths for a community of culture. These truths are embodied in museum artifacts and exhibits. Duncan explains that museums "*work* like temples, shrines, and other such monuments." Museum patrons, Duncan argues, "bring with them the willingness and ability to shift into a certain state of receptivity. And like traditional ritual sites, museum space is carefully marked off and culturally designated as special, reserved for a particular kind of contemplation and learning experience." See Carol Duncan, "Art Museums and the Ritual of Citizenship," in *Exhibiting Cultures: The Poetics and Politics of Museum*

Display, eds. Ivan Karp and Steven D. Lavine (Washington, DC: Smithsonian Institution Press, 1991), 91. Museums are, therefore, viewed as special environments where the highest civic truths are exhibited and articulated. Because of the civic import we give museums, they become important learning spaces where patrons willingly view and absorb community history, values, and ideals. Drawing on this unique relationship between museum and patron, museums often create dynamic and dramatic exhibits that call for audience intellectual and emotional participation. Museum displays are, according to Crane, particularly evocative sites, "where subjective memory and objective historical traces collide." See Susan A. Crane, *Museums and Memory* (Stanford, CA: Stanford University Press, 2000), 7. This participation in a museum exhibit draws patrons into enacting or performing some local community tradition or ideal or value. These forms of participatory museum events draw audiences into a collective gathering of enthusiastic praise for received community structures. Their interactions with the museum function to powerfully legitimize and celebrate the locale's received cultural, sociopolitical, and rhetorical structures.

4. "The Horse and Buggy Doctor" is one of Halstead's most recognizable symbols. This descriptive phrase came from the title of Dr. Hertzler's 1938 autobiography (*Horse and Buggy Doctor*). In this book, Dr. Hertzler devotes an entire chapter to modes of transportation to country patients. He contends: "The means of transportation at the beginning of any practice was preferred in the order named: horse or team and buggy; horse and road cart, a two-wheeled vehicle with a simple and very hard board seat on which no cushion could be fastened; horseback; and finally just plain everyday walking it or pedaling a lowly bicycle." See Arthur E. Hertzler, *The Horse and Buggy Doctor* (Lincoln: University of Nebraska Press, 1938), 61. Others writing about Dr. Hertzler note that "since his practice was a rural one, it was often necessary for him to travel long distances by horse and buggy to see his patients." Jerrad J. Hertzler, "Arthur E. Hertzler: The Kansas Horse and Buggy Doctor: A Biographical Sketch," *Journal of the Kansas Medical Society* 63 (October 1962): 426.

7

Infusing "Spirit" into Community Building: The Kansas Sampler Foundation

As I walk into The Barn's large meeting room, I immediately sense this is not going to be just another business conference. I'm here to attend a "Motivational and Support Gathering" facilitated by the Kansas Sampler Foundation. The informational brochure for "The Gathering" indicated "Community leaders from across the state are invited to take part in an environment of support, motivation, vision-making, idea sharing, and networking." Sounded like a meeting of like-minded souls and so I am here.

We're gathering at "The Barn," the name of a Valley Falls Bed and Breakfast, so named because the proprietor, Tom Ryan, got tired of managing pigs and cattle, and converted their living quarters into a B & B where he could manage people's need for camaraderie and commerce. The meeting room I've walked into appears as a spacious living room in someone's home. Overstuffed sofas and cushioned wicker chairs are arranged around the room. Tropical plants and trailing philoden-drons break up the even, symmetrical look of the meeting hall. As I sit down in one of the oval wickers, I peer out through a bank of floor-to-ceiling windows and onto a spacious, undulating, and unbroken rural Kansas countryside. A wonderful view.

Marci Penner, director of the Kansas Sampler Foundation, walks in, smiling and seemingly chatting with everyone. She moves to the front of the room and asks that the lights be turned down—"to set the mood a bit." "We're here for the next forty hours," she explains in gentle tones, "to address the isolation people are feeling in rural Kansas. We're here to figure out how to help promote the Kansas we all know and love. We're here to give each other energy."

123

Introduction

I believe that a central feature of community-building language is "spirit." By spirit, I refer not simply to the term's narrow interpretation as an individual's association with some organized religious belief system or the varied practices of meditation and prayer. Instead, spirit in the context of this study refers to a broad, transforming, imaginative, and ethical energy and emotion. This form of spirit can be and is possessed by individuals in nearly any context—education, business, politics, religion, and/or community building. I believe spirit becomes materialized in an ethical rhetoric, which is an energy-giving, imaginative, connecting, and unifying discourse. Characteristic of the Kansas Sampler Foundation message is a powerful "spiritual rhetoric." Marci Penner and the Kansas Sampler Foundation work tirelessly to energize and enthuse people throughout and about rural Kansas. This organization asks both Kansans and non-Kansans to explore the state with "new eyes," to view the state's resources in new and different ways. The Sampler works to make connections among people and localities and articulates a message of interdependence. Finally, the Sampler articulates an ethical discourse valuing Kansas' people, their efforts, and resources. More than any group with which I've been associated, the community-building language of the Kansas Sampler Foundation possesses a spiritual tone. In this essay, I will explore both the spirit articulated by Kansas Sampler Foundation rhetoric and how that spiritual message works to build rural Kansas community.[1] But first, I will briefly review the importance of spirit to community building and provide a history of the Kansas Sampler Foundation.

Connecting Spirit to Community Building

While spirit itself is ineffable, resisting naming and definition (Rushing 160), spiritual community-building language is made material in a variety of rhetorics. Initially, a spiritual community-building language is articulated through creative energy. Spiritual rhetoric is energetic, enthusiastic, and emotional—literally drawing citizens into a common vision of community building. As Herman Schmalenbach argues, "communions are borne along by waves of emotion, reaching ecstatic heights of collective enthusiasm" (332). Schmalenbach continues by pointing out, "Emotional experiences are the very stuff [of human communion]. Jubilant followers who swarm around a leader chosen in an inspired flood of passion do not intend to be bound up with him and with one another on the basis of characteristics they naturally have in common. They are bound together by the feeling actually experienced. Indeed, each one is *en rapport*" (335). Thus, community-building spiritual rhetoric is originative, functioning to literally create community-building efforts. This occurs through an enthusiasm, an emotion, and energy articulated by community-building rhetors.

A community-building spirit is imaginative. A spiritual rhetoric is creative, valuing the exploration of community issues from different angles. Spiritual rhetoric asks us to see problems and challenges from multiple perspectives. As Bud Goodall explains, "Spirit calls, pushes, nudges, comically points to and dramatically shoves us into an awareness of imaginative capacities. . . . Spirit enables us to relearn forgotten or covered-up sense-making abilities, to cull from the ineffable, the imagistic, and semiotic possibilities" (*Divine Signs* 213). A spiritual rhetoric encourages us to read and write of community building in the poetics of the extraordinary and prose of the everyday. It refrains from making all community decisions based on the variable analytic studies of science and the bottom line of cost-benefit business models.

A spiritual community-building rhetoric is also ethical. Many community scholars have arugued that a value system or an ethic is characteristic of healthy communities and central to those ethics is concern for humaneness. Examples of humaneness in community-building ethics include: (1) Bellah et al.'s discussion of our culture's "second language"; (2) Buber's notion of the "community of otherness" and "the narrow ridge" (quoted in Arnett); (3) Rousseau's argument that key to community is "altruistic love"; (4) Jason's concept of "true communities"; (5) Morgan's writings about spirit in the workplace. Each of these humane ethics would agree with Rousseau, who argues that "morally right actions are those that build community" (106), and with Morgan who contends that spirit is "the life-giving dynamic that happens between people" (7). In each of these ethics, a concern for other is paramount. Community-building values would include: taking responsibility for one's actions; treating people with dignity, creativity, courage, service, integrity, trust, joy, interdependence and clear purpose; and creating communities that provide a place for people to live that is protected and nourishing.

Part of a humane community-building ethic is a language of interdependence and connection. Janice Hocker Rushing, for example, argues that spirit is a "guide toward wholeness," "the realization of the interrelationship among all things," and that "spirit transcends all oppositions" (161). Bud Goodall argues that spirit is "the holistic force for connecting ourselves to Others, for connecting our interests to better interests of community, for connecting our communities' interests to the best interests of the Earth" (*Divine Signs* 212). Likewise, Thomas Berry writes that spirit is the "supreme mode of communion [existing] within the individual, the human community, within the earth-human complex" (40).

This analysis, then, explores the way that a specific organization—the Kansas Sampler Foundation—materializes "spirit" in their rhetoric of community building. Before examining this spiritual discourse, however, it is important to gain some historical perspective on the Kansas Sampler Foundation.

The Kansas Sampler Foundation

In the early 1990s, Marci Penner returned home to Inman, Kansas, from the University of Wisconsin and Philadelphia, Pennsylvania, where she studied and worked in counseling. Moving from work in guidance counseling to writing counseling guides about viewing Kansas, Marci and her father, Mil Penner, toured the state to catalog places, events, and attractions for their Kansas guidebooks.[2] As they would journey and explore across the state, they would routinely stop in small towns and ask the locals what there was to see and do in town. Waitresses in local cafes, clerks in convenience stores, and service station attendants often responded, "there's nothin' in this place to do" or "we're in the middle of nowhere doing nothin'." The Penners were disturbed that so many in rural Kansas did not recognize the wonderful resources their localities possessed and that so many Kansas communities were in decline both in enterprise and energy.

When they finished the *Kansas Weekend Guide* and the *Kansas Event Guide* in 1991, the Penners invited the communities they explored to attend a book signing at their Inman farm. The Penners encouraged these communities to bring examples of their local commerce and customs so that others from around the state could "sample" Kansas's wonderful gifts. The occasion was such a success that the "Kansas Sampler" festival was born and became an annual event. In 1993, the Penners created the nonprofit Kansas Sampler Foundation and hired Marci Penner as its director. The Sampler's fundamental goal is to promote and preserve rural culture and communities in Kansas. The Sampler pursues this goal along two tracks: (1) they strive to educate those who wish to understand and experience the diversity, beauty, and drama of Kansas, and (2) they work to network rural community leaders.

One path toward the Sampler's goal of promoting and preserving rural Kansas culture and community is education of Kansans about Kansas. Initial education efforts appeared in the Kansas guidebooks. Information in the guidebooks then became symbolic grist for slide shows about Kansas and a trivia game about Kansas entitled "Go Kansas!" Marci Penner now takes these informational tools across the state to let Kansans know of the wonderful resources that exist all around them. The Sampler's hope is that Kansas's citizens will begin to recognize and promote the value of rural culture and the contributions rural communities have made to the history of Kansas and to the ongoing drama of rural life. The ambition of the Sampler is that these education efforts will foster awareness and nourish pride in rural Kansas. As Jeri Harder explains, "The hope of the foundation is, that as communities take more pride in knowing and telling who they are and what they have, more people will visit these towns for an authentic experience, that dollars will be turned over, and that this will help keep rural communities alive and vibrant" (12).

The second path the Sampler Foundation takes toward its goal is to network rural community efforts. The Sampler promotes a cooperative spirit within and among Kansas communities so as to enhance the chance these rural towns will survive and thrive. The Sampler has engaged in a number of specific projects to better network rural community leaders. They continue to conduct the annual Kansas Sampler festival—the festival has now outgrown the Penner farm—rotating it to various communities around the state. An annual retreat for nonmetropolitan community leaders, known as "The Gathering," was created in 1993 and has become a powerful forum of ideas for the Sampler and rural Kansas. This retreat is a time for rural community leaders to gather together and reflect on rural Kansas—its strengths, opportunities, challenges, and threats. It also a time for brainstorming about ways to better "tell the story" of rural Kansas. This annual retreat has been a significant catalyst for progress toward Sampler goals. From "The Gathering," the Kansas Explorers Club was founded, a group that works to inspire, educate, and encourage the exploration and appreciation of Kansas.[3] Kansas Explorers now number over 1,300 members and have become an important energy and communication source for the Kansas Sampler Foundation. From another motivational gathering, the idea of a bimonthly newsletter, *We Kan!*, emerged. This newsletter serves as an information source to assist community leaders and friends of Kansas to develop their unique identities, tell their local stories, and energize their communities. From yet another gathering came the eight elements of rural culture—history, architecture, geography, art, commerce, cuisine, customs, and people.[4] These elements now form the basis of all the Sampler's rural education efforts. The Sampler highlights each of the rural culture elements in all of its communication. The elements are used in seminars and presentations conducted by the Sampler. And at yet another "Gathering," the informational Kansas trivia game, "Go Kansas!" was developed.

The Sampler Foundation has transformed from an idea conceived by Marci and Mil Penner as they traveled and explored the blue highways of Kansas to become a significant force in promoting Kansas culture, community, and tourism. The educational game show, "Go Kansas!," and the Kansas Explorers Club have been featured on Kansas public television across the state. The Kansas State Office of Tourism hired the Sampler Foundation as a consultant to catalog the state's resources relevant to culture and tourism efforts. In fact, the Sampler Foundation has been influential in creating the Kansas tourism themes that the state now promotes in all publicity materials.

The Spirit of the Kansas Sampler Foundation

Through their rhetoric, the Kansas Sampler Foundation in general and Marci Penner in particular articulate a compelling community-building spirit. By examining the articulated discourse of the Kansas Sampler Foundation ranging from talk at "The Gathering," to the *We Kan!* newsletter, to books and articles written by and about the Sampler, one begins to see the powerful spiritual quality of Sampler rhetoric.

Creating Energy

Spirit is initially a creative force, and "The Gathering" and the Sampler Foundation are viewed as the crucible for community-building efforts throughout Kansas. "The Gathering" and the Sampler are constructed by Kansas Explorers as a life-force, both possessing life qualities itself and giving life qualities to others. The Sampler is, for example, depicted by the owner of a Hutchinson video company as "pretty magical. It has a soul." And the Sampler, as life-force, is perceived as also giving emotional and community life to others. Nearly all "Gathering" participants report that they come to the meeting to be rejuvenated, revitalized, reinvigorated, reborn. One participant contends that the Sampler "has given this group of [community developers] life. We have a heartbeat because of you." Another participant avers, "You [the Sampler] have given new eyes for Kansas," while yet another participant explains that "The Gathering" gives us "emotional sustenance." The owner of The Barn told Marci Penner, "When I'm looking about Kansas, talking up our local community, your voice echoes through my mind." "Gathering" participants report that Marci Penner and the Kansas Sampler Foundation literally give life to their rural work as they receive emotional sustenance, a heartbeat, eyes to see, and a voice to use from the Sampler's spiritual message.

But besides giving "individual life" to those who work daily and doggedly to preserve and promote rural development, narratives told by "Gathering" participants also reveal the Sampler provides "community life." The following three narratives, told by "Gathering" participants, illustrate the power of the Sampler's life-force message.

Jim "Cowboy" Gray of Ellsworth looks and lives the part. From head to toe, Cowboy dresses as if he just walked in from a 1890s Wild West cowtown. At today's meeting, Jim wears a black, Will James Stetson pulled down over a face highlighted by a broad, cowhand-style mustache; a wild rag of blue bandana is wrapped around his neck and lays against his duckins canvass vest. Underneath his vest, Jim wears a white bib-front shirt to "stave off the consumption chill." Black frontier pants are tucked into his knee-high, brown Coffeeville boots. His E. Garcia spurs announce his presence as he jangles into our meeting room. Jim Gray owns the Drover's Mercantile in Ellsworth, a haberdashery of vintage cowboy clothing. In addition, he runs a cattle ranch and is the founder of the C.O.W.B.O.Y. Society.[5] He is also featured riding his horse and driving a cattle herd in a Kansas tourism video highlighting Kansas's Wild West history. At one meeting, Cowboy told everyone about the genesis of his work in cowboy culture:

> This meeting at The Barn was the spark for me. It gave me the courage to step outside with my ideas. Everyone gets discouraged. Just hang in there, just keep poundin' away. I did and now we have the Drover's Mercantile in Ellsworth. We have the C.O.W.B.O.Y. Society. And we're influencing the community too. They have approved and are going to support the Chisolm Trail project. They're going to support the cowboy get-together in Ellsworth. The cowboy heritage story is

going to be part of Ellsworth's 130-year celebration. You just have to live it, live your dream.

Jim Gray's story is typical of many that are told at "The Gathering." Many participants report that the Sampler and "The Gathering" have been instrumental in providing the energy, the spark, the courage, and the life for their community business and development. Jeri Harder credits the Sampler and "The Gathering" for helping her start the *Tour Kansas Guide*, the "most complete calendar of events" in Kansas. Jan and Winston Summerfield and Marge and Bob Wan talk about how they walked out of "The Gathering" in 1997, energized from the meeting, and formed their business Country Boys Carriage and Prairie Adventures. But beyond simply generating new Kansas commerce, "The Gathering" and the Sampler infuse community building as well. As Jim Gray points out, the community of Ellsworth has embraced the cowboy theme and has used it to create a more identifiable image. Jim Gray's work, given expression through his interaction at "The Gathering" and with the Sampler, is now a significant part of that created community image.

Besides providing energy for rural commerce and then hoping that commerce energizes rural community rebirth, the Sampler also works directly to sustain rural communities. This work is reflected in a narrative from Delores Landry. Delores looks like someone's grandmother, but acts like somebody's kid sister. Delores is active and spirited, especially as she energetically promotes north central Kansas. She has championed the area as a distinct tourism district, promoting both the general attraction of the region as well as the value of specific attractions. Delores describes herself through the metaphor of a round, green bucket. Round because she is well-rounded, involved in many things. Green for promoting growth. A bucket also has a handle to grab "a hold of," and Delores feels like she's a handle for people to grab a hold of when they need help. The bucket's flat bottom symbolizes stability, and Delores believes she doesn't get easily upset or tipped over.

Delores Landry was, however, terribly upset a few year ago. She was concerned she was going to lose Ames, Kansas—her hometown—as an identifiable place. She tells the following story of how "The Gathering" and the Explorers spearheaded the effort to preserve her small town:

> Well, when we were here a number of years ago, that's back when the post office was doing some reshuffling and they said they were going to get rid of some of these little post offices. Well, our postmistress had passed away and the local post office had blown away during a tornado. Well, I was sharing this story to all of you and told everyone that from now on my address would be Concordia instead of Ames, and Tom came up off his seat and said, "That can not be! We can't let these little towns just fade away! We've got to do something about that." He got on the phone to the Omaha post office, got everything talked up there, and he told everyone that was here, "When you go home, you write a letter or a note or something to Delores at Ames so they will know they're getting mail there." So we went home and talked to the people in Concordia. They said, "Well, yes, we've received word from Omaha and you can continue to use Ames, but be sure to use Concordia's zip

code." So, I have to wear my Ames sweatshirt. And thanks to Tom, we're still Ames.

Characteristic of the Kansas Sampler Foundation and those explorers who gather at The Barn is the support they provide for Kansas's people, projects, and places that need help. The Sampler believes in the inherent value of rural communities and works vigorously to help others who are also trying to preserve rural culture. Besides support from "The Gathering," the Sampler Foundation uses its newsletter, *We Kan!*, to highlight local efforts to promote and preserve rural culture. *We Kan!* functions as a clearinghouse of information about rural community development. It provides information about grant opportunities, how to work with local and regional media, how to connect with state tourism officials, and upcoming rural conferences. Through *We Kan!*, the Sampler announces "Explorer" work days where Explorers show up from around the state to help a particular rural community in need.[6] The newsletter publicizes specific development efforts of rural towns as they work to establish local business, festivals, or protect local culture. *We Kan!* highlights local businesses and communities and encourages explorers to support these various rural communities and commerce as a method of sustaining rural Kansas communities. The Kansas Sampler Foundation functions very clearly and purposively as a spirit of promotion and preservation of rural Kansas.

The Sampler also infuses spirit into rural Kansas by encouraging local civic responsibility. A narrative by Jay Yoder is illustrative of the energy given by the Sampler and then the local results of that energy. A man of forty-some years, Jay is solid and muscular with long black hair. His regular forty-hour-a-week job takes his time, but not his heart. Instead, his soul is located in his business—The Wooden Anvil Mercantile—where he builds red cedar furniture and in his south central Kansas hometown, Partridge—"a good place to be from." Jay Yoder is a quiet man, a man of few words whose goal for the new millennium is to improve his speaking and writing communication skills. Yet, Jay is already a recognized civic leader in Partridge, a cocreator of the Partridge Community Park, and a doer in community affairs. Jay speaks from the heart, talks with uncommon sincerity; and the narratives he tells at "The Gathering" are among the most powerful told. He credits his community commitment and his civic voice to the energy and support he has received from the Sampler and "The Gathering" as he explains in the following narrative where he describes how he and others reinvigorated the Partridge Community Association. According to Jay:

> We had a meeting of our association. We were dwindling, and we just didn't have a response to it anymore, and so we had a goal-setting meeting. Well, there might be a dozen people come to our regular meeting, there might have been 25 at our goal-setting meeting. We were packed. We set some goals and then a committee decided to see what direction we needed to go to get these goals met. As we were doing that, we decided that we could not make decisions based on this small amount of people, so then we decided to go with this survey to make sure we hit

everybody. So, I just took the survey around the community, door to door. I wanted everybody to talk. If they didn't want to respond, that was fine, some people just got mad.

One result was, we wanted to a way to educate people. So I just thought of the rural culture elements and for three or four months picked somebody in town to talk about, say, Partridge geography, somebody to talk about the history. So, that's how we picked programs for our assocation and it picked up how many people come out to the association meetings.

Marci Penner points out that when Jay Yoder first came to "The Gathering," "he was so shy, sat on the back row, we didn't hear much from him, but he kept doing these things that were wonderful." Gradually, Jay became more personally committed to working to improve Partridge, taking real responsibility for enhancing his town. He became involved with the Partridge Community Association, worked on enhancing the community park, planted trees, lobbied to stop "over pumping" of well water. From the Kansas Sampler Foundation and "The Gathering," Partridge, Kansas, gained a real civic voice and force in Jay Yoder. His story, however, is not unique, as others have taken the Sampler's spiritual energy and transformed that energy into civic action. Clearly, the spirit of the Kansas Sampler Foundation infuses energy into Kansas's people, projects, and places. It literally provides the life spark for rural community development.

Articulating Imagination

Inherent in a spiritual message is an articulation of imagination that calls on rhetors and auditors alike to speak and hear and see in new ways. Through imagination, conventional wisdom is challenged and traditional perceptions are questioned. The Sampler's spiritual rhetoric, in fact, attempts to reshape citizens' perceptions of rural Kansas. Too often, according to a common Sampler lament, "Kansans don't take pride in the wonderful gifts their communities possess." The Sampler contends that Kansans need to highlight their uniqueness, "to take the cobwebs off of who we are and what it is we have and invite people to come share this part of us" (Penner, personal e-mail). Kansas's communities possess real treasures, according to the Sampler, and citizens just need to realize and highlight these local riches. The Sampler's hope is that by adjusting local perception, pride in one's local community will increase, and that this newfound pride will concomitantly lead to increased community building and development. It is the idea that one is more likely to sustain and improve something he or she is proud of than something not held in esteem. The Sampler also believes it important for Kansans to define themselves through their own words and work, rather than be defined through representations of Kansas imposed from individuals and corporate entities outside of Kansas.

Thus, Sampler spiritual rhetoric works to change standard perceptions of Kansas. The Sampler labors to alter the received view of Kansas as "that great historic rectangle of discomfiture" (Heat-Moon, "Great Kansas Passage" 196), as a "hot, flat, treeless, boring, and God-forsaken hellhole," as a "fly-over" state, a state to drive across fast and preferably at night, and a state whose most famous image is the drab home of Dorothy until she is swept heavenward by a killer tornado into the colorized Land of Oz.[7]

To accomplish this perceptual conversion, the Sampler argues that Kansas's communities offer "authentic explorer experiences" as opposed to "mediated and designed tourist experiences." The conversion begins with "attitude." It begins with an imaginative valuing of places and things not normally valued in mass-mediated America. Marci Penner writes, "It's all an attitude. It's a mindset we're selling. We want to help people see the beauty of our subtle nature; we want Kansans to feel pride in who they are and that it is worth sharing" (personal e-mail). Speech communication scholar Bud Goodall, though not talking about Kansas, also argues observation of otherness is about attitude. When writing about "tourist" as a metaphor for observing others, he writes, "So the question then quickly becomes one not of direction—for all roads do in fact lead somewhere—but of the *attitude* we take when we travel" (*Living in the Rock N Roll Mystery* 222; emphasis mine).

Fundamental to a change in attitude is the process of viewing Kansas. A primary Sampler mantra counsels people to "see Kansas with new eyes." The Sampler encourages people to look for authentic experiences; that the exploration and the search are as vital as experiencing the attraction itself. As Marci Penner writes, "people who enjoy the authentic experience appreciate the journey as much as, if not more than, arriving at the destination" (personal e-mail). Instead of viewing otherness through the speed of our drive-through culture, the Sampler urges stepping outside the role of hurried tourist, rejecting the tendency to know Kansas from the concrete turnpike and instead becoming intimate with one's destination. As Mil Penner admonishes in a chapter entitled "New Eyes for Kansas,"

> Put on "new eyes" when you explore Kansas. Let go of preconceived ideas of empty space and turnpike boredom. The state's beauty, its secrets, and its history are often subtle, wrapped in a veil that yields to patient exploration. Kansas's charm is like a prairie rose at dawn glowing through iridescent dewdrops; you must be there at just the right moment to see the dazzling beauty. (8)

The Sampler works to alter one's observational strategies. The Sampler counsels "new eyes," patience, and letting go of preconceived ideas and traveling blue highways so as to notice the unique and subtle beauty in the quiet, rural Kansas character.[8] The sojourn is as important as the final destination.

Beyond emphasizing the importance of the journey, the Sampler also works to distinguish the characteristics of the authentic experience from the mediated tourist attraction. According to the Sampler, the authentic is found in local communities. The authentic is in the drama of the everyday, the subtle, the unique, and the journey of getting there. While the authentic can be found everywhere across Kansas, an example would be in the work of Tobe Zweygardt. Tobe—as in robe—is a well-worn man of some eighty years, living in Cheyenne County, the most northwestern county in the state and named after the northern branch of the Cheyenne Native American tribe. He created a Native American iron sculpture in the heart of Cheyenne County to commemorate the Cherry Creek encampment site following the Sand Creek massacre of the Cheyenne Indians. His motivation was neither money nor praise, but rather his "heartfelt emotion for the Sand Creek survivors" and the preservation of their memory (Penner, personal e-mail). Mr. Zweygardt wanted this significant part of his county's history preserved and honored. He wanted to help tell his county's story, and he hopes a few folks will travel by and think just a bit more about this part of Kansas's rich history.

The mediated tourist attraction, in juxtaposition, is found in the glitz, the wholesale, the mass-marketed tourist-designed experience. An exemplar of the mediated tourist stop is symbolized in the Wizard of Oz theme park moving forward toward construction just southwest of Kansas City, Kansas. This $761 million tourist attraction, proposed and promoted by a California group, seeks to capitalize on Hollywood's connection of Kansas to the Land of Oz.[9] Once completed, the theme park will provide a mediated version of a 1939 mediated version of Kansas and its fantasy characters. Promoters argue the theme park will be a special place. The park will be a "destination"—a place of unusual attractions, a place of superior technology, a place that includes other activities such as a golf course, an RV park, and resort hotel (Hobson). Oz does not exist for the journey of exploration, but rather becomes a "destination" for a "designed experience." According to scholars Dan Nimmo and James Combs, "a designed experience is not something one normally does in everyday life, but [is a] planned and constructed event," where the purpose of the event becomes both entertainment and therapy (7). Rather than talk in terms of historical preservation or enhancing community identity, park promoters talk in terms of technology, publicity, marketing, and profits. As one of the Oz promoters concluded, "The overriding principle is, if you build a high-quality themed attraction, people will come" (Hobson). Rather than highlighting the unique, the subtle, promoters compare the Oz park to other mediated attractions such as Branson, Missouri, Disney World and Disney Land, and Six Flags over Texas.

Connected to this aspect of spirit is Daniel Kemmis's concept of "grace." Kemmis writes, "grace has to do with a manner of acting in the world that is strikingly appropriate to the time and place" (*The Good City* 25). Spiritual rhetoric in community building, then, asks citizens to recognize an interdependency among people, businesses, localities, and their environments as they go about building communal relationships. Certainly, Tobe Zweygardt's local work is graceful as he takes his inspiration from local events, places, and people and manifests that inspiration in the narrative his iron sculpture tells. His sculpture comes from his imagination and his hands and gracefully connects to the local environment to tell local history. The Oz project, by contrast, takes a national tourist model, adds virtual worlds and fantasy characters, offers local connection via a mass mediated message, and locates the themed park not near the historical site in southwest Kansas that inspired the story, but near Kansas's largest population base for maximum profit opportunity.[10]

Valuing the Humane

A community-building spirit also values the ethics of the humane. The humane ethic is expressed in the variety of scholarly writings identified above. Characteristic of each, however, is the perspective of connection, of wholeness. Scholars writing of a spiritual ethic argue that our deeds are a connection to others and the environment around us and that to exhibit the humane, we need to respond to others in recognition of our impact on their lives. The Sampler's humane ethic is materialized through its rhetoric of connection. It promotes both a connection between rural communities and a recognition of connection of community and environment.

The Sampler articulates a community-building spiritual rhetoric that is unifying and connecting. This component of spiritual discourse, related to the imaginative, recognizes and celebrates interrelationships and wholeness. The Sampler works hard to point out connections between localities, arguing that identifying and exploiting commonalities provides a path for rural community survival. The Sampler, in fact, utilizes a connecting rhetoric in several ways. It highlights cooperative, connected projects. These projects illustrate commonalities of interests and needs among rural communities and show how rural leaders have addressed those interests and needs to sustain and build community. Additionally, the Sampler offers ideas of thematic tourism and themed events that communities might utilize. Again, the goal is to enhance local community. Finally, the Sampler serves as a clearinghouse, providing useful information to rural leaders around the state on issues of common interest. The Sampler strongly believes that cooperation and connection are fundamental components of rural community building.

The primary strategy in the Sampler's unifying rhetoric is to highlight successful, cooperative rural projects in which communities have worked together to help one another. Examples of this strategy routinely appear in the *We Kan!* newsletter. This example appeared in the February 24, 1996, issue:

> Abbyville (pop. 142), Partridge (pop. 230), Plevna (pop. 124), and Sylvia (305) are Reno County communities joined by U.S. 50 and are located within an 18-mile stretch. They recently decided to get together to figure out how they could pool their resources. It might be for a joint event, it might be for recreation. They don't know yet. What they do know is that a collective energy might take them further than they can go by themselves.
>
> Cooperative efforts and each person taking responsibility for being a positive influence is what will keep our rural communities alive and thriving. In this case, it took the inspiration of one to make this meeting happen.
>
> Good luck, you four small towns. We'll be anxious to hear how your meeting goes and we'll be cheering you all the way. (Penner 1)

Another example is provided in the June 16, 1997, issue of *We Kan!*:

> The Heartland Network is an association of twelve community clusters of over 100 farm families across Kansas and northeast Missouri who are working together to

find ways to improve profitability on their farms while protecting and conserving resources, and improving their quality of life. (Penner 2)

In both these examples, as well as a variety of others reported in *We Kan!*, the Sampler describes instances of cooperation based on mutual interest and need. The ultimate purpose in both instances is to sustain local community.

"How can we get visitors into our towns and encourage them to continue to the next town?" is a rhetorical question often posed by the Sampler. The question, though, is a serious source of concern for rural Kansans. "Promote thematically" is the response given by the Sampler Foundation. The idea offered by the Sampler is to identify commonalities across the state in terms of the rural elements and then encourage localities to coordinate tourism efforts around those connecting issues. The Sampler believes that coordinated thematic tours is a likely avenue to draw visitors and is also a way for local citizens to actively develop and promote their own community. Numerous examples of thematic activities are offered by the Sampler. Examples include a museum and dining experience centered around the remaining "Harvey Houses." Fred Harvey developed chain restaurants called "Harvey Houses" across Kansas for early Santa Fe railroad passengers. Today, several of those houses remain and have been converted into museums and/or local restaurants *(We Kan!*, November 1998, 2). Another example offered by the Sampler is to "encourage a giant shopping trip across the state" by listing in the newsletter specific local business across the state where citizens can shop and purchase unique items such as dulcimers, pipe organs, authentic Western wear, and stained glass *(We Kan!*, January 2000, 1). A third example provided is a "thematic tour" to visit, tour, and explore the historic Kansas courthouses *(We Kan!*, February 1999, 3).

A third way the Kansas Sampler Foundation functions to connect rural communities and leaders is to serve as a clearinghouse for information relevant to local communities and individuals and groups promoting those communities. The Sampler tries to provide rural leaders notice of issues, people, and events that might help in their local community development. Just some of the examples of information the Sampler provides include tax credits for historical preservation, grantwriting seminars, granting procedures and deadlines, seminars on historical performance, state tourism officials and their contact addresses, telecommunications forums, and media exposure opportunities.

Kenneth Wilkinson writes that one cannot talk about healthy rural communities without promoting "ecological well-being." According to the humanist approach to community building, there is an interdependent relationship between social life and the surrounding environment that supports that life *(The Community* 75). The Sampler does not routinely preach about the social/environmental connection, but rather their position can be viewed in the issues and projects they value as well as those they do not value. The Sampler Foundation values the local, the small; the business or event that integrates itself into the local environment, that does not sap natural and social resources. As an example, the Sampler encourages explorers to bypass the national, franchised, and mass-marketed megabusinesses. They argue these corporate conglomerates have snuffed out the local cafes and main street businesses as well as obliterated in their wake local history, color, and pride. In Sampler rhetoric, for example, Wal-Mart and the various fast-food chains destroy local commerce ecology while corporate farming besmirches the local natural environment.

Conclusions

The Kansas Sampler Foundation articulates a powerful spiritual message of rural community building. The Sampler is literally the genesis for much community development in Kansas. Whether it be Marci Penner's enthusiastic persona, the supportive messages in *We Kan!*, the energy spread by the Kansas Explorers Club, or the ideas generated from "The Gathering," the Kansas Sampler Foundation gives birth to much rural community development in Kansas.

The Sampler also works to convert the way individuals perceive Kansas. The Sampler asks people to see and think about Kansas imaginatively. They urge Kansans and non-Kansans to see the state with new eyes, to value the journey as much as, if not more than, the destination, to value the local and the subtle. Through this perceptual shift via imaginative exploration, the Sampler believes that Kansans will reclaim pride in their localities and subsequently build stronger communities.

Finally, the Sampler articulates a community-building rhetoric based on a humane ethic. The ethic argues that Kansans are linked in interest and need and that connection and cooperation are crucial for community development and survival. The Sampler also values the local over the national, the subtle over the gaudy, Main Street over Madison Avenue.

In the end, Sampler rhetoric is a creative, imaginative, and ethical discourse that ultimately seeks to restore pride in Kansas and promote a "can-do" attitude for all Kansans working in community development.

Notes

1. I first met Marci Penner in March 1996, at a seminar sponsored by Kansas State University's Kansas Center for Rural Initiative. Marci was presenting a forum on the Kansas Sampler Foundation. I was intrigued by her very positive message regarding rural community building. Following her presentation, I contacted her and told her of my interest in rural Kansas success stories. I told her I was interested in narratives of small towns overcoming obstacles, that I was interested in communication strategies used by rural Kansans to promote their communities. Marci told me about an annual motivation and support gathering. So, in January 1997, I attended my first "Gathering." I have attended this annual meeting ever since. All data reported in this chapter come from the "Gathering" as well as other Kansas Sampler Foundation publications, my participant observation with Kansas Explorers, and personal interviews and correspondence with Marci Penner. This data collection has occurred since

my first meeting with Marci Penner in 1996.

2. Marci and Mil Penner wrote three books in the early 1990s. See Mil Penner and Marci Penner, *Kansas Weekend Guide* (Inman: Sounds of Kansas Press, 1991); Mil Penner and Marci Penner, *Kansas Event Guide* (Inman: Sounds of Kansas Press, 1991); Mil Penner and Marci Penner, *Kansas Weekend Guide Two* (Inman: Sounds of Kansas Press, 1993).

3. The Kansas Explorers Club is an organization that makes an art of "seeing Kansas with new eyes." Their membership fee is $18.61 (Kansas's birthday). There is a secret ritual of initiation. The club encourages members to (1) feel good about spending money in rural communities, (2) support local, hometown businesses, (3) "dare to do dirt" (in other words, drive the back roads so as to see the "real" Kansas, not just the interstate or the large communities), (4) be curious and explore communities via the eight rural culture elements, (5) leave rural towns stronger by encouraging locals to also "see their own community with new eyes."

4. The Sampler's notion of rural culture comes not from culling and reporting of academic source information on the topic, but from a poolside brainstorming session at the 1994 "Gathering." Explanation of each rural culture element is intentionally left somewhat vague, allowing citizens to form their own conception of each element. General statements about each element can be found in Kansas Sampler Foundation reference materials and in Marci Penner and Pat Villeneuve, *Seeing Our Communities with New Eyes* (Topeka: Kansas State Department of Education, 1999), and Mil Penner, *Exploring Kansas* (Lawrence: University Press of Kansas, 1996).

5. C.O.W.B.O.Y. stands for "Cock-eyed Old West Band of Yahoos" and the C.O.W.B.O.Y. Society works to promote cowboy interests around the state and country.

6. An example of this type of support is found in the following notice appearing in the April 17, 1997, issue of *We Kan!*: "The Kansas Explorers Club is initiating a clean-up day in Elk Falls . . . on Saturday, April 26. The work crew will include folks from the Friends of Elk Falls, Kansas Explorers and friends, and Southern Kansas Telephone volunteers. Several dozen are expected to trim branches, paint signs, pick up trash, weed the famous Elk Falls garden, haul debris from a caved-in building, groom pathways, and more" (Penner, "Roll Up Your Sleeves" 1).

7. After finishing my M.A., I took my first teaching job at a private college in Nebraska. A college tradition at the first faculty meeting was to hear from faculty who had been on sabbatical or a research fellowship the prior year. At my first meeting, a faculty member described his summer research fellowship at the University of Kansas as residing in a "hot, flat, treeless, boring, and God-forsaken hellhole." I have often marveled at his powers of distinction as he also regarded Nebraska as a "garden on the plains."

8. "Blue highways" is a term coined by William Least Heat-Moon in his book of the same title. According to Heat-Moon, "On the old highway maps of America, the main routes were red and the back roads blue. Now even the colors are changing. But in those brevities just before dawn and a little after dusk—times neither day nor night—the old roads return to the sky some of its color. Then, in truth, they carry a mysterious cast of blue, and it's that time when the pull of the blue highway is the strongest, when the open road is a beckoning, a strangeness, a place where a man can lose himself." See William Least Heast-Moon, *Blue Highways: A Journey into America* (Boston: Little, Brown and Company, 1982).

9. Frank Baum, an actor who passed through Kansas in 1882, wrote *The Wonderful Wizard of Oz* in 1900, and Judy Garland starred in the film, *The Wizard of Oz* in 1939. Since that time, Dorothy and Oz have arguably become "the state's most identifiable icon." See "Is 'Oz' Image Good for Kansas," *Manhattan Mercury*, 1 February 2000.

10. The area of Kansas depicted in first scenes of *The Wizard of Oz* is identified as the area around Liberal, Kansas. Liberal, in fact, proclaims itself as the site of Dorothy's Kansas

home. Liberal has a "Land of Oz" exhibit complete with a Yellow Brick Road and replicas of Dorothy's farm, celebrates an "Oztoberfest," and runs "Dorothy's House Museum." It is, however, a community of only sixteen thousand and is located in southwest Kansas some four hundred miles away from Kansas City. Thus, the profit orientation guiding the Wizard of Oz theme park disconnects the attraction from what little historical roots that do exist.

Part III

Community-Building Lessons

8

Lessons Learned

This text has slowly taken shape over the last fourteen years. It has emerged through the displays of Halstead Heritage Museum, through the performance of Victorian Days, in the strategic planning meetings of Lincoln and Mitchell counties, through the Ten Commandments conflict in Manhattan, and in my work with the Kansas Sampler Foundation and the Kansas Center for Rural Initiatives. Through these projects and during this time, I have worked on numerous rural issues, met many wonderful people, collected reams of data, and thought extensively about the way rural Americans work to construct and sustain their local communities. Ultimately, however, it has not been enough time to fully immerse myself in the enormous task of building and sustaining rural community. That is literally a full-time, forever job.

As I completed writing the book, the inevitable question from friends and colleagues arose: "How *do* people go about communicating to build community?" That is a difficult question to answer and presents the central goal of this project and chapter—to cogently summarize the lessons learned from these years of rural projects and analysis. In this chapter, I attempt, with some trepidation, to organize and discuss the lessons I have learned on a variety of rural community-building topics.

Initially, this has been a text exploring a symbolic process by which citizens and agencies in small towns work to construct a sense of community and concomitantly seek to build a positive identity for their town. Local community remains an important source of human connectedness, in socializing citizenry, in developing communication skills, and in trusting or loathing civil government. Community is likewise the social crucible of identity formation and value education. But community building is especially critical in rural America. Rural America faces incredible challenges ranging from a lack of services to youth flight to a loss of capital to an eroding infrastructure. Building community provides a necessary, if only a preliminary, step to reclaiming and sustaining rural towns.

While this text has examined community within the context of rural towns, I believe community is ultimately a sense of interconnectedness we feel with others, whether that interconnectedness occurs within the confines of city boundaries or across the cyberspace of the Internet. As a result of my work, I am convinced that community is a feeling of connection, of support, of the fulfillment one senses in the presence of other, like-minded individuals. I also believe that community involves a moral dimension. For community to exist, there needs to be not only a concern for individuals at a humane level, but also at least some level of value agreement between people.

Lessons Learned about Civic Communion

Civic communion is both process and method, event and heuristic. It is both a significant moment of community interaction and a powerful lens through which scholars can examine that interaction.

Civic Communion as Community Event

Several community-building scholars have written about the structural and symbolic practices I label civic communion. Kenneth Wilkinson, for example, writes that "When community is experienced consciously, it can arouse feeling, and this cognitive and emotional response to the experience of community is communion" (*The Community* 110). Likewise, Daniel Kemmis writes about renewing a culture of cooperation—essentially building the form of community I advocate. "We need to spend time in such [centennial] celebrations," Kemmis argues, "in such remembering. But this should not be merely an exercise in nostalgia. At its best, such recalling can serve . . . to remind us, in an active, creative way, of what we have in common" *(Community* 69). Finally, Bellah and his coauthors, in their informative text, *Habits of the Heart,* refer to "practices of commitment" in which citizens "participate in the practices—ritual, aesthetic, ethical—that define the community as a way of life" (154).

I believe, however, that this text serves to fill out our understanding of the community-building processes discussed by these scholars. In this book, I have provided detail about the various characteristics and practices of civic communion and have then highlighted those characteristics and practices through a series of case studies.

Moments of civic communion provide the interrelation of a focused organization and powerful rhetoric which together function to draw individuals into a desired vision of community. Organizationally, civic communions are segmented moments of collective reflection and celebration of community life. These passionate, yet transitory, moments are organized and led by civic leaders and involve widespread participation by the citizenry at large. The rhetorical and performative dimensions of civic communion ultimately function to construct the bonds of interconnectedness.

Rhetorically, civic communions are emotional celebrations of community social and organizational structures. Civic communions are created to achieve some purpose. With the possible exception of a community's response to some unexpected tragedy, all moments of civic communion are conceived, planned, and produced with some civic goal in mind. Some particular civic group provides organization and direction for creation of the event. As they organize and direct the civic communion, this group's vision, perspective, and interests infuse the civic communion event. Yet, I also believe every civic communion functions to offer open, permeable, rhetorical spaces in which citizens may discuss a variety of civic visions. Certainly, civic communion rhetoric is generally dominated by one or a few civic groups. Still, I believe civic communions provide a structural mechanism—a rhetorical space—for alternative views of community. In Waterville, the organizing committee has expanded and diversified the Victorian Days performances as the festival has evolved. Strategic planning offers structured and managed opportunities to articulate a variety of community visions. Public conflict clearly features differences of opinion about the values, purpose, and vision of a community. Decisions about museum displays are made in the crucible of debate where a diverse views are articulated.

Civic communions do label situations positively or negatively, name appropriate and inappropriate behaviors and values, and identify both community heroes and villains. The result of this civic rhetoric is to cluster groups of citizens together, solidifying citizen coalitions, and arranging those groups hierarchically. Civic communions become sociopolitical touchstones for the community, functioning as a source of collective memory.

Finally, the performative component of groups of individuals working together establishes connectedness. Whether producing community celebration, participating in community planning, organizing coalitions to engage in community conflict, or engaging in festival activities, groups of people are drawn together through the sheer act of interacting with one another toward a common civic purpose. Through this communion performance, certain histories, values, and people are celebrated while others are ignored or devalued.

A critical point in the understanding of civic communion is that the organizational and rhetorical structure of civic communions manifest themselves in a variety of civic contexts. In this book, I have identified several contexts including community planning, community festivals, community conflicts, and heritage museums. One can also imagine other civic communion moments. Examples might include community response to local tragedies such as a hurricane, flood, tornado, or the untimely death of a noteworthy citizen. Celebration of community-funded, public works projects such as a downtown renovation or the dedication of public art would also likely provide moments for collective reflection.

Ultimately, however, I believe civic communions are generally conservative rhetorical and performative moments. As John Bodnar explains, "Commemorative activities ... almost always stress the desirability of maintaining the social order and existing institutions, the need to avoid disorder or dramatic changes, and the dominance of citizen duties over citizen rights" (19). As civic communions are organized and directed primarily by community elites and focused toward celebrating some community individual, history, or vision, the tendency is to promote stability and highlight the traditional. Thus, I believe civic communions ultimately work to reify existing community structures.

Civic Communion as Heuristic

Civic communion also functions as a powerful heuristic for examining community processes and community sociopolitical structures. In the tradition of ethnography of communication, civic communion provides a lens for exploring the rhetorical and performative complexities of the community-building process. By collecting ethnographic data from interviews, participant observation, and community performances as well as by examining a community's rhetorical documents, scholars can study community building from a multiplicity of perspectives. Through civic communion, community-building researchers can explore community settings, participants, goals, community-building acts, agencies, norms of interactions, and genres of civic communions.

Civic communions offer an additional methodological benefit as these community moments are clearly "delimited, blessed, adorned" as compared to everyday community life (Falassi 4). Falassi refers to moments of civic communion as "time out of time," as possessing "a special temporal dimension devoted to special activities" (4). In rural communities, civic communions are clearly "set apart" from normal activities. Significant numbers of the community work toward the realization of and participation in the communion. Real time essentially freezes. Consequently, this bracketed moment of community reflection and celebration offers researchers a profitable moment for study of community-building processes.

Civic communion as heuristic has a prismatic quality. Because of the complexity of civic communions, scholars can focus the crystal of analysis in different directions, calling attention to not only the pragmatics of community-building communication, but community sociopolitical structures as well. This analytic focus can move back and forth from an examination of symbolic structures to the study of sociopolitical structures. In this text, for example, the performance of festival was examined and gender roles were explored through those performances. Sociopolitical relationships between rural and urban interests were explored through a narrative analysis of the civic communion of strategic planning. The opportunities for this type of analysis are wide ranging. Sociopolitical structures such as dominance, power, gender, and social roles can be explored through the study of civic communions constituted by myths, ideographs, narratives, rhetorical fantasies, and/or values. Civic communion as method reflects back and forth from analysis of the rhetorical and performative characteristics of community building to the study of a locale's sociopolitical structures.

Lessons Learned about the
Rhetoric of Community Building

To sustain and build community, communication is obviously critical. Citizens interested in constructing a sense of connectedness must communicate in a way that celebrates commonalities and in a way that draws others into a communal vision of the community. I believe there are several specific and interrelated community-building rhetorics embedded in civic communion events. Those include: (1) historical presence comprised of value talk, ideographic talk, and history talk; (2) appeals to interdependence; and (3) a spiritual rhetoric. These rhetorics have no primacy over one another and I believe that they can be used singularly or in a variety of combinations. These rhetorics do not provide a list of apodictic strategies for successful community-building efforts, but rather offer an index of community-building language strategies which would direct citizens toward a more communal existence. Recognizing that these community-building rhetorics are often interrelated, I will try to discuss the characteristics of each individually and illustrate how together they might be used in a particular combination.

Communal feelings are initially enhanced as people more clearly understand local history, important values, and political ideals. I label the interaction of these three community cognitions "cultural presence." These elements constitute the factual or dominant views that give identity to a locality. Historical issues of local commerce, the sociopolitical genesis of the community, and area geography all interact to give an identity to the town. Enacted values and political ideals also provide identity to the locale. As Daniel Kemmis writes, "In any genuine community there are shared values" (*Community* 78; see also Fisher 206). Values such as perseverance, religious tolerance, and innovation can be associated with the image of community and give that town or area a particular identity. Similar to a community's values are its political ideals or ideographs. Celeste Condit writes that ideographs are "a kind of 'ultimate term'—special words or phrases that express the public values that provide the 'constitutional' commitments of a community" (*Decoding Abortion Rhetoric* 13). Ideographs would include examples such as "freedom," "property," and "individualism." These ultimate terms are always politically contested by differing community groups and are often protected in some form by civil governments. Again, the types of ideographs a community celebrates and protects give identity to that community. Philip Selznick explains the process by which cultural presence becomes a community-building tool:

> The bonds of community are strongest when they are fashioned from strands of shared history and culture [and the] quest is for principles latent in the community's culture and history. Once formulated, such principles become resources for internal dialogue. They are instruments for reflective morality, that is, they are authoritative standpoints from which to criticize and change specific beliefs, norms, and practices. At the same time, the principles express a distinctive ethos and a special experience. (197)

Kemmis argues that "What makes a city a good city is . . . the way in which it creates presence" (*The Good City* 21). Kemmis' statement reveals that community building comes from more than simply understanding cultural presence. It comes from the creation of that presence. Bellah et al. explain:

> People growing up in communities of memory not only hear the stories that tell people how the community came to be, what its hopes and fears are, and how its ideals are exemplified in outstanding men and women; they also participate in the practices—ritual, aesthetic, ethical—that define the community as a way of life. (154)

I argue one way communities practice the construction and performance of cultural presence is through symbolic moments of civic communion. Indeed, much of the talk during moments of civic communion is either contested discussions or celebrations of the history, values, and political ideals important to a town's existence.

In addition to creating cultural presence, community building also involves the communication of interdependence and cooperation. Philip Selznick argues, "Community begins with, and is largely supported by, the experience of interdependence and reciprocity" (198). Appeals to interdependence are made on a variety of levels. At the most basic level, interdependence is cast as citizens pooling talents and labor to accomplish social and community tasks. Indeed, Kemmis explains the values of a community are materialized through practices of interdependence and cooperation (*Community* 79). Interdependence is further articulated through the argument that all segments of a community are fundamentally interconnected. Thus, attention to quality of life issues—development of parks, pools, arts centers—concomitantly enhances commercial interests as businesses and companies are interested in their employees' ability to enjoy life in the local community. Likewise, education interests can work with tourism interests to develop informational materials to promote the local community. Appeals to interdependence can also communicate how the local community and economy are interconnected to regional, national, and international forces—cultural forces, economic forces, and political forces.

Spiritual communication is also critical to community-building efforts. This form of community-building discourse is multifaceted, involving (1) a rhetoric of grace, (2) an articulation of imagination, and, finally, (3) creative energy. A rhetoric of grace is essentially an argument or appeal to citizens and communities to act in a manner "that is strikingly appropriate to the time and place" (Kemmis, *The Good City* 25). Other scholars have labeled this mode of acting consistently with one's place in the world "harmonious interconnectedness" (Burkhardt 72). The appeal to grace or harmonious interconnectedness is an argument for the intersection of a locale's cultural presence with its economic or cultural development. Leonard Jason, for example, writes that to build supportive communities, "we should develop traditions, norms, and values that are tied to the settings or communities in which we live" (75). There are many community-building implications for a rhetoric of grace. Many small towns hold strategic planning meetings resulting in the decision to pursue business expansion. Their solution is to seek one big company or business that will hopefully turn the town around economically. Referred to as "chasing smokestacks," this economic development strategy works against the notion of grace. Small towns often do not have the capital, the infrastructure, or the potential workforce to attract and keep large companies. To attract large businesses, small towns often must give away huge tax incentives to that business, ultimately costing the town revenue and frustrating local small business owners. These communities and citizens often become frustrated and angered by their lack of success in attracting large-scale business, when the more appropriate action would be to attract or develop more small-scale or homegrown businesses.

Also inherent in a spiritual rhetoric is an articulation of imagination that calls on rhetors and auditors alike to speak, hear, and see in new and innovative ways. Through imagination, conventional wisdom is challenged; traditional perceptions are questioned. The hope is that by adjusting local perception, pride in one's local community will increase, and that this newfound pride will concomitantly lead to increased community building and development. It is the idea that citizens are more likely to sustain and improve something they are proud of than something they do not hold in esteem. It begins with an imaginative valuing of places and things not normally valued in mass-mediated America. Speech communication scholar Bud Goodall, though not talking about rural America, argues that observation of otherness is about attitude. When writing about "tourist" as a metaphor for observing others, he writes, "So the question then quickly becomes one not of direction—for all roads do in fact lead somewhere—but of the *attitude* we take when we travel" (*Living in the Rock N Roll Mystery* 222; emphasis mine). The sojourn is as important as the final destination. The authentic is in the drama of the everyday, the subtle, the unique, and the journey of getting there.

The final component of a spiritual community-building rhetoric is creative energy. Eileen Stuart, John Deckro, and Carol Mandle write that spirit "is thought of as transcendent energy," often conceptualized of in terms of "a flame that burns," "a spark within us," and as "a vital force" (36). In each of these descriptors, spirit is connected to energy. And, in fact, critical to building communal bonds in rural areas is a creative and burning energy exhibited by local leadership and volunteers. In each of the case studies presented in this text and in numerous other rural projects with which I have worked, there is one person or a small group of people who impel community-building efforts. In each of the case studies, individuals work tirelessly in the service of the community. In Waterville, it was LueAnn and Ruth Ann Roepke, Sandy Harding, Pam White, and the entire Victorian Days committee. In the Lincoln and Mitchell counties strategic planning efforts, it was Bob Crangle. During the Ten Commandments conflict in Manhattan, Karen McColloh became the lightning rod for the separation of church and state position while Don Rose was the driving force behind the group urging the monolith to remain on city property. In Halstead, the Historical Society's Board of Directors—Larry Murray, Carolyn Williams, Eva Lee Butin, Craig Souter, and Irene Sommerfeld—work actively to promote, raise funds, and maintain the Heritage Museum. Finally, Marci Penner, director of the Kansas Sampler Foundation, appears to possess limitless energy as she crisscrosses the state promoting rural Kansas. Each of these individuals communicates a positive, enthusiastic, and energetic vision of their community, drawing others into their community-building efforts.

Beyond the creative energy of civic-minded leaders, however, is the necessity of securing assistance for community-building efforts from the local population. Desire and energy to work toward community building for the larger public comes from various motivational sources and leaders should recognize and address these motivations. These motivational sources vary depending on the local citizenry, the area's history, and the particular community project. Leaders may attempt to energize citizens through appeals to civic responsibility, through appeals to service, appeals to fun, or appeals to friendship or tradition. Ultimately, it is important to find the proper appeals particular communities can employ to energize volunteers to assist in community-building efforts.

Endings and Beginnings

I get a call. Sue Padilla from St. John, Kansas, is on the line. She's looking for someone to come and speak about the power heritage museums have in telling the community story. It seems the town has just started constructing their own museum from an abandoned building on their town square and is now looking for someone to come out and provide some thoughts on how to best proceed. "The town Library Board and Lion's Club have joined together to work on the museum project," Sue tells me. "The opportunity for a civic communion moment is presenting itself," I think to myself. "People organizing and planning for ways to celebrate their community, to tell their story." I fire up the computer. "Let's do a little research on St. John," I mutter to myself. I go online and find out that St. John is a town in southern Kansas, about one hundred miles west of Wichita in a physiographic area known as the Arkansas River Lowlands. I also find out that St. John has a population of about thirteen hundred people and seems to be very proud of their downtown Victorian square which features a three-tier foundation and an ornate block wall surrounding the main square. "Sounds interesting." Each year, St. John celebrates the St. John Jubilee over Memorial Day weekend. "Another potential civic communion moment," I think. Knowing the general area of St. John, I'm sure that ranching, farming, and oil production are all important to the local economy. I also see from a map that St. John is framed to the northeast by Rattlesnake and Wild Horse creeks. "What wonderful names. Makes the place sound foreboding, rugged, and forbidding." I also read online that a local book entitled *No Cyclone Shall Destroy* provides a history of St. John. "I've got to find out more about this place," I decide. "Time to do some field research." I grab my legal pad and my recorder. I check my cache of blank audiotapes and the status of my batteries. "I'm good to go," I announce to myself. I walk out of "The Castle" and hop into my car. I'm off toward rural Kansas in search of civic communion.

Works Cited

Books and Articles

Abrahams, Roger D. "The Language of Festivals: Celebrating the Economy." In *Celebration: Studies of Festivity and Ritual*, ed. Victor Turner, 161-77. Washington, DC: Smithsonian Institution Press, 1992.

Adelman, Mara B., and Lawrence R. Frey. *The Fragile Community: Living Together with AIDS.* Mahwah, NJ: Lawrence Erlbaum Associates, 1997.

Adler, Patricia A., and Peter Adler. "Observational Techniques." In *Handbook of Qualitative Research*, eds. Norman K. Denzin and Yvonna S. Lincoln, 377-92. Thousand Oaks, CA: Sage Publications, 1994.

Allison, Eric W., and Mary Ann Allison. "Using Culture and Communications Theory in Postmodern Urban Planning: A Cybernetic Approach." *Communication Research* 22 (December 1995): 627-45.

Altman, Irwin. "Dialectics, Physical Environments, and Personal Relationships." *Communication Monographs* 60 (March 1993): 26-34.

Armada, Bernard J. "Memorial Agon: An Interpretative Tour of the National Civil Rights Museum." *Southern Communication Journal* 63 (Spring 1988): 235-43.

Arnett, Ronald C. *Communication and Community: Implications of Martin Buber's Dialogue.* Carbondale: Southern Illinois University Press, 1986.

Aronoff, Marilyn. "Collective Celebration as a Vehicle for Local Economic Development: A Michigan Case." *Human Organization* 52 (1993): 368-79.

Averill, Thomas Fox. "Flyover Country: An Introduction." *The North American Review* 284 (January 1999): 4-9.

Bakan, David. *The Duality of Human Existence: An Essay on Psychology and Religion.*

Chicago: Rand McNally & Company, 1966.

Ball, R. L., et al. *A Cultural Resource Survey of Lincoln County, Kansas.* Manhattan, KS: Kansas State University, Kansas Center for Rural Initiatives, 1991.

Bauman, Richard. "Performance." In *Folklore, Cultural Performances, and Popular Entertainment: A Communication-Centered Handbook,* ed. Richard Bauman, 1-49. New York: Oxford University Press, 1992.

Bellah, Robert N., et al. *Habits of the Heart: Individualism and Commitment in American Life.* Berkeley: University of California Press, 1985.

Bender, Thomas. *Community and Social Change in America.* New Brunswick, NJ: Rutgers University Press, 1978.

Berry, Thomas. *Creative Energy: Bearing Witness for the Earth.* San Francisco: Sierra Club Books, 1988.

Bhattacharyya, Jnanabrata. "Solidarity and Agency: Rethinking Community Development." *Human Organization* 54 (Spring 1995): 60-69.

Blankenship, Jane, and Deborah C. Robson. "A 'Feminine Style' in Women's Political Discourse: An Exploratory Study." *Communication Quarterly* 43 (Summer 1995): 353-66.

Bodnar, John. *Remaking America: Public Memory, Commemoration, and Patriotism in the Twentieth Century.* Princeton, NJ: Princeton University Press, 1992.

Bordo, Susan. *Unbearable Weight: Feminism, Western Culture, and the Body.* Berkeley: University of California Press, 1993.

Bormann, Ernest G. *The Force of Fantasy: Restoring the American Dream.* Carbondale: Southern Illinois University Press, 1985.

Bourke, Lisa and A. E. Luloff. "What Influence does She Have in this Town? The Perceived Influence of Women in Rural Pennsylvania Communities." *Journal of the Community Development Society* 29 (1998): 237-255.

Brookfield, Stephen D. *Understanding and Facilitating Adult Learning.* San Francisco: Jossey-Bass, 1986.

Browne, Stephen H. "Reading, Rhetoric, and the Texture of Public Memory." *Quarterly Journal of Speech* 81 (May 1995): 237-50.

Bryson, Bill. "Why Post Rock." *Post Rock* 9 (Summer/Fall 1975): 3, 12, 30.

Bryson, John M. *Strategic Planning for Public and Nonprofit Organizations: A Guide to Strengthening and Sustaining Organizational Achievement.* San Francisco: Jossey-Bass, 1995.

Burke, Kenneth. "Auscultation, Creation, and Revision." in *Extensions of the Burkeian System.* ed. James W. Chesebro, 42-172. Tuscaloosa: University of Alabama Press, 1993.

———. *Symbols and Society.* Chicago: University of Chicago Press, 1989.

———. *The Rhetoric of Religion.* Berkeley: University of California Press, 1970.

Burkhardt, Margaret A. "Spirituality: An Analysis of the Concept." *Holistic Nursing Practice* 3 (1989): 69-77.

Carbaugh, Donal. *Situating Selves: The Communication of Social Identities in American Scenes.* Albany: SUNY Press, 1996.

Clandinin, D. Jean, and F. Michael Connelly. "Personal Experience Methods." In *Handbook of Qualitative Research,* eds. Norman K. Denzin and Yvonna S. Lincoln, 413-27. Thousand Oaks: Sage Publications, 1994.

Cohen, Anthony P. *The Symbolic Construction of Community.* New York: Tavistock Publications, 1985.

Colaw, Emerson. *Beliefs of a United Methodist Christian.* Nashville: Discipleship

Resources, 1987.

Coleman, James S. *Community Conflict*. New York: The Free Press of Glencoe, 1957.

Condit, Celeste Michelle. *Decoding Abortion Rhetoric: Communicating Social Change*. Urbana: University of Illinois Press, 1990.

———. "Democracy and Civil Rights: The Universalizing Influence of Public Argumentation." *Communication Monographs* 54 (March 1987): 1-18.

Conquergood, Dwight. "Rethinking Ethnography: Towards a Critical Cultural Politics." *Communication Monographs* 58 (June 1991): 179-194.

Cooper, Thomas W. "Communion and Communication: Learning from the Shuswap." *Critical Studies in Mass Communication* 11 (December 1994): 327-45.

Cope, Meghan. "She Hath Done What She Could: Community, Citizenship, and Place Among Women in Late Nineteenth-Century Colorado." *Historical Geography* 26 (1998): 45-64.

Crane, Susan A. (Ed.). *Museums and Memory*. Stanford, CA: Stanford University Press, 2000.

Cyr, John. *Strategic Plan for Lincoln and Mitchell Counties*. Author. March, 1992.

Crawford, Lyall. "Personal Ethnography." *Communication Monographs* 63 (June 1996): 158-70.

Daniels, Thomas L., John W. Keller, and Mark B. Lapping. *The Small Town Planning Handbook*. Washington, DC: American Planning Association, 1988.

Denton, Robert E. *The Symbolic Dimensions of the American Presidency: Description and Analysis*. Prospect Heights, IL: Waveland Press, 1982.

Dewey, John. *Experience and Education*. The Kappa Delta Pi Lecture Series. New York: The MacMillan Co., 1938.

DeWit, Cary W. "Women's Sense of Place on the American High Plains." *Great Plains Quarterly* 21 (Winter 2001): 29-44.

Douglas, Jack D. *Investigative Social Research: Individual and Team Field Research*. Beverly Hills, CA: Sage Publications, 1976.

Duncan, Carol. "Art Museums and the Ritual of Citizenship." In *Exhibiting Cultures: The Poetics and Politics of Museum Display*, eds. Ivan Karp and Steven D. Lavine, 88-103. Washington, DC: Smithsonian Institution Press, 1991.

Duncan, Hugh. "Axiomatic Propositions." In *Drama in Life: The Uses of Communication in Society*, eds. James E. Combs and Michael W. Mansfield, 30-38. New York: Hastings House, 1976.

Duncan, J. S. "The House as Symbol of Social Structure." In *Home Environment. Vol. 8. Human Behavior and Environment: Advances in Theory and Research*, eds. Irwin Altman and Carol M. Werner, 133-55. New York: Plenum Press, 1985.

Durkheim, Emile. *The Division of Labor in Society*. Trans. George Simpson. Glencoe, IL: The Free Press of Glencoe, 1933.

Effrat, Marcia Pelly. *The Community: Approaches and Applications*. New York: The Free Press, 1974.

Emerson, Robert M., Rachel I. Fretz, and Linda L. Shaw. *Writing Ethnographic Fieldnotes*. Chicago: University of Chicago Press, 1995.

Etzioni, Amitai. "Holidays, the Neglected Seedbeds of Virtue." In *The Monochrome Society*, ed. Amitai Etzioni, 113-40. Princeton: Princeton University Press, 2000.

Ewert, D. Merrill, Thomas G. Yaccino, and Delores M. Yaccino. "Cultural Diversity and Self-Sustaining Development: The Effective Facilitator." *Journal of the Community Development Society* 25 (1994): 20-33.

Falassi, Alessandro. "Festival: Definition and Morphology." In *Time Out of Time: Essays*

Works Cited

on the Festival, ed. Alessandro Falassi, 1-10. Albuquerque: University of New Mexico Press, 1987.

Farber, Carole. "High, Healthy, and Happy: Ontario Mythology on Parade." In *The Celebration of Society: Perspectives on Contemporary Performance*, ed. Frank E. Manning, 33-50. Bowling Green, OH: Bowling Green University Popular Press, 1983.

Fine, E., and Speer, J. "Tour Guide Performances as Sight Sacralization." *Annals of Tourism Research* 12 (1985): 73-95.

Fisher, Walter R. "Narration, Reason, and Community." In *Writing the Social Text: Poetics and Politics in Social Science Discourse*, ed. Richard Harvey Brown, 199-217. New York: Aldine de Gruyter, 1992.

Fitchen, Janet M. *Endangered Spaces, Enduring Places: Change, Identity, and Survival in Rural America*. Boulder, CO: Westview Press, 1991.

Fitzgerald, Don. *Pleasant Valley: Waterville, Revisited*. Waterville, KS: A Yellowjacket Book, 1987.

Flathman, Richard E. *The Philosophy and Politics of Freedom*. Chicago: University of Chicago Press, 1987.

Fuller, Wayne E. *The Old Country School: The Story of Rural Education in the Middle West*. Chicago: University of Chicago Press, 1982
———. *One-Room Schools of the Middle West: An Illustrated History*. Lawrence: University Press of Kansas, 1994.

Fuoss, Kirk. "'Community' Contested, Imagined, and Performed: Cultural Performance, Contestation, and Community in an Organized-Labor Social Drama." *Text and Performance Quarterly* 15 (April 1995): 79-98.

General Accounting Office. *Army Training: Various Factors Create Uncertainty About Need for More Land*. Washington, DC: Government Printing Office, April, 1991.

Gold, Raymond L. "Roles in Sociological Field Observations." *Social Forces* 36 (March 1958): 217-23.

Gonzalez, Maria Cristina. "The Four Seasons of Ethnography: A Creation-Centered Ontology for Ethnography." Unpublished paper.

Goodall, H. L., Jr. "Casing the Academy for Community." *Communication Theory* 9 (November 1999): 465-94.
———. *Casing the Promised Land: The Autobiography of an Organizational Detective as Cultural Ethnographer*. Carbondale: Southern Illinois University Press, 1989.
———. *Divine Signs: Connecting Spirit to Community*. Carbondale: Southern Illinois University Press, 1996.
———. *Living in the Rock N Roll Mystery: Reading Context, Self, and Others as Clues*. Carbondale: Southern Illinois University Press, 1991.

Gusfield, Joseph R. *Community: A Critical Response*. New York: Harper & Row, 1975.
———. "A Dramatic Theory of Status Politics." In *Drama in Life: The Uses of Communication in Society*, eds. James E. Combs and Michael W. Mansfield, 244-57. New York: Hastings House, 1976.

Hawley, Amos. *Human Ecology: A Theory of Community Structure*. New York: The Ronald Press Company, 1950.

Heat-Moon, William Least. *Blue Highways: A Journey into America*. Boston: Little, Brown and Company, 1982.
———. "The Great Kansas Passage." In *What Kansas Means To Me: Twentieth-Century Writers on the Sunflower State*, ed. Thomas Fox Averill, 193-206. Lawrence: University Press of Kansas, 1991.

Hellerstein, Erna Olafson, Leslie Parker Hume, and Karen M. Offen. "General Introduction."

In *Victorian Women: A Documentary Account of Women's Lives in Nineteenth-Century England, France, and the United States*, eds. Erna Olafson Hellerstein, Leslie Parker Hume, and Karen M. Offen, 1-17. Stanford, CA: Stanford University Press, 1981.

Hertzler, Arthur E. (Dr.). *The Horse and Buggy Doctor*. Lincoln: University of Nebraska Press, 1938.

Hertzler, Jerrad J. (Dr.). "Arthur E. Hertzler: The Kansas Horse and Buggy Doctor: A Biographical Sketch." *Journal of the Kansas Medical Society* 63 (October 1962): 424-33.

Hillery, George A. "Definitions of Community: Areas of Agreement." *Rural Sociology* 20 (1955): 111-23.

Hume, Leslie Parker, and Karen M. Offen. "The Adult Woman: Work." In *Victorian Women: A Documentary Account of Women's Lives in Nineteenth-Century England, France, and the United States*, eds. Erna Olafson Hellerstein, Leslie Parker Hume, and Karen M. Offen, 272-291. Stanford, CA.: Stanford University Press, 1981.

Jason, Leonard A. *Community Building: Values for a Sustainable Future*. Westport, CO: Praeger Publishers,1997.

Jorgensen-Earp, Cheryl R. "The Lady, The Whore, and the Spinster: The Rhetorical Use of Victorian Images of Women." *Western Journal of Speech Communication* 54 (Winter 1990): 82-98.

Kansas State Department of Education. "Certified Personnel Report, State Profile, 2002-2003. www.ksde.org (accessed 1 December 2003).

Karp, Ivan. "Festivals." In *Exhibiting Cultures: The Poetics and Politics of Museum Display*, eds. Ivan Karp and Steven D. Lavine, 279-87. Washington, DC: Smithsonian Institution Press, 1990.

——. "Introduction: Museums and Communities: The Politics of Public Culture." In *Museums and Communities: The Politics of Public Culture*, eds. Ivan Karp, Christine Mullen Kreamer, and Steven D. Lavine, 1-18. Washington, DC: Smithsonian Institution Press, 1992.

Kato, Hidetoshi. "The City as Communion: Changes in Urban Symbolism." *Journal of Communication* (Spring 1974): 52-60.

Katriel, Tamar. "'Our Future Is Where Our Past Is.' Studying Heritage Museums as Ideological and Performative Arenas." *Communication Monographs* 60 (March 1993): 69-75.

——. *Performing the Past: A Study of Israeli Settlement Museums*. Mahwah, NJ: Lawrence Erlbaum Associates, 1997.

——. "Sites of Memory: Discourse of the Past in Israeli Pioneering Settlement Museums." *Quarterly Journal of Speech* 80 (February 1994): 1-20.

Kemmis, Daniel. *Community and the Politics of Place*. Norman: University of Oklahoma Press, 1990.

——. *The Good City and the Good Life*. Boston: Houghton Mifflin Company, 1995.

Klumpp, James F., and Thomas A. Hollihan. "Rhetorical Criticism as Moral Action." *Quarterly Journal of Speech* 75 (February 1989): 84-96.

Lavenda, Robert H. "Festivals and the Creation of Public Culture: Whose Voice(s)?" In *Museums and Communities: The Politics of Public Culture*, eds. Ivan Karp, Christine Mullen Kreamer, and Steven D. Lavine, 76-104. Washington, DC: Smithsonian Institution Press, 1992.

Lavenda, Robert H., et al. "Festivals and the Organization of Meaning: An Introduction to Community Festivals in Minnesota." In *The Masks of Play*, eds. Brian Sutton-Smith and Diana Kelly-Byrne, 34-50. New York: Leisure Press, 1984.

Licuanan, Niza R., Rosintan Panjaitan, and John C. van Es. "Gender and Community: Development in the United States: Does Gender Matter." *Journal of the Community Development Society* 27 (1996): 135-47.

Lindlof, Thomas R., and Bryan C. Taylor. *Qualitative Communication Research Methods*, 2d ed. Thousand Oaks: Sage Publications, 2002.

Lofland, John, and Lyn H. Lofland. *Analyzing Social Settings: A Guide to Qualitative Observation and Analysis*, 3d ed. New York: Wadsworth Publishing Company, 1995.

Lohmann, Roger A. *The Commons: New Perspectives on Nonprofit Organizations and Voluntary Action.* San Francisco: Jossey-Bass Publishers, 1992.

Low, Setha M. "Symbolic Ties That Bind: Place Attachment in the Plaza." In *Place Attachment. Vol. 12. Human Behavior and Environment: Advances in Theory and Research*, eds. Irwin Altman and Setha M. Low, 165-85. New York: Plenum Press, 1992.

Lowenthal, David. "The Pioneer Landscape: An American Dream." *Great Plains Quarterly* 2 (Winter 1982): 5-19.

——. "Pioneer Museums." In *History Museums in the United States: A Critical Assessment*, eds. Warren Leon and Roy Rosenzweig, 115-27. Urbana: University of Illinois Press, 1989.

Luke, Timothy W. *Museum Politics: Power Plays at the Exhibition.* Minneapolis: University of Minnesota Press, 2002.

Mackin, James A., Jr. "Schismogenesis and Community: Pericles' Funeral Oration." *Quarterly Journal of Speech* 77 (August 1991): 251-62.

Manning, Frank E. "Cosmos and Chaos: Celebration in the Modern World." In *The Celebration of Society: Perspectives on Contemporary Performance*, ed. Frank E. Manning, 3-30. Bowling Green, OH: Bowling Green State University Popular Press, 1983.

Marsden, Michael T. "Summer and Winter Festivals in Thompson, Manitoba." In *The Cultures of Celebration*, eds. Ray B. Browne and Michael T. Marsden, 157-70. Bowling Green, OH: Bowling Green State University Press, 1994.

Marsden, Michael T., and Ray B. Browne. "Introduction." In *The Cultures of Celebration*, eds. Ray B. Browne and Michael T. Marsden, 1-8. Bowling Green, OH: Bowling Green State University Press, 1994.

Marty, Martin. *The Lord's Supper.* Minneapolis, MN: Augsburg Fortress Press, 1997.

Mayfield, Lydia. *Halstead: The Early Years.* Halstead, KS: Author, 1987.

McGee, Michael Calvin. "The 'Ideograph': A Link Between Rhetoric and Ideology." *Quarterly Journal of Speech* 66 (February 1980): 1-16.

Melton, Gary B. "Ruralness as a Psychological Construct." In *Rural Psychology*, eds. Alan W. Childs and Gary B. Melton, 1-15. New York: Plenum Press, 1983.

Miller, Lynn R. "Defending Small Farms, Small Towns, and Good Work." In *Rooted in the Land: Essays on Community and Place*, eds. William Vitek and Wes Jackson, 60-65. New Haven: Yale University Press, 1996.

Minar, David W., and Scott Greer. *The Concept of Community: Readings with Interpretations.* Chicago: Aldine Publishing Company, 1960.

Morgan, Marie. "Spirit in the Workplace: A Movement on the Verge of Taking Off." *At Work: Stories of Tomorrow's Workplace* 2 (September/October 1993): 7-9.

Muilenburg, Grace, and Ada Swineford. *Land of the Post Rock: Its Origins, History, and People.* Lawrence: University of Kansas Press, 1975.

Nimmo, Dan, and James E. Combs. *Mediated Political Realities*, 2d ed. New York: Longman, 1990.

Nisbet, Robert A. *The Quest for Community: A Study in the Ethics of Order and Freedom.* New York: Oxford University Press, 1953.

Nubel, Hans U. "Towards a Communion of Communions." Paper presented at "The Ways We Celebrate" conference, Washington, DC, April 2003.

Oliver, Robert T. "Communication, Community, Communion." *Today's Speech* 15 (October 1967): 7-9.

Ott, Gina M., and Beth Tatarko. *Kansas Community Strategic Plans.* Topeka: Kansas, Inc., 1992.

Padwe, Sandy. *Basketball's Hall of Fame.* Englewood Cliffs, NJ: Prentice-Hall, 1970.

Paulsen, Gary. "Start of the Wheat State." Kansas Wheat Commission. www.kswheat.com (accessed 2 November 2003).

Peavy, Linda, and Ursula Smith. *Pioneer Women: The Lives of Women on the Frontier.* Norman: University of Oklahoma Press, 1966.

Penner, Marci, and Pat Villeneuve. *Seeing Our Communities with New Eyes.* Topeka: Kansas State Department of Education, 1999.

Penner, Mil. *Exploring Kansas: A New Look at the Sunflower State.* Lawrence: University Press of Kansas, 1996.

Penner, Mil, and Marci Penner. *Kansas Event Guide.* Inman: Sounds of Kansas Press, 1991.

———. *Kansas Weekend Guide.* Inman: Sounds of Kansas Press, 1991.

———. *Kansas Weekend Guide Two.* Inman: Sounds of Kansas Press, 1993.

Peterson, Tarla Rai, and Cristi Choat Horton. "Rooted in the Soil: Understanding the Perspectives of Landowners Can Enhance the Management of Environmental Disputes." *Quarterly Journal of Speech* 81 (May 1995): 139-66.

Philipsen, Gerry. "Places for Speaking in Teamsterville." *Quarterly Journal of Speech* 62 (February 1976): 15-25.

———. *Speaking Culturally: Explorations in Social Communication.* Albany: SUNY Press, 1992.

Poplin, Dennis E. *Communities: A Survey of Theories and Methods of Research.* 2d ed. New York: MacMillan Publishing Company, 1979.

Popper, Deborah Epstein, and Frank J. Popper. "The Great Plains: From Dust to Dust." *Planning* 12 (December 1987): 12-18.

———. "The Fate of the Plains." In *Reopening the Western Frontier,* ed. Ed Marston, 98-113. Covelo, CA: Island Press, 1989.

Procter, David E. "The Dynamic Spectacle: Transforming Experience into Social Forms of Community." *Quarterly Journal of Speech* 76 (May 1990): 117-33.

———. *Enacting Political Culture: Rhetorical Transformations of Liberty Weekend 1986.* New York: Praeger Publishers, 1991.

———. "The Metaphoric Worldview of Maranatha Ministries: Working God's Harvest on College Campuses." *Speaker and Gavel* 23 (1986): 79-86.

Putnam, Robert D. *Bowling Alone: The Collapse and Revival of American Community.* New York: Simon and Schuster, 2000.

Riley, Glenda. *The Female Frontier: A Comparative View of Women on the Prairie and the Plains.* Lawrence: University Press of Kansas, 1988.

Robertson, James Oliver. *American Myth, American Reality.* New York: Hill & Wang, 1980.

Rose, Dan. *Living the Ethnographic Life.* Qualitative Research Methods Series, 23. Newbury Park, CA: Sage Publishers, 1990.

Rousseau, Mary F. *Community: The Tie that Binds.* Lanham, MD: UP of America, 1991.

Rueckert, William H. *Kenneth Burke and the Drama of Human Relations.* 2d ed. Berkeley: University of California Press, 1982.

Rushing, Janice H. "Power, Other, and Spirit in Cultural Texts." *Western Journal of Communication* 57 (Spring 1993): 159-168.

Samuelson, Bill. *One Room Country Schools of Kansas*. Emporia: Chester Press, 2000.

Schmalenbach, Herman. "The Sociological Category of Communion." In *Theories of Society: Foundations of Modern Sociological Theory. Vol. I*, eds. Talcott Parsons, Edward Shils, Kaspar D. Naegele, and Jesse R. Pitts, 331-47. New York: Free Press of Glencoe, 1961.

Schneider, Raymond J. "Tampa: Tales of Two Cities." *Text and Performance Quarterly* 14 (October 1994): 334-41.

Schwartz, Howard, and Jerry Jacobs. *Qualitative Sociology: A Method to the Madness*. New York: The Free Press, 1979.

Scott, Robert L. "Diego Rivera at Rockefeller Center: Fresco Painting and Rhetoric." *Western Journal of Speech Communication* 41 (Spring 1977): 70-82.

Selznick, Philip. "In Search of Community." In *Rooted in the Land: Essays on Community and Place*, eds. William Vitek and Wes Jackson, 195-206. New Haven: Yale University Press, 1996.

Skocpol, Theda, and Morris P. Fiorina. "Making Sense of the Civic Engagement Debate." In *Civic Engagement in American Democracy*, eds. Theda Skocpol and Morris P. Fiorina, 1-26. Washington, DC: Brookings Institute Press, 1999.

Solomon, Martha. "Robert Schuller: The American Dream in a Crystal Cathedral." *Central States Speech Journal* 34 (Fall 1983): 172-86.

Stoeltje, Beverly J. "Gender Representations in Performance: The Cowgirl and the Hostess." *Journal of Folklore Research* 25 (1988): 219-41.

Stoneall, Linda. "Bringing Women into Community Studies: A Rural Midwestern Case Study." *Journal of the Community Development Society* 14 (1983): 17-29.

Stuart, Eileen M., John P. Deckro, and Carol Lynn Mandle. "Spirituality in Health and Healing: A Clinical Program." *Holistic Nursing Practice* 3 (1989): 35-46.

Tatarko, Beth, David Procter, Carol Peak, and Linda Simon. *Strategic Planning Guidebook*. Manhattan: Kansas Center for Rural Initiatives, 1991.

Taylor, Steven J., and Robert Bogdan. *Introduction to Qualitative Research: The Search for Meanings*. New York: John Wiley, 1984.

Throgmorton, James A. *Planning as Persuasive Storytelling: The Rhetorical Construction of Chicago's Electric Future*. Chicago: University of Chicago Press, 1996.

Tillmann-Healy, Lisa M. "A Secret Life in the Culture of Thinness: Reflections on Body, Food, and Bulimia." In *Composing Ethnography: Alternative Forms of Qualitative Writing*, eds. Carolyn Ellis and Arthur P. Bochner, 76-107. Walnut Creek, CA: Alta Mira Press, 1996.

Trent, Judith S., and Robert V. Friedenberg. *Political Campaign Communication: Principles and Practices*. 3d ed. Westport, CT: Praeger, 1995.

Trujillo, Nick. "In Search of Naunny's Grave." *Text and Performance Quarterly* 18 (October 1998): 344-68.

——. "Interpreting November 22: A Critical Ethnography of an Assassination Site." *Quarterly Journal of Speech* 79 (November 1993): 447-66.

Tuan, Yi-Fu. *Space and Place: The Perspective of Experience*. Minneapolis: University of Minnesota Press, 1977.

Turner, Victor W. "Dewey, Dilthey, and Drama: An Essay in the Anthropology of Experience." In *The Anthropology of Experience*. eds. Victor W. Turner and Edward M. Bruner, 33-44. Urbana: University of Illinois Press, 1986.

Van Maanen, John. *Tales of the Field: On Writing Ethnography*. Chicago: University of

Chicago Press, 1988.

Vicinus, Martha. *Suffer and Be Still: Women in the Victorian Age.* Bloomington: Indiana University Press, 1972.

Walzer, Michael. *Toward a Global Civil Society.* Oxford: Berghahn Books, 1995.

Weaver, Richard. *The Ethics of Rhetoric.* Chicago: Henry Regnery Company, 1953.

Weiss, Richard. *The American Myth of Success: From Horatio Alger to Norman Vicent Peale.* Urbana: University of Illinois Press, 1988.

Wilkinson, Kenneth P. "In Search of the Community in the Changing Countryside." *Rural Sociology* 51 (Spring 1986): 1-17.

———. "Phases and Roles in Community Action." *Rural Sociology* 35 (March 1970): 54-68.

———. *The Community in Rural America.* New York: Greenwood Press, 1991.

Williamson, Margaret Holmes. "Family Symbolism in Festivals." In *Middletown Families: Fifty Years of Change and Continuity,* ed. Theodore Caplow, 225-45. Minneapolis: University of Minnesota Press, 1982.

Wuthnow, Robert. *Loose Connections: Joining Together in America's Fragmented Communities.* Cambridge, CT: Harvard University Press, 1998.

Yang, Sharon R. "Victorian Refashioning: Shakespeare's Rosalind as a Paragon of Victorian Womanhood." *Text and Performance Quarterly* 22 (January 2002): 24-46.

Zelizer, Barbie. "Reading the Past Against the Grain: The Shape of Memory Studies." *Critical Studies in Mass Communication* 12 (June 1995): 214-39.

Zencey, Eric. "The Rootless Professors." In *Rooted in the Land: Essays on Community and Place,* eds. William Vitek and Wes Jackson, 15-19. New Haven: Yale University Press, 1996.

Newspaper Stories, Editorials, Letters to Editor, and Brochures

Aldrich, Mike. Letter. *Manhattan Mercury* 5 May 1999: A6.

Alexander, Chip. "Remembering Rupp." *Orlando News & Observer* 16 March 1997. www.search.nando.net/nao/special/97dean/rupp01.html (accessed 15 November 2003).

Bennett, Gayle. Letter. *Manhattan Mercury* 14 October 1999: A6.

Bidwell, Orville W. Letter. *Manhattan Mercury* 19 November 1999: B10.

Blair, Keith. Letter. *Manhattan Mercury* 6 June 1999: C8.

Bunch, Shawn. Letter. *Manhattan Mercury* 2 May 1999: C8.

Butler, James. "Spare Public Officials Religious Litmus Test." *Manhattan Mercury* 14 October 1999: C8.

Campbell, Dave. Letter. *Manhattan Mercury* 4 May 1999: A6.

Cayton, Rodd. "Ten Commandment Backers Mobilize to Persuade City to Fight Lawsuit." *Manhattan Mercury* 16 April 1999: A1.

———. "Majority Returns Plaque as 'Less Divisive' Course." *Manhattan Mercury* 28 April 1999: A1.

———. "Living Wage Looms as Issue." *Manhattan Mercury* 2 May 1999: A1.

———. "Recall Face-Off." *Manhattan Mercury* 24 November 1999: A1.

"Chance to Vote to Save McCulloh Approaches." Editorial. *Kansas State Collegian* 19 November 1999: 4.

"City's Decision was the Right One." Editorial. *Manhattan Mercury* 29 April 1999: A6.

Crane, Charles H. Letter. *Manhattan Mercury* 3 December 1999: A8.

Crangle, Bob. "Even Small Towns Need their Export Markets." *Salina Journal* 23 February 1995: 4.

———. "Life in the Designer Community." *Salina Journal* 11 March 1995: 4.

———. "Money Maps Would Show Where the Cash Flows." *Salina Journal* 23 October 1993: 4

———. "Resettling of Rural America Happens . . . One by One," *Salina Journal* 1 September 1995: 4.

Crubel, Michael R. Letter. *Manhattan Mercury* 4 May 1999: A6.

Ebert, Ken. Letter. *Manhattan Mercury*: 10 May 1999: A8.

Ebert, Roger. "Picnic." *Chicago Sun Times Online.* www.suntimes.com/ebert (accessed 15 November 2003).

Eichman, Carmen. "God Must Have Hand in Our Government." *Manhattan Mercury* 9 May 1999: C9.

Emery, Darren R. Letter. *Manhattan Mercury* 6 May 1999: A6.

Ernst, Hank. "Standing Our Ground." *Kansas Farmer* 3 June 1989: 7-8.

Felber, Bill. "Voting by Petition: Most Ten Commandments Petition Signers Sat Out the April 6 Election." *Manhattan Mercury* 7 May 1999: A1

———. "Among Jurors, at Least, the Recall is a Bitterly Divisive Topic." *Manhattan Mercury* 28 November 1999: A1.

Fliter, John. Letter. *Manhattan Mercury* 3 December 1999: A8.

Garton, Jan. Letter. *Manhattan Mercury* 24 November 1999: A8.

Garwick, John. Letter. *Manhattan Mercury* 29 November 1999: A8.

Gates, Griffith G. Letter. *Manhattan Mercury* 23 November 1999: A8.

Glasgow, Hillary. Letter. *Manhattan Mercury* 1 December 1998: A8.

Glasser, Jeff. "A Broken Heartland: Nothing Manifest about the Destiny of Small Towns on the Great Plains." *U.S. News and World Report* 7 May 2001: 18-22.

Hall, Linda. Letter. *Manhattan Mercury* 3 May 1999: A6.

Hamilton, James R. "Neutrality on Religion Protect All." *Manhattan Mercury* 5 December, 1999: C9.

Hampton, Kent. "Secular Humanism Behind McCulloh's Vote." *Manhattan Mercury* 21 November 1999: C8.

Harder, Jeri. "It All Started with the Kansas Sampler Foundation." *Tour Kansas Guide* 7 (September 1999): 12.

Harris, Richard. Letter. *Manhattan Mercury* 15 November 1999: A6.

Hayter, Richard B. Letter. *Manhattan Mercury* 3 December 1999: A8.

Heaton, Lou. Letter. *Manhattan Mercury* 22 November 1999: A8.

Herspring, Dale. "Neutrality Tilts Scales Toward Religion of Secular Humanism." *Manhattan Mercury* 22 November 1998: C9.

———. "Monolith Vote Likely to Haunt Commissioners." *Manhattan Mercury* 23 May 1999: C8.

Hobson, Grace. "3.2 Million Oz Visitors: Real World or Fantasy? Experts Examine Crown Projections." *Kansas City Star* 19 September 1999: A1.

Huddleston, Dave. Letter. *Manhattan Mercury* 9 June 1999: A6.

"Is 'Oz' Image Good for Kansas." *Manhattan Mercury* 1 February 2000: A2.

Johnson, David L. Letter. *Manhattan Free Press* 2 December 1999: 5.

Johnson, Deena. Letter. *Manhattan Free Press* 2 December 1999: 6

Johnson, Linda R. Letter. *Manhattan Mercury* 9 May 1999: C8.

Kilborn, Peter T. "Bit by Bit, Tiny Morland, Kan. Fades Away." *New York Times Online.* www.nytimes.com/2001/05/10/national/10town.html (accessed 15 August 2001).

Knight, D. W. "Oppose Expansion." *Salina Journal* 7 June 1990: 4.

Larson, Anne. Letter. *Manhattan Mercury* 2 May 1999: C8.

LaSalle, Mick. "Picnic." *San Francisco Chronicle.* www.thegoldenyears.org (accessed 15 November 2003).

Marshall, Gary. Letter. *Manhattan Mercury* 30 April 1999: A6.

Matthews, Anne. "The Poppers and the Plains." *New York Times Magazine* 24 June 1990: 1-5.

McClure, John D. Letter. *Lincoln Sentinel Republican* 5 December 1991: 3.

McFarland, Marcia R. Letter. *Manhattan Mercury* 26 October 1999: A6.

Miller, Carrie. "Command Performance." *Manhattan Mercury* 20 October 1998: A1.

———. "City's Attorney Says Monument May Stand Legal Test." *Manhattan Mercury* 2 November 1998: A1.

———. "Secular Humanism: Fighting Words." *Manhattan Mercury* 13 June 1999: A1.

Morgan, Linda M. Letter. *Manhattan Mercury* 30 April 1999: A6.

Mrozek, Donald J. Letter. *Manhattan Mercury* 2 December 1999: A8.

Mullin, Robert Evan. Letter. *Manhattan Mercury* 2 May 1999: C8.

Neal, Steven A. Letter. *Manhattan Mercury* 6 May 1999: A6.

Ossar, Michael. "Should Your Views Prevail? Or Mine?" *Manhattan Mercury* 30 May 1999: C9.

Penner, Marci. "They Want to Work Together." *We Kan!* 24 February 1996: 1.

———. "Roll Up Your Sleeves on April 26 in Elk Falls." *We Kan!* 17 April 1997: 1

———. "Farm Families Working Together." *We Kan!* 16 June 1997: 2.

Peters, Carolyn. Letter. *Lincoln Sentinel Republican* 30 May 1991: 3.

"Political Lynching Must be Stopped." Editorial. *Manhattan Mercury* 3 October 1999: A6.

Potter, Greg. Letter. *Manhattan Mercury* 11 May 1999: A6.

Prairie People Tourism Association. "South Central Kansas Explorer's Guide." Advertisement Brochure n.d.: 1-31.

"Reject This Vengeful Recall." Editorial. *Manhattan Mercury* 5 December 1999: C8.

Reitz, Roger. Letter. *Manhattan Mercury* 1 December 1999: A6.

Richter, Linda. Letter. *Manhattan Mercury* 19 November 1999: B10.

Rintoul, David A. Letter. *Manhattan Mercury* 29 April 1999: A6.

Roffler, Rick. Letter. *Manhattan Free Press* 2 December 1999: 4.

Rose, Don. Letter. *Manhattan Mercury* 6 May 1999: A6.

———. Letter. *Manhattan Mercury* 10 October 1999: C8.

Roth, Lindsey. Letter. *Manhattan Mercury* 21 November 1999: C8.

Sampson, Ron. Letter. *Manhattan Mercury* 3 December 1999: A8.

Sanders, Robert J. Letter. *Manhattan Mercury* 25 November 1999: C9.

Sapp, Ancel L. Letter. *Manhattan Mercury* 28 November 1999: C8.

Sarff, Arlin. Letter. *Manhattan Mercury* 15 November 1999: A6.

Satchell, Michael. "Operation Land-Grab." *U.S. News and World Report* 14 May 1990: 32-34.

Sauer, David. Letter. *Manhattan Mercury* 5 May 1999: A6.

Scott, Mark. "Dressing Up the Weaver's Interior." *Manhattan Mercury* 27 August 2003: A1.

———. "Recall Inquiries Surface." *Manhattan Mercury* 29 April 1999: A1.

Seymour, Roger. Letter. *Manhattan Mercury* 3 December 1999: A8.

Shamburger, Samuel L. Letter. *Manhattan Mercury* 11 May 1999: A6.

Shea, J. D. Letter. *Manhattan Mercury* 28 April 1999: A6.

Shoop, Bob. Letter. *Manhattan Mercury* 18 November 1999: A8.

"Shopping Season Is Underway." Editorial. *Lincoln Sentinel Republican* 28 November

1991: 3.

Sills, Jack. Letter. *Manhattan Mercury* 2 May 1999: C8.

Simmons, Rose M. Letter. *Manhattan Mercury* 20 October 1999: A6.

Sisco, Suzanne. Letter. *Manhattan Mercury* 14 May 1999: A6.

Tate, Barbara J. Letter. *Manhattan Mercury* 28 April 1999: A6.

"The Story of Post Rock." *Seattle Times* 17 June 1973: A6. Found in Scrapbook #2, Mitchell County Historical Society.

Thomas, Wilton B. "McCulloh a Caring, Conscientious Public Servant." *Manhattan Mercury* 24 October 1999: C8.

Trussell, Russell. "Post Rock." *Kansas City Star* 3 July 1994: H1-3.

Tummala, Krishna K. "Debate Must Be Based on Reason, Not Religion." *Manhattan Mercury* 30 May 1999: C9.

Ukena, Jerry. Letter. *Manhattan Mercury* 25 November 1999: C9.

Urban, Dianne K. "Remove the Monolith." *Manhattan Mercury* 22 November 1998: C9.

Vogel, David. Letter. *Manhattan Mercury* 13 May 1999: A6.

Von Elling, Bill. Letter. *Manhattan Mercury* 5 December 1999: C8.

"Waterville Celebrates Its Heritage." Supplement to *Waterville Telegraph* 28 April 2001.

"Waterville Man Uncovers 'Buried Treasure' in Home." *Waterville Telegraph* 20 February 1999: 1, 3.

"Welcome to Waterville's Tenth Annual Victorian Days Celebration." Publicity Flier. 29 April 2000. n. pg.

Weston, Todd. "Let's Offend Atheists, ACLU Before We Offend God." *Manhattan Mercury* 18 April 1999: A6.

Williams, Liz. Letter. *Manhattan Mercury* 3 December 1999: A8.

Wisdom, Bill. Letter. *Manhattan Mercury* 30 November 1999: A6.

Zentz, Marvin. "First Amendment's Intent is to Protect Christians." *Manhattan Mercury* 5 December 1999: C9.

Personal Interviews and Communications

Genschorck, Cindy. Personal interview. 21 April 2003.

Harding, Sandy. Personal interview. 17 March 2003.

Irons, Mary. Personal interview. 17 March 2003.

Keckeisen, Robert J. Letter to author. 3 February 1998.

Minge, Dr. Ward Alan. Personal interview. 15 March 1999.

Murray, Larry. Personal interview. 27 April 2000.

Penner, Marci. Personal e-mail. 26 January 2000.

Roepke, LueAnn. Personal interview. 17 April 2001.

———. Personal interview. 24 April 1999.

Roepke, Terry. Personal interview. 21 April 2001.

Stewart, Gay. Personal interview. 7 April 2003.

Tormondson, Scott. Personal interview. 7 April 2003.

Walter, Ann. Personal interview. 17 March 2003.

White, Pam. Personal interview. 6 July 2001.

Whitesell, David. Personal interview. 31 March 2003.

Williams, Carolyn. Personal interview. 5 November 2003.

Index

Abrahams, Roger, 44
Adelman, Mara, 7
Adler, Patricia, 48
Armada, Bernard, 108-9
Aronoff, Marilyn, 60
autoethnography, 23-24
Averill, Thomas, 17

Bauman, Richard, 8, 13
Bellah, Robert, 79, 125, 142, 146
Bender, Thomas, 4
Berry, Thomas, 125
Bhattacharyya, Jnanabrata, 18-19
blue highways, 137
Bogdan, 28, 34, 36
Bordo, Susan, 52
Bourke, Lisa, 56
Browne, Ray, 45, 108
Browne, Stephen, 109
Bryson, John, 68
Buber, Martin, 6, 13, 125; and narrow ridge, 6
Buffalo Commons, 74
Burke, Kenneth, 14, 24

civic communion, 10, 11-15, 19-20, 39, 146; and community building, 142-44; community conflict as, 87-89, 102-4, community festivals as, 44-46, 60-61; as conservative community moment, 144; heritage museums as, 108-9, 119-20; as heuristic, 144-45; strategic planning as, 67-69, 77-78
civic engagement theory, 9
civic values, 45
Clandinin, D. Jean, 25
Cohen, Anthony, 7
Colaw, Emerson, 11
Coleman, James, 89
collective memory, 108-109
Combs, James, 133
communication, as performance, 7-8; as symbolic form, 7-8
communion, 11-12
community, 3-4; and conflict, 83-104; as relational, 5-7, 19; and religion, 21; rural, 16-19, 24, 25-29; and strategic planning, 65-79; as symbolic, 7-10; as territory, 4-5, 65-67

163

About the Author

David E. Procter is an associate professor of speech communication and head of the department of speech communication, theatre, and dance at Kansas State University. He is the author of *Enacting Political Culture: Rhetorical Transformations of Liberty Weekend 1986* (1991) and book chapters examining community building in President Clinton's first inaugural and through community festivals. Procter has also published numerous scholarly essays in the *Quarterly Journal of Speech, Human Communication Research, Women and Politics, Communication Studies,* the *Western Journal of Speech Communication, Communication Research Reports,* and the *Journal of the Community Development Society.* He is also director of the Institute for Civic Discourse and Democracy, a research and educational programing agency that seeks to enhance democratic decision making and community development through improved communication processes.